A DAY I AIN'T NEVER SEEN BEFORE

A DAY I AIN'T NEVER SEEN BEFORE

REMEMBERING THE CIVIL RIGHTS MOVEMENT IN MARKS, MISSISSIPPI

BY *Joe Bateman*

AND *Cheryl Lynn Greenberg*

WITH *Richard Arvedon*

THE UNIVERSITY OF GEORGIA PRESS

ATHENS

Athens, Georgia 30602
www.ugapress.org

Designed by Kaelin Chappell Broaddus
Set in 10.25/13.5 Miller Text Roman
by Kaelin Chappell Broaddus

Most University of Georgia Press titles are
available from popular e-book vendors.

Printed digitally

Library of Congress Cataloging-in-Publication Data

Names: Bateman, Joe B., 1942– author. | Greenberg, Cheryl Lynn, author. | Arvedon, Richard, author.
Title: A day I ain't never seen before : remembering the civil rights movement in Marks, Mississippi / by Joe Bateman and Cheryl Lynn Greenberg, with Richard Arvedon.
Other titles: Remembering the civil rights movement in Marks, Mississippi
Description: Athens : The University of Georgia Press, [2023] | Includes bibliographical references and index.
Identifiers: LCCN 2022020530 | ISBN 9780820363035 (hardback) | ISBN 9780820363042 (paperback) | ISBN 9780820363028 (ebook)
Subjects: LCSH: Civil rights movements—Mississippi—Marks—History—20th century. | African Americans—Civil rights—Mississippi—Marks—History—20th century. | African Americans—Mississippi—Marks—Social conditions—20th century. | Marks (Miss.)—Social conditions—20th century. | Quitman County (Miss.)—Race relations—History—20th century. | Quitman County (Miss.)—Social conditions—20th century. | Bateman, Joe B., 1942– | Civil rights workers—Mississippi—Marks—History—20th century.
Classification: LCC F349.M29 B38 2022 | DDC 976.2/063092 [B]—dc23/eng/20220504
LC record available at https://lccn.loc.gov/2022020530

You brought me to a brand-new day,
a day I ain't never seen before.

—REV. WILLIE MALONE
(he often used these words in his prayers opening civil rights meetings in Marks, Mississippi; the same or similar words were commonly used in prayer by Black southern ministers)

If there is no struggle there is no progress.

—FREDERICK DOUGLASS,
"The Significance of Emancipation in the West Indies," 1857

CONTENTS

ACKNOWLEDGMENTS

Joe

My deepest thanks to the Black community of Marks, Mississippi, for sheltering me from 1964 through 1966 while I worked with the civil rights movement there and for teaching me not only their own history and cultural values but also how people everywhere can struggle for freedom and a better life. My thanks to them again for their help providing information for this book in the years since.

My thanks also to the Franklin family of Marks, who kept me in their home most of the time I was there, for teaching me some of the most important lessons of my life and for providing much of the basic material used here; to Rev. G. W. Ward and Mrs. Sarah Ward for welcoming me into their home when I first arrived in Marks and for showing me the beauty of the Black culture of the South and the dignity people can have under oppression; and to Dr. Demitri Shimkin and Mrs. Edith Shimkin for urging me to write this book and enabling me to visit Marks in 1975—the first time I had been there since 1969. I thank the Shimkins also for their materials on Black family life, which helped me find meaning in my own impressions and memories and in the information the people of Marks provided me.

I am grateful to the following people for sources on Marks and Quitman County:

- Mary Cox and Malcolm Shepherd of the law firm of Anderson, Banks, Nichols, and Stewart in Jackson, Mississippi, for the records of the school desegregation case in Quitman County;
- Jan Hillegas and Ken Lawrence of Freedom Information Service of Jackson for photocopies of reports from the civil rights project in Marks, the Jackson offices of the Council of Federated Organizations, and the Mississippi Freedom Democratic Party (thanks also to Jan for typing the original manuscript);
- Celia Rosebury Lighthill for granting permission to use an article by Mae Ella Franklin of Marks in the now-defunct *Insurgent* magazine;
- the staffs of the University of Oklahoma library and the Wisconsin State Historical Society (WSHS);
- Mr. James Wilson Sr. of Marks for giving me access to his collection of documents and letters relating to his involvement in civil rights and community development;
- Michael Morgala and Nina Wojciechowska of Madison, Wisconsin, for letting me stay at their home while I worked with WSHS materials;
- Dr. Stan Hyland of Memphis State University and Mrs. Keith Hyland for hosting me while I researched back issues of the Memphis newspaper;
- Dr. Charles Williams of Memphis State University for help in my journeys to Marks and for making copies of the original manuscript when rain damaged it;
- Dr. Simon Cuthbert-Kerr of Edinburgh, Scotland, for sharing his research materials with me, including statements that people in Marks and I had made for possible legal cases and reports from the Mississippi State Sovereignty Commission (now online), which spied on us in the 1960s.

My thanks, of course, also go to everyone I worked with in Marks, including the other civil rights workers in Marks and Quitman County:

Richard Arvedon	Rev. L. C. Coleman	James Jones
Willie Bolden	Darrell Fountain	Leo Martinez
Dave Bradshaw	Allan Goodner	Richard Moore
Stanford Brown	David Harris	Frank Morse
Alex Capron	Sam Jackson	Doris Newman

Kate Quinn	Lew Sitzer	Harry Swan
Alex Shimkin	R. T. Smith	Zoya Zeman
John Siegel		

and all the others whose names I don't know.

I also thank Henry Tapp and the City-Wide Sunday School Alliance of Springfield, Ohio, for providing funds for the civil rights project in Marks; and the attorneys Henry Aronson, Al Bronstein, Don Jelinek, Mel Leventhal, Len Rosenthal, Marian Wright Edelman, and others for getting us out of jail and keeping us moving forward.

Finally, there was the long process of preparing this book for publication. I would first like to thank Richard Arvedon, friend and fellow civil rights worker, and Dr. Cheryl Greenberg, historian of the civil rights movement, for transforming my original manuscript draft into this book.

Thanks also to the incredibly patient staffs of the Western New Mexico University library and the Silver City, New Mexico, public library for helping me with the mysteries of computers during the revision process; to Bill Wilson of Norman, Oklahoma, for helping me access the ancestry.com website to find information about my ancestors that I had never known, and to my cousin Nancee Shanks for copies of the wills of our ancestors Isaac Bateman and William Erwin.

And a special thanks to Susan Miller for discovering a copy of my original manuscript when I thought it had all been lost in a flood in Oklahoma.

My main happiness is that the people I worked with and lived with in Marks, most of them deceased now, many of them barely literate, have been able to reach out and tell their stories to others.

I dedicate this book to the memory of one of my coworkers, Alex Shimkin. His father, Demitri Shimkin, a colonel in military intelligence, resigned in 1964 in protest against the U.S. government's escalating war in Vietnam. At about that time Alex, twenty, worked with the Northern Student Movement doing community organizing in Detroit.

In 1965 Alex worked for voting rights with the Student Nonviolent Coordinating Committee in Selma, Alabama. From there he went to Natchez, Mississippi, and then to Marks, Mississippi, where this book tells his story as part of the movement there, much of it in his own words. After Marks he worked in Jackson and then in Holmes County, Mississippi. All this time the Vietnam War was one of his deepest concerns.

Alex went to Vietnam in 1967 as part of International Volunteer Services (IVS), a private Peace Corps–type operation in Vietnamese villages. As he wrote in his application to IVS, "I have no right to be exempt from making sacrifices overseas." He learned to speak Vietnamese. Once in Vietnam, he learned of South Vietnamese soldiers forcing villagers to remove land mines from a road with their bare hands, which caused a number of civilian casualties and deaths. Reprimanded for speaking with reporters about it, Alex left IVS.

He became a reporter for *Newsweek*. In 1971, he and Kevin Buckley, *Newsweek*'s bureau chief in Saigon, learned that during Operation Speedy Express in late 1969 in the Mekong Delta, eleven thousand enemy troops had been killed, but only seven hundred weapons taken. Alex and Kevin wondered, Could all those thousands really have been enemy soldiers?

The two interviewed U.S. pacification officials and talked with participants in the operation. They traveled through the area on foot, by Jeep, and on boats and rafts, interviewing local Vietnamese people. One American they spoke to estimated almost half of the Vietnamese who had been killed there had been noncombatants. Kevin Buckley sent the story to *Newsweek*'s New York office in December 1971. The magazine was not interested. After repeated efforts Buckley finally got *Newsweek* to run a dramatically shortened version of the story, "Pacification's Deadly Price," in June 1972.

A few weeks later Alex was killed when he and another reporter encountered a North Vietnamese unit in Quang Tri province. He was trying to explain who he was when a hand grenade landed at his feet and exploded. He was twenty-seven.

His friends remember his courage and his devotion to all oppressed people.

Cheryl

To Joe's thanks I'd like to add mine to the many archivists and activists who helped me locate documents and photos to undergird the narratives in this story, including Matt Lutts of AP Images, Phil Sutton and Rachel Mosman at the Oklahoma Historical Society (OHS), Meredith McDonough and Amelia Chase at the Alabama Department of Archives and History (ADAH)—and those who tried to find photos, even if they were unsuccessful, including Michelle Duerr from University of Memphis Special Collections, Mallory Covington and Chad Williams from the OHS, Jamie Corson at the Memphis Public Libraries, Lina Ortega at the University of Oklahoma Libraries, Professor Sarah Janda of Cameron University, Kaitlin Bain at Beaumont Enterprise, Melissa Lindberg in the Prints and Photographs Division of the Library of Congress, J. G. at the Mississippi Department of Archives and History, Trinity Library's own Jeff Liska, and Amy from Getty Images. And of course thanks to those institutions and individuals that granted permission to use materials in the book, including Roland Freeman, whose gifts are evident in every photo he took, Shutterstock, AP, OHS, ADAH, Jan Hillegas of the Freedom Information Service, and Steve Cotton of the Southern Courier Association.

My deep gratitude also to Trinity College and to Paul Raether, whose generosity in funding the chair I hold allowed me to pay for permissions and related costs of publication. The Watkinson Rare Books and Special Collections Library at Trinity is a hidden gem with wide-ranging collections that include, among its archives, some of Audobon's drawings and Robert Frost's later manuscript poems. Thanks to Eric Stoykovich and Christina Bleyer of the Watkinson, Joe's papers, including the original manuscript, have now joined those holdings.

I'd like to thank the anonymous readers who made such helpful suggestions for revisions, and the production staff of the University of Georgia Press, who, from start to finish, took such care with every aspect of the manuscript: the quality of the photographic reproduction, the thorough editing, the advertising plans, and instructions on how to best format the complex citations. The best thing about signing with the Press was the opportunity to work with Nate Holly, a prince among editors. He was simultaneously my cheerleader and my wrangler, answering every question with patience and thoughtfulness, even when the questions came multiple times a day. His generosity of spirit, enthusiasm for the project, and breadth of knowledge made this entire process a pleasure. I feel very lucky.

Without Richard Arvedon's deep dedication and hard work, especially his gentle shepherding, his willingness to take on any task, and his careful eye, Joe's remarkable manuscript could never have become a book. After Richard and Joe brought me on board, both embraced me as if I were family. They have been flexible and open in all our discussions of ideas and possibilities for the book over so many years and so many iterations. I am honored by their trust. To have had the opportunity to work with such remarkable and inspirational people as Joe and Richard, two people who live their commitment to justice, has been one of the greatest privileges of my life.

Finally, I want to thank Richard's family and mine. Debbie traveled to Marks and took notes and photos; Emma helped identify and organize photos; and Abe not only located a number of online materials but traveled all the way to the Wisconsin Historical Society to verify quotes from materials the rest of us were unable to find. The clarity and elegance of the maps are thanks to Morgan's steady hand and indefatigable investment in getting every detail right; she also helped verify quotations and statistics. In our house, "Joe's MS," the one constant on my to-do list over many years, has become a buzzword for any project we will not let go of, no matter how long it takes. Both Richard's and my families endured (and even embraced) our obsession with the project, propping us up through every frustration and enthusiastically cheering every milestone—all of them deserve thanks for that, as well as a place in heaven. Perhaps most important, if it weren't for the long friendship of Morgan and Emma, Richard and I would never have met, and I would never have been introduced to Joe and this remarkable material. From beginning to end, this transformation of a manuscript into a powerful book of struggle and hope was truly a family effort and a labor of love.

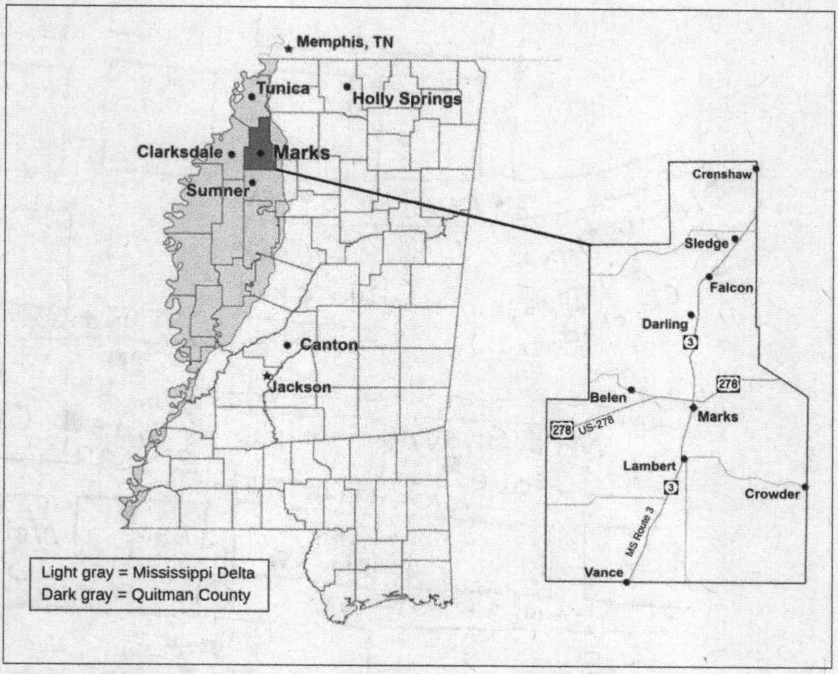

Quitman County, Mississippi.
Map by Morgan Lloyd.

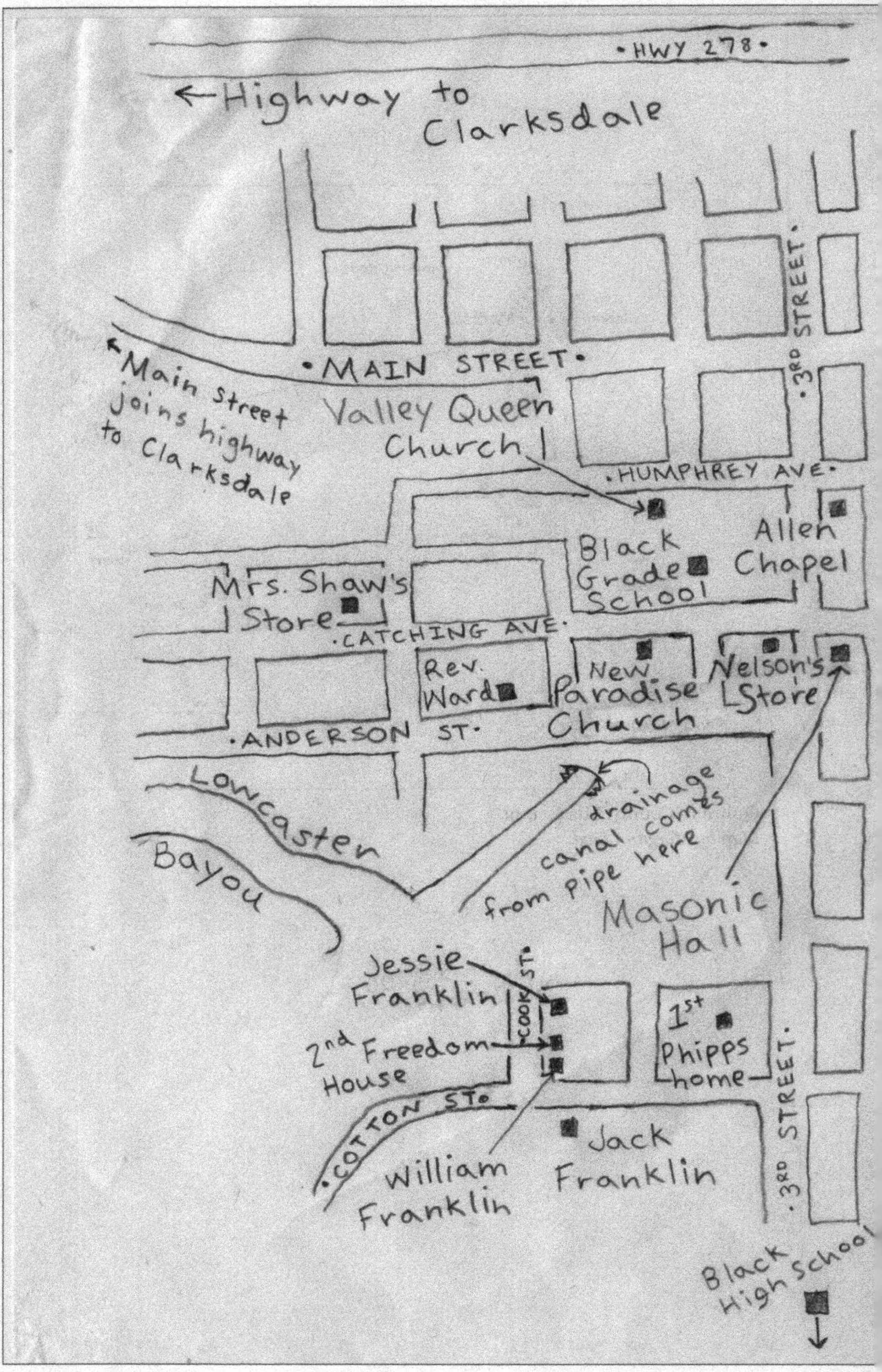

Marks as I remember it.

Map by Joe Bateman and Morgan Lloyd.

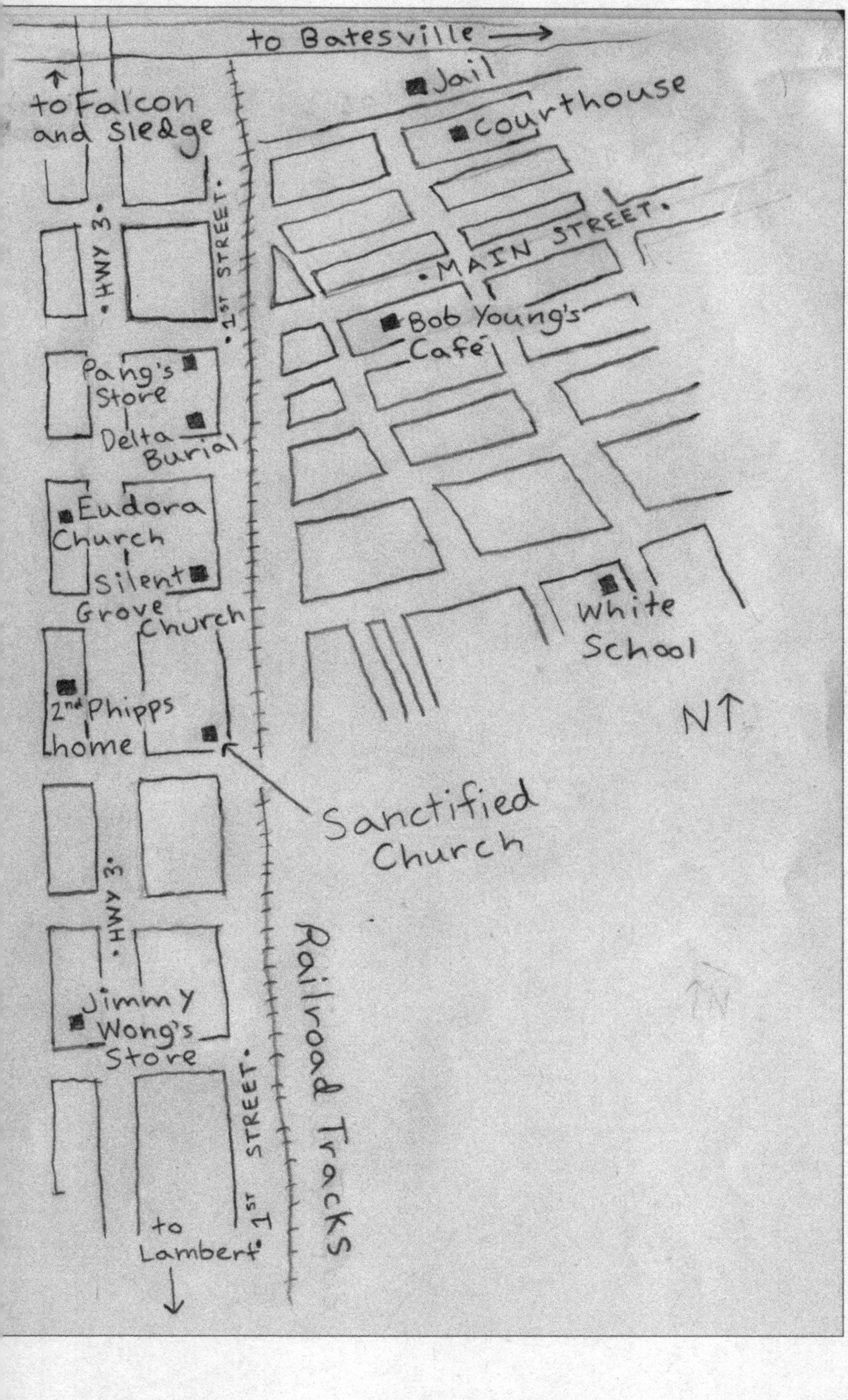

to Batesville
to Falcon and Sledge
Jail
Courthouse
HWY 3
1st STREET
MAIN STREET
Bob Young's Café
Pang's Store
Delta Burial
Eudora Church
Silent Grove Church
White School
2nd Phipps home
Sanctified Church
N
HWY 3
Jimmy Wong's Store
1st STREET
Railroad Tracks
to Lambert

A DAY I AIN'T NEVER SEEN BEFORE

INTRODUCTION

Why another book about the civil rights movement? Too often, we equate the movement with Martin Luther King Jr. or the Civil Rights Act of 1964 or the *Brown v. Board of Education* decision a decade earlier. We might also mention Rosa Parks and the Montgomery Bus Boycott or the sit-ins of the Student Nonviolent Coordinating Committee (SNCC, pronounced "snick"). They are crucially important people and episodes in the struggle for equal rights and opportunities for African Americans. But behind these names are thousands of ordinary people, Black and white, male and female, southern and northern, old and young, who provided the backbone, the spirit, and the power that brought about both the Civil Rights Act and the Montgomery Bus Boycott and challenged the nation to do more. They were the ground troops for SNCC's democratic vision and Dr. King's dream.

We might also picture the civil rights movement as Selma or the March on Washington or Birmingham sheriff Bull Connor's attack dogs. These are also pivotal moments. But behind the dramatic events at these sites are hundreds of ordinary towns and local organizations whose day-to-day struggles and protests made the movement's impact real.

This book is about those ordinary people in those ordinary towns. Rather than simply narrate his own experience, Joe Bateman, a SNCC activist in Marks, Mississippi, interviewed those he worked with, lived with, and fought with and integrated those voices directly into the story.

The result is the collective memoir of the Black community of Marks and of Joe Bateman, a white civil rights activist who worked there and developed enduring bonds with the people and the place.

One of the poorest towns in the nation, Marks, with a population of about twenty-six hundred at the time, came to national attention as the starting point for the Poor People's March in 1968. The brainchild of Marian Wright of the Southern Christian Leadership Conference (SCLC) and enthusiastically embraced by Dr. King (who was assassinated just before it began), the march was intended to focus the nation's attention on poverty and its intersection with race by winding a mule-drawn caravan of people to the nation's capital. There, housed in tents on the National Mall, poor people would speak to politicians and to the nation about their travails.

Marks, a relatively unknown, deeply poor, largely Black rural community, was the perfect place to begin that march. But it was chosen also because its activism had reached the ears of SCLC planners. In other words, Marks was important both for its absence from any spotlight and for its ongoing political engagement.

Joe hadn't intended to go there in 1964; he knew nothing about the town except that it was "rough." Once in Marks he discovered an active if quiet struggle for dignity, opportunity, and civic equality that had paralleled and occasionally intersected with regional and national efforts. Encouraged by Mississippi Freedom Summer in 1964 and the resulting Mississippi Freedom Democratic Party (MFDP) organization, the movement in Marks gained strength and momentum and faced increasing white resistance—again engaging with, but separate from, the larger movement unfolding around it. Marks activists might organize community members to pressure local officials for sewer lines one day and confer with Justice Department lawyers the next. The slow, frustrating, dangerous, exhilarating, and tedious progress of those struggles is recounted here in the words of Marks residents and activists, as they talked with Joe during and after those heady movement days.

That intersection of the local and the national gives this story much of its structure. Neither the civil rights movement nor the Black community of Marks have sharply delineated beginnings, but Jim Crow segregation, an exploitative sharecropping system, educational inequality, and political and social restrictions were firmly in place by the turn of the twentieth century. By the 1930s local activists, sometimes through the National Association for the Advancement of Colored People (NAACP) or other national organizations, worked on voter registration projects, fought for New Deal benefits, and identified educational and economic inequalities, working mostly in secret to avoid white retaliation. Although the 1954 *Brown v. Board of Education* decision ended school segregation in theory, white leaders in Marks and Quitman County, like most in the rest of the South, resisted integration with a combination of creative work-arounds and violence. In Mississippi, white resistance also led to the creation of the Mississippi State Sovereignty Commission, initially to prevent school integration and later to investigate (and undermine) civil rights activity and activists.

Not only did Marks residents know about the vigilante killing in Mississippi of young Black Chicagoan Emmett Till in 1955, local ministers brought many community members to the trial. Although the accused men were acquitted, for most it was the first time in memory that white people went on trial for killing a Black person. The event both reminded Black southerners of the risks of activism and offered hope for progress.

Marks residents also knew of the Montgomery Bus Boycott that began later that year, although both fear and the lack of a bus system made a similar local campaign unlikely. But the student sit-in movement that began in Greensboro, North Carolina, in 1960 (and that became SNCC) led some young people in Marks to attempt to desegregate a local restaurant—which resulted in arrests and white violence.

SNCC focused also on voter registration, arguing that in the South, voting was both the path to power and a potent form of organizing. Meanwhile, especially in farm areas like the Mississippi Delta, mechanization offered a way for white landowners to maintain political power by shrinking their Black sharecropping labor force and dispossessing Black farmers.

By 1963 a new movement strategy had emerged: parallel institutionalism, which organized nonracist but otherwise identical political structures to those already in place, to demonstrate that the Black community was prepared for true democratic participation and to highlight the evils of white supremacy. An MFDP apparatus was set up to mirror the lily-white Mississippi Democratic Party and ran an integrated slate of candidates in a mock election. In 1964, the MFDP formally nominated delegates to the party's national convention to replace the regular party's all-white slate, and the Council of Federated Organizations

(COFO), an umbrella group of civil rights groups, invited activists to come to Mississippi and organize voters. Called Freedom Summer (or the Mississippi Summer Project), the event drew hundreds of northern and southern activists, mostly young college students of all races. Trained in nonviolence, these organizers established Freedom Schools to teach literacy and history and to raise awareness of systemic white supremacy. They led marches and demonstrations and went door-to-door to bring the movement to the people. Often focused in the larger towns, COFO paid less attention to places like Marks. But a few volunteers looking for such sidelined communities, like Joe, waded in, only to discover that local folks had been quietly organizing all along.

The Democratic National Convention refused to seat the MFDP delegation, despite the party's position (and a 1946 Supreme Court decision) against segregated primaries. This decision infuriated many civil rights activists, who viewed this as a betrayal. It provoked many to rethink liberal integration efforts and move toward empowering Black people as an independent power base, which they called Black Power.

While Black Power ideology created rifts in the movement over the role of white workers, many white activists on the ground, like Joe, continued their work in Black communities. There was plenty still to do: continuing the struggle to register voters and integrate local schools, organizing new local programs through President Lyndon Johnson's War on Poverty, fighting for promised welfare benefits, or marching from Selma to Montgomery for voting rights. These local and national events were interconnected—hearing of white violence elsewhere, local activists might organize a protest, which would result in confrontations at home. A student might travel to James Meredith's March Against Fear (to encourage Black voter registration) and be tear-gassed by state troopers, which might radicalize her to become more active locally. A court decision in one town or state launched similar cases elsewhere.

The challenges and achievements of this struggle are told here in the words of participants. This is not the celebratory story of unity we have come to expect. In their own voices, Joe and Marks's Black (and some white) residents describe class divisions, political and ideological conflicts, apathy, and doubt within the community, as well as confrontations with the white power structures outside it. Neither the Black nor the white community was of one mind about either the movement or any particular tactic or goal.

Still, certain overarching themes emerge: the visible inhumanity with which so many whites treated Black and poor people; the universal desire of the Black community for equal opportunity and equal treatment; the willingness of so many to struggle to win that equality, whether openly or in secret; the importance of small communities and largely unknown people to the larger movement; and the fundamental decency of so many who risked everything to help one another and build a better life. And one more rather provocative theme: that the racial binary of white and Black has more to do with ways of thinking and behaving than skin color. When Marks's Black residents insist that Joe is not white, they offer all of us a different sense of how race can be understood.

The last chapters of the book explore the aftermath of the civil rights movement in Marks. Again, the successes and the continued challenges are laid bare as we see greater (but not full) racial equality against the backdrop of ever-bleaker economic realities. Today most Black and white people in Marks have similar opportunities—for unemployment and poverty and the problems that come with them. Yet the commitment of Marks's Black community to build bonds of trust and support, to provide for their families, and to live with decency and integrity is undiminished. The spirit of Marks is the spirit of the civil rights movement, past and present.

—Cheryl Lynn Greenburg

PROLOGUE

Marks Spreads Its Wings

I was back in Marks, Mississippi, where I had been a civil rights worker from 1964 to 1966. Now it was 1975. As I walked through the Black section of Marks, I met up with Rev. Lillian Bobo, a tall woman who preached in several churches in the area. She pointed to the bright-colored, low-cost houses built recently with federal aid, just beyond the shacks where most Black people in Marks still lived. Then she smiled and said, "You see how Marks done spread its wings, ain't it?"

Marks is in the Delta country—a long triangle of almost perfectly flat land between the Mississippi River on the west, the Tallahatchie and Yazoo Rivers on the east, and the Tennessee line to the north.

The people of the Delta are mostly Black. Until the 1960s most of them lived in semi-serfdom on the large cotton plantations. The population has been declining for decades as plantations have mechanized and Black laborers, no longer needed, have migrated to northern cities. Those who stayed behind suffer high unemployment rates. Even today, there is malnutrition among their children.

Marks is the seat of Quitman County, "a stone plantation county," my coworker Alex Shimkin once called it. The county is an extreme example of Delta conditions, with one of the lowest Black median incomes, one of the highest rates of Black unemployment, and one of the highest rates of Black out-migration in the state.

Black people in Marks kept an underground civil rights movement going until Freedom Summer in 1964 when civil rights workers came from outside and the local movement came out in the open. For a long time, statewide civil rights organizations thought of Marks as a low-priority, isolated outpost. A group of Freedom Summer volunteers and SNCC staff went to Marks late that summer, almost as an afterthought. Although James Jones of the Clarksdale SNCC staff in nearby Coahoma County had been in touch with movement leaders in Marks for several months before Freedom Summer, these leaders were almost unknown statewide. Some, like Mr. Franklin and Mrs. Weathersby, were absolutely unknown.

Partly this is because there was such a gap between the poor Black residents of Quitman County and the Black leadership in Clarksdale. Aaron Henry, state head of the NAACP, lived in Clarksdale. He had a pharmacy degree and owned a drugstore in the Black business district. Other leading members of the local NAACP were of similar status. This meant they were very different from the great majority of Black people in Marks.

For example, the week I spent in Clarksdale, I stayed with Mr. and Mrs. Gray. While their home might be modest by the standards of many Americans, it was far ahead of most Black homes in Marks. I paid them ten dollars for lodging. All civil rights workers were expected to pay their host families. In Marks, in contrast, no Black person ever asked me to pay anything. In fact, Alec Dean told me he gave money to civil rights workers staying with him because they had so little. Mr. Dean had not fully paid for his house, so he went several years without electricity to afford the payments. He also had a grandson with a severe thyroid condition living with him and his wife. Mr. and Mrs. Dean could not afford to treat their grandson until the Johnson administration made Medicaid available to poor people in 1965. I believe this class difference is one reason Marks, unlike Clarksdale, had received so little attention from national civil rights groups. Civil rights workers in Marks had the psychology of a small garrison surrounded by hostile whites.

Then, in 1968, just before his death, Martin Luther King Jr. and the Southern Christian Leadership Conference picked Marks as the starting point for its Poor People's Campaign Mule Train to Washington, D.C., because Quitman County had the poorest Black population in Mississippi. For a brief time, Marks had national publicity. Federal programs began to raise the living standard. Then the Nixon administration's cutback of federal aid took away some of the gains the Black people of Marks had won. But they continued to advance slowly and (usually) quietly. They made gains no one can take away from them: greater knowledge of the outside world and how to organize for what they need.

This little town in an impoverished county, with a declining population (Marks lost about 40 percent of its population between 1970 and 2000), and other small southern towns like it have always been important as a home base for groups of Black kinfolk trying to make a living in the North. Now it is more important than ever as so many unemployed Black people are moving back to the South.

I am white and from Oklahoma. Before the Civil War, some of my ancestors were slave owners in Montgomery County, Mississippi, where one hundred years later Mrs. Fannie Lou Hamer would be put in jail in Winona, the county seat. After I had been in Marks a few months, Black people would talk more freely in my presence than they would around most whites. Mrs. Mary Jones, a woman active in the movement, once said, "Well, we all know you can't trust a white person."

I said, "Well, you've said a lot of things around me."

She stared at me and said sharply, "You ain't white! You ain't white!"

Yet I don't begin to understand all about the Black community of Marks. Especially when people talked about the old plantation days, I could only write down what they told me and remember that, as Jessie James Franklin of Marks said to me, "If you ain't been through the motions of a thing, you can't believe it."

I understand what he meant. Mrs. Ora Bea Phipps told me about the work songs she heard in her youth and how hard it is for us to know what lay behind them. "The prisoners used to sing when they was working on the roads. That was back when they was killing the prisoners right and left. The gangs that worked on the railroad would sing the same way. They would all go "Whah!" and come down with them irons straightening the track. I would hear them many a time when we was working in the field along where the track run. They would sing anything like:

> See that gal if she was mine
> She wouldn't do nothing but wash and iron.

And they would sort of make a rhythm for their work singing, but you don't hear them singing no more. I see the whites pattern after the Blacks and the Blacks pattern after the whites, but it takes someone who been under that stress to sing about it. Someone else don't know what it's all about, what it really means, even if they do try to pattern after it."

My Family, Myself, and Why I Went to Marks

One piece of good fortune my brother and I and many other people from old southern families have is a quality I call resonance: connectedness to a past and to a related present. Dr. Demitri Shimkin, the father of my civil rights colleague Alex Shimkin, wrote of listening to a Black teenage girl in Holmes County, Mississippi, reel off the names of over one hundred relatives. My family kept track of these things as well, and the resonance between past and present is everywhere.

My maternal grandmother's maternal grandmother was Kate Birdsong, born in 1850. So my great-great-grandmother is probably related to T. M. Birdsong, the Mississippi commissioner of public safety in 1966. He was in command of the highway patrolmen who tear-gassed civil rights supporters that year on the March Against Fear at Canton, Mississippi. Some of the people in this book were gassed in that incident.

My great-grandfather was born in 1860 and was one-fourth Cherokee. In the 1920 census he was counted as white. In the 1930 census he was counted as Indian. My grandfather grew up in what is now Oklahoma before it became a state. The eastern part was still Indian Territory containing the Cherokee, Choctaw, Chickasaw, Creek, and Seminole Nations. In 1907, the tribal land was incorporated into the new state of Oklahoma. Most of the land went to whites.

The earliest ancestor on my father's side that I know of is Jonathan Bateman, who came to Virginia from England in 1671 as an indentured servant. At the end of his indenture he moved to Tyrell County, North Carolina. By 1833 the Bateman family had slaves: two men, Peter and Thomas, and a woman named Clou. Jonathan's descendant, my great-grandfather Joe Bateman, married Harriet Holtzman. Her great-grandfather was William Erwin, who owned slaves. It is strange to read William Erwin's 1815 will in which he disposes of seven human beings and some furniture in a few sentences. Less than fifty years later, William Erwin's grandson was killed fighting to preserve this slave society. In 1965, 150 years after William Erwin wrote his will, I was in jail for a civil rights demonstration in Marks, and I am his great-great-great-great grandson. In 2009, a Black man became president. His wife and daughters are the descendants of slaves. They lived in the White House, which was built by slaves.

In 1918, my grandfather Bateman married Fay Baker. Her great-grandmother owned two slaves, Brit and Kit. Brit and Kit had three children, a son named Pierce and two daughters, Louisa and Rainey. I knew my great-grandmother, who remembered her grandmother. So in my lifetime a relative knew my slave-owning ancestor. I lay awake one night thinking how close the world of slavery was to me.

I do not feel guilt that I am the descendant of slave owners, but the shadow of slavery still falls over me and over most southerners, Black and white. A white friend of mine once said he thought whites in the civil rights movement were "fighting someone else's battles," but I think I fought not only to help free Black people but also to help lift the burden of history off southern white people—to free myself from a whole set of institutions for racial control that was very oppressive for all of us, white and Black. As just one example, racial attitudes and the whole set of institutions for racial control kept all southern workers out of labor unions and kept wages lower there than in the rest of the country. There were plenty of southern whites who saw this as well. At the SDS projects and the New York SNCC office, I met many who had in effect been exiled from their homes because of their support for the movement.

This brings me to my own life and the world I grew up in. I was born in Duncan, Oklahoma, in 1942. Ten miles away were the little towns of Comanche and Marlow, where Blacks couldn't stay after sundown. In 1923, when my mother was an infant, a hotel owner in Marlow hired a Black man to carry luggage and sweep the place. A mob killed both the Black man and the hotel owner.

I was in my first demonstration in April 1961. I was visiting Chicago when I encountered supporters welcoming the San Francisco–Moscow Peace Walk. I followed the marchers to a hotel where A. J. Muste, the grand old man of American pacifism, spoke. I ended up on their mailing list, which meant I also got on the mailing lists of a dozen different organizations. One of these was the Student Peace Union.

That same week my parents got divorced. My father was strongly opposed to my civil rights efforts. My mother identified as a political conservative and would not think of herself as a feminist. Even so, in 1966 my mother had to leave Duncan, in part because after I was arrested for civil rights activity in Mississippi she started getting threatening phone calls late at night. Dr. Shimkin said people know about the hardships civil rights workers endured, but no one talks about what their parents went through.

I had been reading about the peace movement and the civil rights movement and a new organization, Students for a Democratic Society (SDS). I was very excited by all of it. I was at the University of Oklahoma in Norman, where ROTC was compulsory for two years. I flunked my last semester of ROTC and didn't want to take it over. I dropped out of college and went to Chicago to work with the Student Peace Union. Most of the people I met there were in the Young People's Socialist League, and I began to think of myself as a socialist too. I returned to Norman later that spring to enroll for summer courses and attended the founding meeting of the school's SDS chapter on May Day 1963. All these organizations were interconnected, and many of us moved freely between them.

My first civil rights activity was a sit-in at an Oklahoma City amusement park that refused to admit Black patrons. We were arrested but released within a few hours. The sit-in was led by Clara Luper, a Black schoolteacher and local NAACP leader. She had started her sit-ins in 1958, two years before the sit-ins in Greensboro, North Carolina that launched the Student Nonviolent Coordinating Committee.

In December 1963, the SDS national newsletter described the upcoming Mississippi Summer project, and I decided to apply. I wanted to do something with my life, and I didn't have anything to stay in Oklahoma for. I was accepted and went to Jackson, Mississippi, to the office of the Council of Federated Organizations (COFO), the civil rights coalition running the Summer Project.

COFO continued my political education. Even before the Summer Project, COFO workers, Black and white, were becoming economically radicalized. I remember Emmy Shrader, a white woman who worked in the Jackson office, saying, "People are not talking as much about integration any more, as social revolution." Any civil rights worker in Mississippi at the time, seeing the conditions there, could agree.

I went to the Mississippi Summer Project orientation in Oxford,

Ohio. While I was there my father called the orientation office saying that if I went down to Mississippi he would come down there after me "with some Oklahomans who really know how to integrate." Three civil rights workers, Mickey Schwerner, James Chaney, and Andrew Goodman, had already disappeared near Philadelphia, Mississippi. We all believed that they had been killed, and security concerns were all-important. Dottie Zellner, a white SNCC worker, told me I could not go to Mississippi that summer. So instead I headed south to work on a union organizing campaign in Kentucky. Before I arrived there, though, the sheriff's department had shut the campaign down. I spent a few weeks in the national SDS office in Chicago and then hitchhiked to New York City in August 1964 to work in the SNCC office. SNCC was one of the main groups behind the Summer Project.

All of us from the SNCC office went to Atlantic City, New Jersey, in the third week of August for the Democratic National Convention. We were there to demonstrate for the MFDP delegation to be seated as the legitimate delegation from Mississippi. Black people had tried to attend precinct meetings of the all-white regular Democratic Party of Mississippi in the early summer, but they were not admitted. So they organized their own Freedom Democratic Party and held their own precinct meetings. There they elected delegates to an MFDP state convention, which chose delegates for the Democratic National Convention. Of sixty-eight delegates, four were white. One of them, Bob Williams, was a former Klansman from Biloxi. The MFDP argued that it, not the segregated traditional delegation, was the only representative of all Mississippi Democrats.

We demonstrated in support of the MFDP all day and all night every day of the convention. If we got tired we were allowed to sit on the boardwalk but not to sleep there. Instead we were taken in shifts to a church to sleep in the pews. But there were so many of us that I only got one shift sleeping on a hard wooden pew. After a few hours, other activists came banging on the pews, and we had to get up and go back to the boardwalk. Although I probably ate something that week, all I remember were the cans of soda pop from Women's Strike for Peace, who were picketing at the convention for nuclear disarmament.

Many of the MFDP delegates had risked their lives to take part in the political process. One of them was Fannie Lee Chaney, mother of James Chaney, the twenty-two-year-old civil rights worker whose body, with Schwerner's and Goodman's, had been found in Mississippi just the week before. I stood in the picket line next to twelve-year-old Ben Chaney, who was holding a large picture of his murdered brother.

But President Johnson was unwilling to seat the MFDP delegation. He feared that doing so would provoke several southern Democratic delegations to walk out of the convention and that he might then lose these states in the November election.

One MFDP delegate, Fannie Lou Hamer of Sunflower County, testified before the convention's Credentials Committee on national TV. On June 11, 1963, she recounted, she, Euvester Simpson, James West, Annelle Ponder, June Johnson, and Rosemary Freeman were on a bus returning from a voter-registration conference. They refused to sit in the back of the bus, and in Winona the sheriff put them in jail. Annelle Ponder was beaten because she would not call the sheriff "sir." Mrs. Hamer was severely beaten because Sunflower officials told the sheriff she was an agitator. Euvester Simpson shared a cell with Mrs. Hamer. She applied cold towels to Mrs. Hamer's bruises and swellings, afraid Mrs. Hamer might not revive. As it was, Mrs. Hamer never recovered fully.

This happened in Montgomery County, Mississippi, where my great-great grandfather had grown up in a slave-owning family. Almost one hundred years before Mrs. Hamer was beaten, in order to have his citizenship restored after the Civil War, he had taken an oath to support the U.S. Constitution. At the Democratic convention of 1964, Lyndon Johnson, the head of that same U.S. government, called a hasty press conference in the middle of Mrs. Hamer's testimony with the deliberate aim of getting her off TV.

Johnson told Senator Hubert Humphrey of Minnesota that if he wanted to be vice president he had to get the MFDP and the all-white Mississippi delegation to accept a compromise. In a passionate speech to the 1948 Democratic convention, Humphrey had declared, "I do not believe that there can be any compromise on the guarantees of . . . civil rights . . . The time has arrived in America for the Democratic party to get out of the shadows of states' rights and to walk forthrightly into the bright sunshine of human rights."[1] But in 1964 Humphrey offered the MFDP two "delegates at large" who would sit with the Illinois delegation. The other MFDP delegates would be "observers" sitting in the visitors' gallery.

Unanimously the MFDP delegates refused. Senator Humphrey persuaded the MFDP's lawyer, the well-known white liberal Joseph Rauh, to urge them to take the two "at large" seats. The MFDP then fired Rauh. Mrs. Lula Belle Johnson, one of the MFDP delegates, pointed to the sky and told me, "Our only lawyer is up there." One of the demonstrators for the MFDP, a white youth who had spent the summer as a civil rights volunteer in Mississippi, started singing new words to a civil rights song: "Ain't gonna let no phony liberals turn me 'round."

Senator Humphrey told the all-white Mississippi delegation that they could be seated if they would swear to support Johnson for president instead of Goldwater and admit Blacks to their delegations at future conventions. Most of them refused and walked out.

Bob Williams, the red-headed former Klansman, stood beside Black SNCC staffer Stokely Carmichael. Both of them were hollering at a group of delegates entering the convention hall. Stokely shouted, "These segregationists from Mississippi have more integrity than you do! I hope Goldwater wins so you can find out what we have to go through in Mississippi!" I went up to Stokely. He was the director for civil rights projects in the Mississippi Delta. I asked him if I could go to work that fall in one of those projects. He said yes. As soon as the convention demonstrations were over, I hitchhiked straight to Holly Springs, Mississippi.

Nothing much was going on in Holly Springs, so Pete Brett and Steve Sokoloff, two white volunteers, gave me a ride to Clarksdale, one of the largest towns in the Delta. Nothing much seemed to be happening in Clarksdale either. Late one afternoon I met up with Dave Bradshaw and Dick Moore, two white civil rights workers who worked in the project in Marks, seventeen miles away. They told me Marks was a rough place and said they had to go back north in a couple of days. I was captivated by the idea of taking their place in a difficult town, and Bradshaw and Moore took me back to Marks with them. When they left, I stayed where they had been, with Rev. G. W. Ward and his wife Sarah. Later that fall I moved in with William Franklin and his family. Mr. Franklin had a profound influence on me. He showed me the potential of people in the most difficult circumstances.

Early the next year, John Siegel, a white civil rights worker, and I moved back in with Reverend Ward and Mrs. Ward. In February we learned that the United States had begun a massive bombing campaign against North Vietnam. The Vietnam War radicalized me. I became convinced the war was wrong, but most Americans still supported it.

That summer I began attending antiwar rallies in Oklahoma, and I remember the terrible feeling of aloneness we had.

I returned to Marks, Mississippi, that fall. Alex Shimkin showed up there as a civil rights worker in early 1966. That spring Alex and I were working to get a Head Start program for Quitman County from the same Johnson administration that was devastating Vietnam. Both of us felt strange about it.

Now that this country has gone so far right that liberals are called "the Left," I think it is important to remember the break with liberalism that Vietnam forced on activists of my generation. We had been badly shaken by Johnson's failure to seat the MFDP. The escalation in Vietnam was the final blow. In 1966 I left Mississippi because I wanted to do something against the Vietnam War.

Being a civil rights worker could be very tiresome at times, but for me it was the most educational and personally satisfying experience of my life. For thirty years or so after I left Mississippi I would travel back to Marks to visit people and talk with them. My coworker Richard Arvedon visited in 2015, and I remain in contact with some of those I knew there. But this book isn't just about my experiences as a civil rights worker. It is really about the people of Marks and the lives they lived, how they engaged with the civil rights movement, and the differences they made.

PART I

BEFORE THE MOVEMENT

CHAPTER 1

"God Promised You a Living and a Killing"

One day in 1975 I was standing in front of Jimmie's Grocery in Marks listening to Willie Thomas, a Black man nearly seventy. He was bemoaning the hard times—prices so high, and you couldn't raise your own vegetables and hogs like you could when people lived on the plantations during the Great Depression. And everything was so cheap in the 1930s.

"Was it better back then?" I asked.

He looked at me like I had lost my mind.

"No!" he said. "That was when we was under the white man!"

Origins

For many older Black people in Marks, slavery was not a condition that had been ended by the Civil War. I often heard phrases like, "Back in slavery time around 1930—"

"I been a slave," William Franklin of Marks told officials in Washington at the Poor People's March of 1968. When I came to Marks in 1964, most Black adults knew someone born into slavery. Many of the elderly were the children or grandchildren of legally enslaved people. They recognized the continuities between the pre–Civil War days and the sharecropping days that came later. The last slave owner in Quitman County died in 1935. Until his death, Black people addressed him as Mahz, and they still referred to him that way in the 1970s. In 1964, while organizing, David Harris and I met a formerly enslaved man in the all-Black community of Falcon twenty miles north of Marks. He signed up to participate in the Freedom Vote that fall.

Words used in slavery times still survived. A Black man giving me a ride from Clarksdale to Marks pointed to the brick homes for the faculty of all-Black Coahoma Junior College as we passed by. "You see the new quarters there?" he asked. It was still common to hear a Black woman say "I got five head of children," from the time masters valued slaves as human cattle.

Jack Brown, ninety years old when I spoke with him, remembered those times: "It was slavery when I was born in 1885, but they had eased up a bit. My father was a Black soldier in the Civil War. He was on a plantation, but the Yankees put him in the navy. He say he got tired of what he was doing to people, so he run away from the navy. He used to sit me down and tell me about it.

"He was about eighty when he died. I was about sixteen. I remember I was plowing. I found out he was dying when I was in the middle of a row.

"I lived on the Buckhalter place—bred and born there, married there, children born there. It was a small plantation, about ten or twelve families. It look like we got by pretty nice. 'Course in them times you had to be satisfied with what they give you. If you wasn't, you had to make out like you was. I've done that a lot of times, made out like I was satisfied when I wasn't. I minded it, but I had to do it in them times. White people been nice to me all my life. I seen them beat a lot of colored people up.

"We raised all our food: hogs and things, our bread and everything. Money went for clothes and coffee and sugar. We got money once a year. That was when they settle with you when they clear your crop. But we didn't get it all. We ain't getting it all today."[1]

The history of Marks, and of the region, is embedded in discrimination. The Choctaws were the original inhabitants. In the 1830s, the U.S. government forced most of them to move west to Indian Territory—now Oklahoma—to make room for whites and their slaves. A few Mississippi Choctaws received land allotments in Neshoba County and established a reservation there.

Alec Dean's family were Choctaws who moved back from Oklahoma to Mississippi in the early 1900s. He lived in Marks until his death in

1979. His wife Elnora was a Black woman. "My daddy was a Choctaw," Alec told me. "My mama's mama was a full-blooded Choctaw, but her daddy was a Nassau, a mixed nation." "Nassau" was a word usually used for a West Indian, but Mr. Dean probably meant he was of mixed racial ancestry.

"He had straight hair in front like mine, but bad hair behind where it was coarse. He was part African. I don't believe I'm on the tribal roll. It's a heap of Indians ain't on the roll. The difference between one nation and another is just the color. You bleed just as red as me. A man's a man, and a woman's a woman, I don't care what nation they are. We all the same."

The town of Marks had its own history of racism. It was named for Leopold Marks, a German-Jewish immigrant who had arrived in New York in 1868 penniless at age seventeen. In the early 1870s Marks took a boat up and down the rivers of Mississippi's Delta country selling goods. He bought land where Marks is now at forty cents an acre but had difficulty getting it registered as a town site because he was Jewish. (Marks was not officially incorporated until 1907, three years before he died.) He built a store to serve the tiny community and at twenty-five became the first representative in the state legislature from newly organized Quitman County, a 412-square-mile area in the northwestern part of the state.[2]

Quitman County was named for John Anthony Quitman, a general in the Mexican War of 1846–48, a war supported by slavery interests and opposed by a freshman congressman named Abraham Lincoln. Quitman, originally from upstate New York, owned a plantation and slaves near Natchez, Mississippi. He became governor of Mississippi, and, after he died on a visit to Washington, D.C., in 1858, there were rumors he had been poisoned by abolitionists.[3]

Marks became Quitman's county seat in 1906 although it remained small—670 people in 1910, 1,258 in 1930.[4] Many came after a 1927 flood devastated the nearby town of Belen, settling around Leopold Marks's (and later his son Sammy's) store. Beatrice Humphreys remembers that when she came as a child with her family they first found shelter from the flood at the Silent Grove Baptist Church, still one of the largest Black churches in Marks. Another person who came from Belen seeking refuge was a young white man named Billy Turner who would, as justice of the peace in 1964, send me to jail.

Most of the county was forest. Beginning around 1900, large numbers of Black settlers began moving from other parts of Mississippi into the Delta to clear farms there. That first year of the new century, 5,435 people lived in the county. Ten years later that number had doubled, and by 1920 the population had reached almost 20,000. In the second year of the Depression, the census reported 25,304 residents, a number that remained roughly the same through the 1950s.[5]

The great majority of those African Americans who moved to Quitman and other Delta counties in the early twentieth century came in the ultimately futile hope that they would have land of their own and thus control of their own lives. Although more Black than white people owned farms in the county, white-owned farms were, on average, much larger.[6]

Mississippi had made it illegal to teach enslaved people to read, and that same desire by whites to keep Black people ignorant lasted past the Civil War. Well into the twentieth century, segregated Black schools never had enough funding, enough textbooks, enough teachers, or a long enough school year. Many Delta planters didn't like their sharecroppers going to school at all. Black people were kept from voting by literacy tests and poll taxes, so whites controlled the political and legal systems.

Since they were often illiterate and always legally helpless, African Americans were cheated and intimidated out of their land by whites who set up the usual southern plantation system. In the Hills region, the rolling country east of the Delta, many Black families continued to own small farms. But the soil there is poor, and soon there were too many people for the land to support.[7] Many moved to the Delta and became sharecroppers or day laborers on white people's plantations. More than 80 percent of Black people engaged in farming in those years were tenant farmers or sharecroppers.[8]

The planter was the source of almost all that could pass for legal authority, and he used it to keep his sharecroppers working as hard as physically possible. Some families were so poor they could not even afford to take care of their own children and had to send them to white families' homes to be servants or to tend the whites' children.

These conditions lasted into the 1960s, when I first arrived as an organizer. When I came back in 1975 to ask them about their early lives, there was no strident outrage and little bitterness in their voices. Yet there was great feeling. Sometimes they laughed—deep, sure laughter. Through their voices you heard strong people who adapted themselves to the system when they saw no choice but were ready to struggle against it when they found the opportunity. Many of these people with the tradition of the independent Hill farmers later became leaders in the civil rights movement.

Every family has a different story, but they all reflect the struggle to survive. William Franklin, born in 1913, told me his story. "My daddy broke away from there in Kosciusko in the Hills 'cause he couldn't raise cotton. The Hills was bad then—forty acres of land, and he couldn't raise but two bales of cotton. We moved to the Delta when I was a year old.

"You search and you'll find Negroes borned in the Hills, they ain't dependent on the white man like in the Delta. A Negro borned in the Delta, he's dependent on the white man and he'll help him out. It's like childrens raised by two different daddies.

"We come to Hushpuckena in Bolivar County in the Delta. Put up some years on one white man's place. And they run us off because my daddy tried to send us to school. They told my daddy they didn't bring us here to go to school. They brought us here for to work. So we moved to another place where they let us go to school three months. But we didn't go much. We had to cut corn stalks, break ground, cut cotton stalks. We went to school about one-and-a-half months a year in a old church house. My daddy kept the oldest ones at home to work and let the youngest go to school. The reason some of us have what education we got is their daddy when he got a good crop in, he'd have enough money to send his child to stay with his brother or cousin in Chicago and go to school there. That's how my brother Jack's wife got what education she got, slipping away up there."

William's brother, Jessie Franklin, took up the story. "My daddy said the Negro come here first. He told me the white man come here walking. He didn't have nothing, but he had a better education. He put a hat on his head and told the Negro to call him Mr. So-and-so: Mr. Ike and Mr. John. And the Negro did it.

"My daddy learned me how to work in the field and take care of cattle. Didn't no white man learn me. So the white man didn't like me 'cause when he come to me and told me, 'Do it so,' I'd say, 'I can't do it that way. My daddy told me to do it this way,' and I'd wait for my daddy to come. He was my boss man.

"Education ain't everything, but it's good to have. If you and me both got education, I can't spend your money and you can't spend my money. We'll have to look for some fool we can both live off of. The song say,

'This is a mean old world to live in.' And the stone's in your road till it looks lonesome. And the big wheels want to be your father. God ain't pleased with that."

"I born in 1900," Jack Franklin told me. He was the oldest of the Franklin brothers. "It was amazing, all that journey through different things. I remember when the houses was built of logs. They had a chimney made of sticks. Somebody told me some day I would see a tractor in the air, and that's the airplane. And it would be a tractor going on the road, and that's a car. We called a T-model Ford a T-Mammy.

"My father's father was under slave. My mother's father was a white man working on the railroad, but they put the poor white under like they did the Black. They rung a bell in the morning for you to go in the field, and they rung a bell at night for you to come out. If you didn't want to go to the field, they kill you and put you in the hole. I drove mules and oxen all over this country. You had to tie a piece of ribbon to your mule's tail to see him in the morning. And the white man was waiting on the fence, waiting to see you come out.

"I can't see why one man want to run the world by his self. Where do hatred come from? What do they have against colored people? I think it's like the big rich folks. You white, I'm colored, and we can work together. I *think*. People say, 'That old n——, he don't think nothing,' but ain't no n——. Jesus didn't make no two bloods. Jesus didn't make no two fleshes. Jesus made one blood."

Alec Dean told a similar story. "My father brought me here from Indian Territory when I was a baby. He come to Cruger, Mississippi, in Holmes County and built the first steam gin there. The gin at Cruger, it was a mule gin before. The mule went round and round, kind of like a molasses mill. You had to stomp the cotton lint down like you stomp the cotton in the wagon when you pick it now. Then you tie it up with a rope to make the bale. You didn't have no strop like you do now to make the bale.

"My mama was a herb doctor. I took sick when the big flu epidemic come in World War I, but she cured me and many a sick person.

"I always worked hard for what I got. I didn't never have a tater already peeled. I had to grow it and peel it. I drove one of the first kinds of tractor they had when I was twelve years old. It was a Forster.[9] They didn't use it to cultivate, just break ground and pull stumps. They used coal oil instead of gasoline and castor oil to oil the machine.

"I went to school when they had schools in the church houses. I kept going till I got promoted to third grade, and I had to quit to take care of my mama. I had to get a job. Back then jobs was plentiful. I have picked cotton for two bits a hundred pounds. I have worked for a dollar a day from sunup to sundown. 'Course that was a long time ago, and I done come out of that. I don't let nobody pull my eye tooth—that means go into debt."

Gilbert Hamer, born in 1910, added his own description of life during Marks's early years. "If he ain't above twenty year old, he don't know nothing about them plantations. But them forty-year-old and fifty-year-old, they can tell you so much about it, how it's a whole new world here.

"Black folks drifted on down here when this was wasteland, just a path in the woods with a shack here and there. It was a forest with bears and panthers. Many a Black man lose his life cleaning land. These white folks just took land. You know no one man can buy seven thousand acres of land. They took it. I know plenty of colored folks had land when the land was first cleant up. Black people cleant it up with axes, and the white folks took it. You see every white man around here that's rich, he made it off the Black man, and now they say we lazy. Anybody lazy that ain't getting enough for what he doing. I know so many colored people and poor white people raised forty or fifty bale of cotton, and the rich man took it all. You never raised forty or fifty bale of cotton without going into debt. It's a whole lot better since this civil right movement started."

Beatrice Humphreys, a year older, shared similar memories. "Mama had twenty-one children, and ever one of them was raised by white folks. I remember when wasn't nothing here but trees. The woods was full of panthers. They wasn't but a couple of houses here in Marks and two stores—the Self family store and Sammy Marks's store.

"My mama lived to get 103 years old, and she died in 1965. She told all of us about slavery. She said the white man brought us here from across the water. They brought us like horses and cattle. You couldn't leave the farm without permission from the white folks, not even to go to a funeral. And you had to be back chopping cotton in the field when the funeral over." Chopping is hard work—it means weeding the plants with a hoe.

"I've chopped cotton many a time for forty cents a day. But we lived better back then even if us didn't have no electric light. We raised gardens: corn, greens, cabbage, cows, billy goats. When I were going to school back when I were young, I didn't learn too much. I didn't get to go to school too much, because I had to nurse the white children.

"I was living out on the plantation over near Belen, three miles and a half from here. I was raised and born in Quitman County. My husband, Reverend Humphreys, helped put the highway through Marks. He poured concrete on it. Ruth Figgs and the other girls toted grass seed to plant along the highway. They named Humphreys Street in Marks after my husband. He was the oldest man on the street. I worked for Mrs. Franks for fifty-three years. From age thirteen. And Beatrice Humphreys is still kicking!"

"People used to not know the months," Lula Belle Weathersby remembered. "So a lot of times you ask, they say they born in potato digging time or when Mandy the milk cow had her calf. That's true of people over forty out on the plantations.

"See, what it was, we lived on sharecropping. Half went to the Man and you paid all the debts out of your half, like the fertilizer. One of us worked for ourself and the other one was working for the Man. And he wasn't satisfied with his half; he'd make you pay more out of your half so you didn't get nothing. We was raising hogs and big gardens then. 'Cause we didn't get the furnish till March—that was a little credit he'd let you have with the grocery store till work time." Landowners often provided credit to their sharecroppers and charged high interest for repayment. Keeping their workers in debt was one more way to maintain control.

Inside a dimly lit shack, Jessie Franklin and Ora Bea Phipps told me about the not-very-old plantation days. "The planters, they wanted to make you work," said Jessie. "It was like the John Henry days. They'd whup you."

"It was slavery then?" asked Mrs. Phipps's fourteen-year-old daughter Carol.

"No. It wasn't slavery," her mother explained. "It was like the penitentiary. They would put people across a barrel and whup them, I hear. I know a old man, he says they put him across the barrel many a time. But they never whup my father."

"They never whup me neither," Jessie agreed. "They told me they'd whup me." He paused. "When sundown come, I runned off! I never give them a chance to whup me."

"We stayed on a pretty fair plantation," Ora interjected. "They never did no whupping."

Jessie continued. "They said make my children get on out in the field. They said, 'If you can't chop cotton on the Fourth of July, you know what to do.' That meant move. That meant if all of you wasn't working, they'd whup you. In 1938, a agent for the planter said he would whup me. I grabbed him up under my arm and carried him to a concrete post to knock him in the head. But I put him down. Then I runned away."

Ora frowned. "If you'd a stayed there, he would a killed you, huh?"

"No," answered Jessie. "I was going to get my mule out to plow at eight o'clock, and he come out on his horse, and he said, 'How come you so late getting out the mule?' And he got off his horse with his short riding whip and said he was going to whup me, and I picked him up. Then a planter threatened to whup me. I left the plantation and come to Marks. I been here ever since.

"Somehow or other they didn't like me much on those farms. See, I wouldn't borrow money like they wanted me to. He wanted to make me get out there and do the same work the other people did when they owed him two hundred or three hundred dollars.

"I worked when people was working for sixty-five cents a day loading logs. Seven or eight of us, we'd tote logs to the pile with the man riding on them. He was a white man, a little old low fellow. He was the whipping man. He'd be balancing on the logs holding onto your heads with his hands."

Henrietta, William's wife, joined the conversation. "You know when the bell ring, you better get out of the house and go out in the field. If you don't, they come to the house and beat you out. I ain't talking about what I heard, I'm talking about what I saw. I saw the planter's agent beat the eyes out of a man's head.

"My brother was in the house. He had just got married. He stayed in the house till nine o'clock. The man come and kicked the door down. He give my brother one good whipping. My brother run to the field with his pantses in his hand. And you better not get sick! He say, 'That boy ain't sick! That gal ain't sick!' He just want to get you into the field.

"Back on them plantations you got to go out to the field before sunup," Jessie remembered. "The white man follow you on his horse. His horse's head be in your back. He be following you to see if you gone work. Or else he get down and whup you. You'd see more peoples leaving by night than a little. Me and my brother come up through that. But our mama and daddy didn't let us say nothing about it. All they do is just kill a chicken and make ice cream for the preacher on Sunday. Children now that ain't been through it can't believe it. It's better than it was when I come along."

Willie Thomas, born in 1907, offered his memories. "You talk about chopping cotton, Joe, you ought to seen me chop cotton. Dirt come up over my hoe about this high." He indicated a spot about two feet off the ground. "You work like that all day, and you get about an hour lunch. You couldn't plow in boots. That dirt be too boggy. You got to roll your britches leg up and plow barefoot. The ground be cold, but you don't know what cold is, you be working so hard. I come in so tired, I set down at the table to eat, I knock the table over and go to sleep. My wife can tell you that."

"I seen people plow in the fields and they'd have the pellagra on their hands and they'd grease them over with meat-grease," Jessie confirmed.[10] "And they'd plow barefoot. I did many a day. My foots would get so sore I could hardly walk to my mule. People would plow barefoot till their feet busted open in the early frost."

Willie shook his head. "You used to not be able to go to church on Sunday 'cause you ain't got no good clothes. You better not wear no white shirt. What you talking about! The white folks wouldn't let you have nary one. You couldn't have no big funeral—about two or three to bury, and they took about an hour and a half, then you got to be back at work at evening. If you take too long, they ain't gonna aks you why. You got to make up a story, like you run into a storm. If they had more of a funeral, it would be at night. You'd go over to the church by lamplight for someone to say something over the dead."

I wondered about how they got paid. "Now, you talk about the plantation commissary," Ora Phipps responded. The commissary was the plantation store. "I remember when all you had to eat come from the commissary."

Jessie nodded. "They had 'doodlum books.' They looked like a food stamp book. That was your furnish."

"When you go to the commissary they tear out a stamp from the 'doodlum book,'" Ora explained. "They'd tell you how much things cost."

Needless to say, the prices at the plantation commissary were subject to change without notice. The "doodlum books" ended only after World War II when planters signed their sharecroppers up to receive government commodities (food distributions) every winter. From what I was told, that involved the planter going down to the commodity office with his sharecroppers and vouching for them as they signed up.

I asked how they all managed to survive. "Back then you hardly had use for money except to buy a little sugar and a little flour," explained William. "Getting you stuck on that money, that's about the worst thing in the world. My mama made the best old lye soap out of hog fat. That stuff so strong, it about burn you in two. You could fair see the dirt drop off. My uncles in the Hills, they still raise about everything they need. We had a plantation doctor on the big plantations. The small ones didn't have none. Every man that had two or three thousand acres had a doctor. You go to the boss man, tell him you need a doctor, he call a doctor. They didn't have the equipments they got now, but you could see a doctor. You could go to him better than you can now."

Still, everyone understood how unjust the system was. As Jessie explained, "I made cotton and corn for a lot of people 'round this Delta. I know how every white man in this area come by his money. I can tell how they used to fool Negroes out of their lands. The Negroes come to the Delta to live on their own land. They got off at the station with they own mules and cows and hogs. They moved here from way in the Hills. They bought the land. Then the white folks took the land from them. The white folks hired n——s to shoot in them people's houses and run them away to Chicago."

Ora pointed to her daughter. "She's too young to remember any of this stuff, and we never told her none of it before."

I asked Ora how people kept going despite that kind of treatment. "They had sound judgment then," she mused. "Lots of people now kill themselves. Times now is a little bit better, but they kill themselves. You used to not hear of that nearly so much. I don't see why people don't wait for someone else to kill them. God promised you a living and a killing."

Marks residents remembered good times too and ways they found to enjoy themselves despite their poverty. "Back on the big plantations they used to get together at the end of the week's work and have Saturday night balls," Ora told me. "They would have house parties at one house or another. They might play one of them wind-up grouchyphones with a big trumpet. Didn't everybody have one. And they would play a bass made of a tub or a old wash board."

William Franklin described a different kind of entertainment. "Right down close to here, a planter had one of the biggest jukes you ever seen for Negroes. Used to make $700 or $800 on a weekend. I used to go play the guitar for him. He trained the Negro how to do everything excusing work. Trained you how to steal.

"First we learned how to make pot-cotch—old white whiskey. Negroes would make whiskey and sell it fifty cents a pint. Then the white man, he said, 'Look, man, I got some cocaine. It'll get you drunk.' All us Negroes that couldn't make whiskey would buy the stuff from him. You put about ten drops of that liquid cocaine in Coca-Cola and you be drunk. That old stuff make you sick in the head and don't do nothing but embalm you. I got sick of that cocaine.

"They used to sell liquid cocaine in the store here. You never seen none of this dry stuff. I guess it was legal because they sold it in the stores. They sold it reasonable, four dollars a can. You buy it, put it in Coca-Cola, put it in whiskey. A can of it last you about a month."

The federal government had made cocaine illegal in 1914, but that hadn't stopped local store owners from selling it. "People was chopping cotton for fifty cents a day," Mr. Franklin explained. "Coffee cost a nickel a pound. We drank it to cure us hunger. You bought most everything on credit then, but not that cocaine. The government finally stopped them from selling it around 1928 or 1929."

Will Haynes remembered taking trips outside Marks on the Illinois Central Railroad. "They had what they called excursions for Black people, round trips from here to Memphis for a ball game and picture shows. I mean that train would be bloated too. I think the last one they had was in the fifties. That was when television begin to come out. The business they used to do on the railroad! They used to have passenger trains stop four times a day. But now the trucks done come in and took the business away. It's only one passenger train on the main line at Batesville and none here. Time does bring about a change, don't it, Joe? I remember when they had what they called butcher boys going on the train selling grapes and cold drinks and bananas."

Trains played an important role in Black economic life. Although the railroads had kept Black people from working in any but the worst jobs, A. Philip Randolph organized a union of Black train car workers in 1925 to demand better working conditions and opportunities.[11] "The Union of Sleeping Car Porters did a lot of good things," Will remembered. "I hear that before I got on, the whites was shooting Black brake-mens to get them to quit. They didn't get rid of them, but they hurt a few. The Black man has come a long ways."

A New Deal?

The Great Depression of the 1930s brought even harder times for Black Mississippians. Crop prices fell along with earnings, and many who had owned land lost it. With President Roosevelt's New Deal and the rules set up to prevent racial discrimination, many Black sharecroppers hoped for help. In theory, they got it. The U.S. Department of Agriculture sent checks to sharecroppers as well as planters for taking land out of production. But the planters often seized the checks, and the sharecroppers had no legal recourse.

A few white families were able to take advantage of the New Deal's loan opportunities. For example, the Self family, which had owned a store in Marks, became more powerful. They supplied groceries to the plantation commissaries, where the sharecroppers bought them with the "doodlum books" the planters issued. Then the Depression sharply cut the price of cotton and land became cheaper. With the money they made, the Selfs became the biggest landowners in Quitman County. By the end of the Depression the proportion of Black people who owned farms had dropped from 25 percent (in 1930) to 10 percent, and their average size dropped to just under twenty acres. The number of farm-owning whites rose slightly, and the average size of their farms almost doubled from fifty-five acres in 1930 to ninety-five ten years later.[12]

Gilbert Hamer remembered those days: "People talk about depression. It ain't no depression now at all. I remember that one back in 1930. They didn't have no Social Security or welfare. It wasn't no grease to cook greens or peas or cornbread, maybe just a little salt.

"It was back in [President] Hoover's time that the hunting license started. It cost $1.25. We called a rabbit a 'Hoover pig.' It's good times now to what it was back then. I made fifteen dollars a month then, less than fifty cents a day. I know enough bad from that time to write five books. Back as late as '42 they was ringing bells to get you to go to work in the field at daybreak. You wouldn't be in no house when no daylight come. So dark you have to feel for the mule to catch him.

"I know Reverend Saddler, a Black preacher in Marks, bought himself a Cadillac, and they wouldn't let him drive it across to the white side. They wouldn't let you drive a car except some old rattletrap. Things have come up from then and changed around so it's a new world. It's gotten better mostly since this civil rights thing started, better and better."

Alec Dean agreed. "You can talk for your rights now, but you couldn't back then. Back in 1935 when the government sent checks to the sharecroppers, we was on Self's place. He took all of our check but five dollars and said it was for the church. A storm blowed down our church, and he give us stuff to build it back with. They had seventy-five or eighty families on the place, and he got all our checks. Don't you know that white man made a lot of money off them people? You didn't talk for your rights, or they'd kill you if you was a poor man—hang you or drag you behind a car. They killed poor white mens too, but mostly it was the colored got killed.

"Roosevelt didn't do much for the poor man," he concluded. "Maybe the middle class."

James Wilson Sr. nodded. "Old Mr. Self's daddy used to live here. He was poor as I is. Mr. Self had a small plantation. He started to furnish the people at other plantations, and, when they couldn't pay for the groceries, he foreclosed them. He taken what he got."

In the midst of the Depression, the Black country singer Charley Pride was born in Lambert, just south of Marks. He grew up in nearby Sledge. When he was five, his parents took him to the courthouse in Marks—the same courthouse where I was sentenced to jail twenty-four years later—where they went to get "relief food" as it was called then. He had to use the bathroom. But there was no bathroom Black people could use in those days, not even a segregated bathroom. Charley had to pee in his pants.

I learned this from a documentary biography of Charley Pride that played on CMT (Country Music Television), directed largely at a southern white working-class audience. One consequence of the civil rights movement is that this program assumed that the audience who saw what happened to the young Charley Pride would think it was unfair. Today the stretch of highway that runs through Lambert is called the Charley Pride Highway.

One night, Willie Thomas and I were watching the movie *Sounder* on his TV. *Sounder* is a drama of Black life on plantations in the 1930s. Mr. Thomas was deeply moved and in distress at some of the scenes, but he said the movie didn't show conditions as bad as they really were.

It wasn't just the poverty or even the cheating that made conditions so bad. Almost all older Black people in Mississippi also recalled violent attacks by whites. The memory of these attacks kept Black tenants and sharecroppers under planters' control long after they stopped being common. "Yeah, this was a dirty state then," Lula Belle Weathersby recalled. "When I was a child I have seen white mens load up in a car and take a colored man and drag him up and down the road until he die. I was a child the first one I seen, eight or ten years old. Yeah, I seen it more than once. The white men was in the car drinking and hollering and acting a fool. I was so glad when the Black man stopped hollering. It didn't seem so bad when he was dead.

"You know what I have seen, Joe? I have seen them take a colored man who was what they called 'going to the barn.' That means he was late to work. This was back in Yazoo County. The boss man took this man among the other Blacks to warn them and tied him down on the ground and set a fire on his back and poured gasoline on him. Burnt him up! Alive!

"I remember another incident in Yazoo County. I have seen one or two hundred white folk take after one colored man and mob him. This wasn't just the poor whites. This was the *leading* class of white folk among them. My daddy was a deacon. I have seen my daddy go and plead and beg for the man's life. You couldn't stop him. I would be so scared for him. They let the man live that time. It had got just a little bit better when I came to the Delta in 1949."

I asked her what made white people act like that. "That was what we couldn't understand. The Black people, you know, was scared of the white people, and they was normally submissive to them. But the white women would tell tales on them. They claimed the Black man was courting a white woman, but the white people next door said it wasn't him. Them's facts too, Joe. It kinda hurt too when I think back then." She laughed sadly. "Oh, it's much different now. They called it lynching back then. They did a lot of lynching. But then one Black person after another kept up and finally forced them to pass that no-lynching law they got now in Mississippi.[13] I believe it was back in the latter part of the thirties. But ooh, child, it's so much better than back then."

Beginnings of Change

Even during the Depression there was some resistance to the economic exploitation. The civil rights movement of the 1960s built on what had come before. In the early 1930s an organization called the Southern Tenant Farmers Union tried to win minimal rights for sharecroppers and landless farm laborers so that they could survive.

When President Franklin Roosevelt launched his New Deal in 1933, the Southern Tenant Farmers Union sent Rev. Claude Williams, a white Presbyterian minister, on a tour of rural Black and white churches in Arkansas. He explained to sharecroppers that they had a right to a share of the checks the Agriculture Department was sending to those who took land out of production. Jessie Franklin, who lived in Arkansas in the late 1930s, remembered Reverend Williams as "a wise man who taught the peoples." In Mississippi, repression was too great for the union to be active. William Franklin remembered that when he got his check at the Sunflower County Courthouse in Ruleville, his landowner was waiting outside and simply snatched it out of his hand. Reverend Wilder of Marks, who was active in the civil rights movement of the 1960s, had also worked for the Southern Tenant Farmers Union in Arkansas in the 1930s. So while the STFU was largely unable to operate in Mississippi, it sowed some of the seeds that led to the civil rights movement in Marks.[14]

Progressive ideas came from outside the South too. From the 1920s onward, hard times led thousands of Black people to move from the Delta to Chicago and other northern cities, part of a movement so vast historians call it the Great Migration. Those who returned, like William Franklin, brought back new ideas about race relations. In the same way, World War II opened many Black soldiers to new possibilities.

"I went up to Chicago when I was about twenty-nine years old in 1940," Mr. Franklin told me. "The first time I went up, I stayed about six months, and I come home. Then I went there and stayed about a year. About five years later I moved back to Mississippi and moved out on a plantation making a crop. I kept moving back and forth till my mother and father was sick. Then I come back to Mississippi and been here ever since.

"Whenever you could make enough of that little money off of day work stuff, you went up North to pile up more money. And to my mind that's where the Negroes first learned you didn't have to say that 'yes, sir' and 'no, sir.' That was the first place, to my way of knowing, that I learned it. You had to give the planter 'yes, sir' and 'no, sir,' but I looked into it a long time, and I figured we didn't have to do it here, but if we didn't do it, we'd be in particular trouble. That give me to know that if you didn't say 'yes, sir' and 'no, sir,' he'd get a clue at you and hurt you. It looked right funny to me that when I'd get up North and say 'yes, sir' and 'no, sir' the fellow said, 'No, you don't have to do that up here.'"

James Wilson Sr. learned a similar lesson. "I been in Quitman County practically all my time other than seven years in Detroit and three in the army. Traveling in the service was a great experience for peoples needing information. In the war I went through Africa, and the people there would tell us colored, 'You ain't as good off as we is. We got our own country, and you ain't got none.'"

"I tell you what opened a lot of Black people's eyes was the army," Ora Phipps agreed. "Because they was going through the world seeing different things. It opened my brothers' eyes. Because they was on the plantation working from sun to sun. There wasn't no system. They caught it a lot harder than I did, because they was older. My brothers got better treatment in the army than they ever did at home." These ideas would eventually help change Marks and the South for good.

On the Eve of the Movement

Despite greater awareness of Black people in Mississippi that their rights were being violated, whites maintained their political and economic control. As a result, even after World War II life for most Black people remained as impoverished and subjugated as ever. What did change was the nature of Black farm work. Mechanization increased, and cotton-picking machines and tractors began to replace hand labor and mule-drawn plows. This lessened the demand for labor, and thousands of sharecroppers were kicked off the land. Some left the county: Quitman's population declined to 21,019 in 1960, of whom 63 percent were Black, a population drop of about 19 percent in ten years. By 1970, the population had fallen further, to 15,888, 57 percent of whom were Black.[15]

Many who stayed moved to towns like Marks and did day labor in the cotton fields. Plantation managers—mostly whites—would bring truckloads of these Black laborers from town to work in the fields and be paid at sundown. Until 1966, Black schools were open in the summer and closed in the fall so children could pick cotton.

As former sharecroppers moved off the plantations, their deserted shacks were brought into town and rented to Black families by white landlords like the Selfs. Annie Belle Stuart, born in 1913, boasted that when she moved to Marks, hers was "the first house built here on this street—in 1945."

"This was a cotton patch then. Then they drug houses in here from the country. Some of these houses look like they been here fifty years, but they was drug here and sot here. I bought the land this house is on from Mr. Self. He owned all the land around here. Lots of people was afraid to buy from him because when he got his finger on you, he kept it there. You would make a payment and he call it paying rent. He wanted it where when you died, the land would go back to his children. A lot of them did it. But I nursed his children for twenty years, and they crazy about me. I got too many little nieces and nephews to leave this house to the Self children.

"When I moved in this house I built a bathroom, and the city tried to get me to take it down in 1955. They didn't have no sewer line through here, but they wanted to dig up my cesspool. I told them they had me to fight if they tried that. When I come here, they didn't have electric light, they didn't have gas, didn't have water—didn't have a road paved, just a old field road. They put the lights and the sewer line through in the '50s, and they paved the road in 1960."

As a result of the population shift off the plantations, the population of Marks grew from 1,818 in 1940 to 2,572 in 1960.[16] There were an additional three hundred people or so, all Black, in the areas around Marks that were not legally annexed. But the city did not provide sewer lines to many Black areas, whether within Marks's legal boundaries or not. When I stayed with Rev. G. W. Ward in the fall of 1964—within city limits—I used a "night pot" and in the daytime went to the outhouse.

But enough displaced Black sharecroppers moved North looking for new work that southern planters faced labor shortages at harvest time. As a result, wages for farm laborers rose a bit, although they remained very low. This enabled a few Black families to finally buy their own land. Most, however, continued to live in desperate poverty.

For Joe Collins, economic changes brought improvement. "In '33 I stayed on [one man's] place, and he paid seventy-five cents a day, but he put half of that in your account, and you couldn't draw on it. In '39 we stayed on [another man's] place and he didn't pay even fifty cents a day, no matter what you were doing, baling hay or anything. We never heard nothing about civil rights then. I didn't know nothing about voting until a few years ago when we had the registering. The white folks back then did what they wanted, but it's been a big change. You couldn't leave a person's place if they didn't want you to. You had to run away at night, you had to slip out. But that's been done away with. [But thanks to rising farm wages,] I cleared a little amount of money, and I put it down and put it down and put it down, and we bought this land in Marks and built this house. It's not fancy, but I like it. We moved in this house in '55."

William Franklin told a more sobering tale: "I managed a plantation in '48 and '49. The planter expected me to carry his work on, and that was a lot of doing. I hauled labor in a ten-wheel trailer truck in the mornings and the evenings. I'd land them in the mornings, put them in the fields, go on and get my tractor, and go to work. I hauled cotton choppers, cotton pickers. They was glad for me to come and get them. I was easy on them.

"The planters still had mules then, but the biggest of them had tractors. They kept mules a long time. In the place where the tractors couldn't do the work, they'd put mules out. They didn't get rid of the mules just because they had tractors. They used mules in wet time, not in dry weather. The planter where I managed had about twenty-five head of mules. People used to get in the cotton patch and sing, whoop, and holler. Was the planter fair? No. You couldn't make nothing with him. Nothing but that little two dollars a day.

"What brought me out of the cotton patch?" he mused. "I made a crop, and the man didn't give me but fifty dollars, and I didn't have enough to support my family with. Once when I was moving off a plantation in 1955, because I was moving, he killed my hogs—shot my daddy's hogs. But when I moved off of the place this time in 1958, I didn't have no hogs. When we come to Marks we worked in the fields by the day, picking and chopping cotton."

His wife Henrietta continued. "Joe, you know what I had to do? I had to put meal in the bottom of the skillet to cook my cornbread with. We didn't have no money to buy no grease. Me and the children had to get out in the mud and water to pick cotton to buy us something to eat. Cold! It be ice on the ground! We cooked a handful of beans in a bunch of water to make soup. It be dry beans. And that's why we had to leave that man's place. We didn't have nothing to eat."

The combination of discrimination and poverty meant few Black adults in Marks had much education. In 1960, only 3 percent of Black Quitman County residents over twenty-five had graduated from high school, compared with almost a third of whites. Black adults' median education level was four and a half years—just over half that of whites. Only four Black adults in the entire county were enrolled in college.[17]

But even these figures exaggerate the amount of education Black people had. Until World War II, many children, Black and white, might go to school only three months a year. Teachers were sometimes as young as sixteen. Many teachers had only an eighth-grade education. Even after the war, the Black school principal in Lambert (who was a servant in the house of the white principal) asked the white school administrator for a course in civics for the Black school. He was given a small booklet titled *Citizenship for Negroes*. It contained the national anthem, the Pledge of Allegiance, and other patriotic statements. Many people forgot how to read and write because it wasn't necessary to know how on the plantations.

After 1954, when the Supreme Court ruled that "separate but equal" schools were unconstitutional, Mississippi passed a law saying schooling was not compulsory. That was not changed until 1977.[18] For generations of Black and poor white children there was no pretense of an attempt to keep them in school.

Once when I was going with the Franklin family to Ruleville, in nearby Sunflower County, sixteen-year-old Mae Ella Franklin pointed out the one-room country school she had attended from first to fourth grade. On Sundays it was a church. She had walked there several miles from her home on the plantation, even on rainy days, while the white children went to school in buses. Then, in 1958, a big modern consolidated high school was built in Marks for Quitman County's Black children, and an addition was built onto the Black grade school there. The Black schools got a fleet of school buses. All this was to show the Supreme Court that Mississippi Black children got a "separate but equal" education. They didn't, of course, but school integration would have to wait for more than another decade. One thing is sure: most of the older Black people in Quitman County—and many younger ones—were not very literate in 1960. From my experience, many poor white people were also illiterate or nearly so.

This was how things stood in Marks on the eve of the civil rights movement. In 1960, the census reported that Quitman County Black families had one of the lowest median incomes of any Mississippi county: $891 a year, making them one of the poorest groups in the poorest state. Black men had median earnings of $558, and Black women $322. Overall, close to three-quarters of all Quitman County residents lived in poverty. For Black households that figure was 94 percent.[19]

Black unemployment in the county was low: 4 percent for men and 7 percent for women. It was their low earnings that left so many in such dire straits. Strong families helped; more than four-fifths of Black families had both parents at home. But a large number of people depended on that income. Only about 24 percent of Black Quitman residents held paying jobs, indicating that many children and the elderly were being taken care of by a small number of people of working age, plus the contributions of those who had moved North to find work.[20]

Even though the Black rural population had declined, farm labor, whether full- or part-time, was still the most important source of income. The next largest occupation was domestic service, followed by machine operation, probably working at the Self family's cotton or soybean oil mills.[21]

Of the forty-four Black professionals in the county, virtually all were teachers.[22] Mrs. Flora Shaw, a Black woman who owned a grocery store in Marks, told me with disappointment that the only job young Black college graduates could think of preparing for was teaching. There were no Black doctors or lawyers anywhere in Quitman County. In fact, in 1964 I was told there were exactly four Black lawyers in the entire state of Mississippi. This was the setting for all the Marks people who tell their stories in this book. This was the reality that civil rights workers like me, who came from outside Marks, saw every day.

PART II

THE MOVEMENT IN MARKS AND BEYOND

CHAPTER 2

"I Got Tired of White Folks on My Back"
1955–1964

"I remember when I first met you, Joe," William Franklin said. "You come up to my place, and you started talking. I never heard no white man before talk like you. You kept saying, 'Oh, Mr. Franklin, I know we can do it.' So I decided I'd go in on it with you. And then, when all the fuss was over, I got to thinking—it was a bunch of times on this stuff when it's a wonder I didn't get shot—you and me both."

Organizing in Secret

Mr. Franklin's amazement that he had survived made a great deal of sense because the work we were doing went to the heart of white supremacy in the South. We wanted to challenge the rules the white power structure had established after slavery that had kept Black people from voting. We built on the efforts of the NAACP, which had been operating secretly to increase Black voting and challenge discrimination for almost a decade.

Nationally, NAACP members tended to be older, better off, and better educated than other African Americans. This might make it seem like a more "moderate" organization. However, in Mississippi, there was hysterical opposition to the NAACP because whites wanted to keep the old racial order. As far as whites were concerned, NAACP members might as well have been communists. Unfortunately, white officials in

Marks were more effective at barring Black people from voting than the NAACP was at getting them registered to vote.

Most Black adults in Mississippi were not allowed to vote until the federal Voting Rights Act of 1965. The 1890 state constitution had established criteria for voting that most Black people could not meet. Black disenfranchisement became a cornerstone of the power of planters over sharecroppers.

To vote in Mississippi before 1965 you had to pay an annual poll tax of two dollars per voter. Most poor people did not have that kind of money. You also had to interpret in writing any passage of the state constitution the county circuit clerk chose. That clerk was the sole judge of whether you interpreted the passage correctly. There were over 360 sections in the Mississippi state constitution, and all the circuit clerks were white. Many Black teachers were told they had failed and could not register to vote, although white illiterates passed and were allowed to register, including one Quitman County official I can think of.

In 1960, only 6.5 percent of Black adults in Mississippi were registered to vote. In Quitman County, only 316 out of 5,673 eligible Black adults were registered. This was better than neighboring Panola County, with just 13 registered Black voters, although over half the people in the county were Black.[1]

Once I went to the courthouse with Reverend Hooks, a Black minister from Marks who was taking the registration test. The circuit clerk opened the state constitution at random and read a section about how the state of Mississippi will not be a fiduciary to municipal bonds. I had been to college, and I had never heard the word "fiduciary" before. Later I found out it means someone who will provide the financial guarantee for a loan. But for a while, some of us civil rights workers used the term jokingly among ourselves: "Some damn fiduciary took all the pencils." Reverend Hooks was not permitted to register.

Whenever someone attempted to register, his or her name and address appeared in the local paper every day for a week. In theory, this was to allow the public to submit any information they had against the "moral character" of the would-be voter. In practice, it let white employers know their Black employees had tried to register and therefore fire them.

Even the few Black people who were registered—mostly teachers, ministers, storekeepers, and their families—might encounter difficulties if they tried to vote in Marks. It was even worse outside Marks.

There were few Black landowners or business owners in the rural areas. If a white planter learned his sharecroppers had registered to vote, he would likely put them off the plantation.

Christean Parker, a Black woman from Darling, five miles north of Marks, described her attempts. "I registered to vote in 1952. I paid the Mississippi poll tax for 1951, and in 1953 I tried to pay for 1952 and '53, but the registrar said I could not pay an overdue poll tax. I paid again for 1954. When I went to the polls in the general election in 1954, sometime in the afternoon, I was told that I had come too late. I paid my poll tax for the next six years. By the time of the general election of 1960, I went to vote in the morning. The white woman at the polls said I had come too late. I have been informed since that the polls in Mississippi are open from 7:00 a.m. to 6:00 p.m."[2]

Most Black people I talked with when I first arrived in Marks in 1964 had no idea what a senator or representative was or what Congress was. The elected officials they knew about were the five road supervisors, five constables, and the sheriff. Each Mississippi county was divided into five "beats," each with a supervisor and a constable. They were called beats because before the Civil War each one was the territory assigned to a patrol that watched for runaway slaves. Now they are called districts, but in 1964, the slavery-time word "beats" was used. Even today local districts are sometimes labeled that way.

The most important elected official was the sheriff, who was also the tax collector. Often he was called the high sheriff, and his deputies were referred to as sheriffs. When the movement began Gordon Darby, a poor white man, was Quitman County's sheriff. Even those too young to remember the plantation days remembered Sheriff Darby. Ruby Lee, twenty-two-year-old grandchild of a minister in Marks, reflected on Sheriff Darby's time in office: "It's more freedom now."

Her friend Geraldine Phipps agreed. "Yeah, it's a lot better since when Mr. Darby was sheriff. He didn't like the girls wearing shorts. He'd cuss them out and make them go back home and put on long dresses, something more decent. And he didn't like Black men wearing mustaches."

Ruby's brother Robie echoed, "When he arrest them he shave the mustaches off or pull them out with pliers."

"And he beat them up," added Geraldine.

Ruby elaborated on the sheriff's views about Black women. "He didn't like the women wearing lipstick. He tell them, 'Get that sorry stuff off your face.' He didn't mind white women wearing it—just Black women."

"They'll be talking about Sheriff Darby twenty years from now," Rev. S. A. Allen told me. He was an older man. "On a Saturday night about seven o'clock, all the Negroes would remove from here to Tutwiler in the next county because they was afraid Sheriff Darby would be after them. You take all the towns around here, they knowed Sheriff Darby. I had people in Clarksdale tell how he treated them. He'd ask for their license, and when they give it to him, he dropped it on the ground, and when they bent down to pick it up he'd kick them."

By the time I got to Marks, Mr. Darby was no longer sheriff. But he and his predecessor, L. V. Harrison Sr., were the major reason that the NAACP was a secret organization in Quitman County. Marks is seventeen miles from Clarksdale, where Dr. Aaron Henry, the state president of the NAACP, had his drugstore. Clarksdale is in Coahoma County and was (and is) the largest town in that part of the Delta. More than half its population was Black. While there was still plenty of police harassment there, it had a long-established NAACP chapter. A few Black community leaders in Marks stayed in secret contact with Dr. Henry so the NAACP could operate in Marks.

Whites were not aware of Marks's NAACP's activities. We know this from the files of the Mississippi State Sovereignty Commission. Established in 1956 to promote Mississippi's official position against school desegregation, it quickly became a spy agency, collecting information on African Americans or anyone else who might challenge the traditional racial order. Even out-of-state travel could provoke scrutiny by commission investigators, who feared that while Mississippi citizens were away they might meet with suspicious contacts who would encourage civil rights.[3]

According to the records, in 1959, Zack Van Landingham, a commission investigator, asked Sheriff Harrison about civil rights activity in Quitman County. The sheriff appeared completely unaware of the existence of the local NAACP. "On March 5, 1959," investigator Van Landingham wrote to the director of the Sovereignty Commission,

> I talked with Sheriff L. V. Harrison Sr., Marks, Mississippi, relative to the racial situation in Quitman County. Sheriff Harrison advised that there was no NAACP chapter in the county, that there were no Negro agitators to his knowledge, that he anticipated no trouble whatso-

ever along racial lines. He said that everything was very quiet and running smoothly. He did advise that there had been 2 or 3 Negroes in the county who were regarded as agitators, but they had moved away.

Sheriff Harrison stated that there were approximately 200 Negroes in Quitman County registered to vote. He promised to immediately advise the State Sovereignty Commission should there be any development along racial lines in his county.[4]

Gordon Darby had a slightly more accurate picture of NAACP activity in Quitman. On July 14, 1960, commission investigator Tom Scarbrough reported that according to Darby's chief deputy, Austin Martin, "most . . . trouble stems from agitating negroes outside of their county over at Clarksdale, which is only 17 miles away. . . . [Q]uite a few of the Quitman County negroes could belong to the NAACP, but of course kept it a secret and in all probability were members in Coahoma County. However, Martin said that Sheriff Gordon Darby was doing an excellent job of keeping the negroes in their place in Quitman County and he felt that so long as Darby remained sheriff no negro trouble would occur in Quitman County."[5] Scarbrough noted that L. V. Craig, the Quitman County superintendent of education, had assured him that "so far as he knew he did not have a single negro schoolteacher who was a member of the NAACP or any other left wing organization and that if he had knowledge that one belonged to such an organization he would dispense with his services as a teacher immediately."[6]

Scarbrough also reported on the number of Black eligible voters, according to the deputy circuit clerk. "There were about 250 negroes in Quitman County who had paid their poll taxes, but . . . only about 60 of the 250 had qualified as voters, the rest having failed to pass the intelligence test required of voters in order to qualify. The Deputy Clerk also stated that at one time there were perhaps 1,200 negroes voting in Quitman County, but they had been gradually reduced until at this time only 60 are qualified to vote."[7]

Under such hostile conditions, it is no wonder that to rural Black people like Lula Belle Weathersby, the NAACP was mainly a rumor at first. "I'll tell you what started this movement—maybe not here in Quitman County, but it shoved it off every place in Mississippi. It was a Black woman, and she was a schoolteacher, and she wanted equal pay with the whites, and they beat her up. They tried to kill her, but she escaped. That was the first thing that erupted, and then it kind of died down, but then one or two more kept coming along until there was enough to make a big push with it."

She was talking about a set of legal cases in Virginia. In 1938, the NAACP had filed a petition with the Norfolk, Virginia, Board of Education on behalf of Aline Elizabeth Black, an African American teacher who argued that the lower salaries paid to Black teachers violated their guarantee of equal protection. The text of that petition was carried by many Black newspapers. Although the state courts ruled for Norfolk, and Black lost her job, the NAACP persisted in its fight for equal pay with a mass protest march and a second suit, filed on behalf of another Norfolk teacher, Melvin Alston. He won that case. Although the state asked the Supreme Court to review it, the high court refused, and the pay equity ruling stood.[8] The victory raised the NAACP's profile across the South and prompted many similar efforts.

Mrs. Weathersby continued, "The teacher come along in the forties. Then after that the NAACP was secretly borned in Mississippi. It was a secret organization where the white man wouldn't even know it existed. They was afraid to have it out in the open. I wasn't a member, but I would hear them whispering about it. They was *very* secret about it. It wasn't easy, but our leaders put it in our minds that it would get through. More and more people began to come into the light with it, and they got killed, but then someone else come along."

Unlike in many Mississippi counties, Quitman officials made no physical attempts to intimidate voters during elections. However, as the Sovereignty Commission files showed, county authorities kept their eye on those few who had successfully entered the voting rolls. These generally moderately well-off Black registrants had organized into the Voters' League, and officials would question local people to learn who the active members were. The white leadership found Black voting, even by these more conservative people, to be intolerable and hoped to stop it.

When I was in Marks organizing for voting rights, we always believed some Black residents were reporting to white authorities on our activities. County Attorney Ben Caldwell once made a point of telling me that he often talked with Percy Nelson, a conservative Black grocer. However, the Sovereignty Commission papers reveal that local white leaders had only sketchy and inaccurate information. Mr. Nelson and others may have spoken with Caldwell, but they never disclosed much of what was going on.

I learned more about the NAACP's early local history from Rev.

Ezra Towner, former head of the Quitman County NAACP. "I've been a member of the NAACP when many people did not want to acknowledge they was a member, but now things seem to be unified, and everybody acknowledges that it's a good organization for Black people and for all people.

"I've been in Quitman County since 1940. I've been a registered voter since 1949. We started off with a Negro Chamber of Commerce, of which the late Percy Nelson was president, and that emerged into the Voters' League in the early 1950s. We've never had much open objection to the Voters' League by the whites in this county. In election years in the '60s, we've had candidates visit us. It used to wasn't many in the Voters' League who belonged to the NAACP, but now I'd call them about the same. It used to be a big difference between them, but now many of them is NAACP members.

"I guess that the best thing about this county that I know of is that there never was objection to Black people voting. Our job was just to explain to Black people why it was important to register to vote. I didn't receive any threats, although I was at all civil rights meetings. I was never at any of the marches. That's the facts of it from my statement."

Rev. Willie Malone, who managed a plantation near Clarksdale and chaired the Voters' League, became involved in voting rights efforts through his religious engagement. Church leadership was important because often the church was the only Black community organization whites permitted.[9] "I began to be a leader in the church when I was fifteen years old," he told me. "I was appointed deacon when I was seventeen. I was crowned deacon in 1930 when I was twenty-one. I always was leading."

Reverend Allen, the League's vice chairman, interjected that, given Malone's relative youth and the fact that he had, in Malone's words, "nary a year of school," Malone's church position showed he had the respect and support of the community. The church elects its deacons, Reverend Allen explained. "It takes the church to crown him, and the minister usually be's in on that deal and catechizes him. [Then] they call on ministers of other churches to help crown him." It was Reverend Malone and community leaders like him who made the civil rights movement possible in the rural South, but because of their limited educational credentials or lack of formal writings most have been forgotten.

Malone continued his story. "I joined the NAACP about 1950, long before this integration thing started. When the NAACP was first started by Dr. [T. R. M.] Howard down at Mound Bayou in Bolivar County, it was secret. It hadn't broke out yet. I joined under Dr. Howard. And they run him away from there.[10] It wasn't called the NAACP then. Reverend Allen was the one started them to voting registering in that political test and the one getting them to join the NAACP, but I was getting them before he was."

The danger was real. Reverend Malone explained how Sheriff Darby had used violence to keep African Americans from doing anything to threaten the system of white control. Once he mentioned Darby in a sermon. "Old man Darby said, 'Why are you talking about me?'

"I said, 'Might I ask you what I was talking about? That four-year-old boy you whupped up for breaking some glass?' The boy was too little to have broke the glass. Darby told his mother to whup him. Then he said she wasn't whupping him hard enough and he whupped the baby hisself with his belt. Made the baby's daddy set on the bed too scared to say anything.

"Sheriff Darby told me, 'Coldwater River's wide enough to hold you, ain't it?'

"I said, 'Yes, sir.'

"'And deep enough?'

"'Yes, sir.'

"'And we got enough gin belts to hold you down where you never rise again?'

"I told him, 'I hope not.' We was standing there in the road, and he told me to go off, that he had searched my record, and if he could find *anything* against me, he was going to put me *under* the jail."

Reverend Malone had several such stories. "Mr. Bob Young, a white man at the store here told me he would let me buy anything on cash, but he wasn't going to sell me nothing on credit because I belongs to the NAACP.

"I said to him, 'How do you know I belongs to the NAACP?'

"He said, 'I know you do, I know you do!'

"One day he said to me, 'Preacher!'

"I said, 'Sir?'

"He said, 'One of these nights you won't be able to get out of the house for the smoke!'

"I said, 'Mr. Young, sir, I know you wouldn't be the one to do that.'

"He said, 'You don't know what I'd do.'

"I said, 'Mr. Young, sir, just 'cause my car is at my house don't mean

I'm there, and just because it's gone don't mean I'm gone. So I be there when you don't think I am. And at night it so dark I can't tell Black from white. And any man that pour coal oil on my house to set it afire, I'm going to do something about it. Because I care just as much for my house as you do for yourn, though mine is a piece.'"

Reverend Allen told me about another kind of intimidation whites also used. "The governor told the teachers if they joined the NAACP—if they joined anything excusing the church—they couldn't teach school no more in this state. That scared them from joining. Some of them is still too scared to join. I think if they had all joined the NAACP at once there wouldn't have been nobody to teach school, so they all should have said, 'Yes, I belong.'" I asked Reverend Allen how he had the courage to do all this. "Just [had] grit in my craw," he told me.

Malone continued his story about the early NAACP: "I had it rough before y'all civil rights workers got here. 'Course the people removed me from being leader of the NAACP. They didn't have the nerve I did, I reckon, so everything kind of quietened down until [1965 when William] Franklin and them broke out down on Cotton Street."

Most Black people in Mississippi knew about the NAACP. In 1955, Emmett Till, a Black teenager from Chicago, was visiting his relatives in Mississippi about fifty miles south of Marks. He had some harmless interaction with a white woman, and for that he was lynched.[11] That was one more reminder to Black people of how dangerous it was to do anything openly to resist white control. But what made this case unusual was that it went to trial, and several Black people testified for the prosecution in open court.

Of course, the lynchers were acquitted. Mother Grace, one of the two Black women ministers in Quitman County, was still indignant about it when I got to Marks nine years later. She knew some of Emmett Till's relatives who had to leave the state because they were willing to testify. Once, before the murder, she had given some food and clothing to help the family of one of the white men who later committed the crime. She referred to the lynchers as n——s. The fact that they were acquitted was probably one of the factors that inspired Mother Grace to join the NAACP.

For the Black people of Quitman County, the Till case was the first time they had ever seen white men prosecuted for killing a Black person. A good number had seen Blacks slain by whites before their eyes with no legal consequences. They had never seen a Black person testify against a white person in a serious criminal case. Reverend Allen, Reverend Malone, and Rev. Panola Carter took carloads of Black people from Quitman County to the trial, an act of courage and an important breaking of racial barriers.

As Mrs. Weathersby remembered, "Lord, it wasn't easy! Used to be if you said what was on your mind, you got killed. Then, when the Till boy got killed in 1955, it was the N double A that pushed for a trial. That was the first time I ever heard that a white was on trial for killing a Black person. Used to, the whites just killed them and that was that. The whites got off free at the trial, but at least they had a trial. You got to take these things step by step.

"After Emmett Till was killed—whoo, Lord! So many Black people left here for Chicago they had to have the laws at the bus station some places to stop them so they wouldn't lose all their labor. You know there was a lot of Black people attended the trial."

Reverend Allen described it to me. "I took a carload of people to the Emmett Till trial every day of it that God send. It sure is a lot of Blacks there. I wasn't scared at all, for it was some foreigners there and they called me and questioned me in a colored restaurant. And they asked me what they thought of a Negro in the state of Mississippi. And I told them that they thought of a Negro as a mule or vomit or something like that.[12]

"And a colored lady was sitting near us, and she told me, 'Mister, you tell them the whites cussed me because I went to the trial instead of going to the field.'

"I said, 'You can do that yourself.'

"But there's always Negroes who have to tell tales to the white man. There was one old gray-headed Negro from Jackson who was always watching us and reporting to the white man. A friend of mine, a preacher who went to the Emmett Till trial, was run out of the state. And Reverend Carter, every time he'd drive down there with a gang of people to the trial, the white people would holler at him and moo at him. One day some whites with guns stopped him and searched his car and cussed at him. That trial was one reason why Dr. Howard had to leave Mound Bayou, because he brought a gang of witnesses in there to testify. It wasn't so hard to get people to organize at that time. Of course, it was in secret."

Both the growth and the secrecy of the NAACP are easy to understand. It wasn't just the Till trial. In the late 1950s, when many Black county residents first got electricity, they also got TVs. Television brought increased interest in politics and civil rights. They began joining the NAACP in slowly growing numbers. But always they faced the hostility of whites who threatened them. Quitman County's white leadership had been defying the *Brown* decision since it was announced in 1954. The court ruling, together with the uproar over Emmett Till's murder, made white leaders suspicious that any Black resistance might be an organized conspiracy.

So it is not surprising that so many of the Black community leaders were ministers. They had an independent power base, organizing experience, and were respected by the communities that selected them as their pastors. Reverend Allen preached to people who were to a great degree isolated from the modern world. Many of them were illiterate, or nearly so, and depended on word of mouth for their news. As an NAACP member, Reverend Allen was their link to a larger world where people were concerned about their rights, to a world where people even imagined that they had any rights.

But in the early 1960s only some local ministers supported the civil rights movement. One large Black church received donations from the wealthy white Self family. This church owned a plantation, and a former business manager there told me the church had been more severe in its exactions from its sharecroppers than many white planters. Not surprisingly, the head pastor was hostile to the movement.

Usually the supportive ministers were from smaller, mostly rural churches who lived in Marks. Maybe it's because they were less beholden to white folks for their living. Many others who took part in the movement came from families active in church work, like the Collins family at Reverend Towner's Silent Grove Church.

"Reverend Towner of the NAACP is my pastor," Lee Dora Collins told me. "I've been in the NAACP since the year of '60. Ooh, it was so secret, we was so scared. We never had a meeting here. We had to go to Clarksdale to meet with Aaron Henry. We didn't have no more than a little get-together in Reverend Malone's house. We couldn't have a meeting then like we do now." I asked her why she had joined. "They said if you needed a lawyer you should. They said it's some good lawyers in the NAACP." However, she reported, "I ain't used nary one."

Dr. Howard, who had recruited these ministers, had seen their potential early on, even though they often lacked formal education. Reverend Malone and Reverend Allen had been preaching in other ministers' churches for almost twenty years at the time of Emmet Till's killing. Reverend Malone became the pastor of his own church in 1955, the year of Till's trial. Dr. Howard, a highly educated man, played a major role in trying to bring Emmett Till's killers to justice, but he depended a great deal on local leaders like Reverend Malone.

Voting Rights Go Public in Marks

Still, the majority of the Black population of Marks had little contact with the civil rights movement. Then, in the fall of 1962, President John Kennedy sent federal troops to Oxford, Mississippi, about eighty miles east of Marks, to protect the right of African American James Meredith to attend the University of Mississippi. White students rioted, and two people, a French reporter and a local white man, were killed.[13] Suddenly everyone knew something about the movement.

"The first I was for knowing about the civil rights was when James Meredith went to Ole Miss in 1962 and the killing started over there," William Franklin told me. "I knowed James Meredith when I lived out on the plantation. His family had they own little farm. I got tired of white folks on my back and my children's back telling me what to do and daring me what not to do."

At the time that federal troops were at Oxford protecting Meredith, local whites made some small concessions. Mr. Franklin remembered that the eye doctor in Oxford let him come in through the front door instead of the back for the first time. More Black people got the opportunity to vote, while white scrutiny of those voters also intensified. The Sovereignty Commission tracked the increase in Black voter registration in Quitman and probably other counties as well.

Reverend Malone told me that in 1962 he became Quitman County's first Black poll watcher. "The white at the poll told me to leave. The marshal what be there in the poll looked in the book and told me they better let me back in there. He said they better get ready to have a whole lot of Blacks there. But my boss told me I'd better get out of there, or I'd be dead before night."

That same year, the Student Nonviolent Coordinating Committee began voter registration work in the Delta at Greenwood, fifty miles south of Marks. SNCC was a grassroots organization of Black college students and a handful of whites who went into Black communities to organize.[14] Each staff worker got a subsidy of ten dollars a week. As time went on, some local people were also given subsidies.

In Mississippi, SNCC focused primarily on voter registration. The organization's strategy was to teach Black people about the state constitution at citizenship "schools" they established and persuade them to try to register to vote. SNCC staff workers would accompany them to observe any irregularities. The object was to demonstrate a pattern of discrimination against African Americans trying to register, to convince the federal courts to end the constitutional interpretation test. SNCC succeeded in getting the test abolished in Panola County, next door to Quitman, by early 1964. Gwen Gillon, a Black SNCC worker, told me that she got a job chopping cotton in Panola so she could talk with the laborers there about registering to vote. They got the Justice Department on it, and Black registration in that county went from thirteen to over one thousand in a few months.[15]

In the fall of 1963, SNCC joined with the NAACP, the SCLC, and the Congress on Racial Equality (CORE) in a coalition, the Council of Federated Organizations (COFO). Using a strategy called "parallel institutionalism"—modeling inclusiveness by building integrated institutions identical to existing all-white ones—COFO hoped to establish Black fitness for voting by setting up its own election structures. That November, COFO ran Aaron Henry for governor of Mississippi in a mock election, with Tougaloo College chaplain Rev. Ed King, a white man, for lieutenant governor. Mock ballot boxes were set up in Black churches, stores, and living rooms, and Black residents were urged to take part to show that many more Black people would vote than were allowed by the constitutional interpretation test. While fewer than 7 percent of Black Mississippians were officially registered to vote, more than 80,000 of the 425,000 Black residents of voting age—more than 18 percent—voted in the mock election.[16]

In Marks, the rapid rise in civil rights activity caused a split in the Voters' League. Those who wanted to openly identify with the movement left the organization and set up the Quitman County League, with Reverend Allen as its head. The two groups did not reunite until 1966. As Lula Belle Weathersby told it, "In 1963, the Southern Christian Leadership came to Quitman County, and things really started picking up. That was when they had the big March on Washington in August, and a few from Quitman County went on it. Then the NAACP and the Southern Christian Leadership merged [to form COFO]. Most of the preachers and teachers was scared to take part except for Reverend Malone and a few others. So they put most of the work on Mr. Franklin. He's not a preacher or a teacher or nothing, but he's got all kinds of nerve. I wouldn't want no better leader."

After the success of the voting experiment, COFO held a conference in Jackson on April 24, 1964, to organize the Mississippi Freedom Democratic Party.[17] The MFDP's purpose was to provide a statewide network allowing full political participation by Black people. COFO planned to conduct a full primary election with its own, integrated slate of delegates, to occur at the same time as the traditional Democratic primary that excluded Black voters. COFO hoped that the national Democratic Party would recognize the MFDP as its official state representative at its national convention in place of the all-white Mississippi Democratic Party, since segregation violated the 1946 Supreme Court decision barring all-white primaries.

The MFDP held a state convention on August 6 to nominate a slate of candidates. Reverend Allen's wife Georgia, Quitman County's official delegate, attended that convention, as did William Franklin and Reverend Carter. The MFDP candidate for senator was Victoria Gray, a Black teacher from Hattiesburg. In the Second Congressional District, where Marks was, the MFDP candidate for representative was Fannie Lou Hamer, a Black woman who had been thrown off a plantation about fifty miles south of Marks for registering to vote. She had been beaten severely by police when she was returning from learning how to organize a Freedom School.[18]

After the convention, Mrs. Allen was fired from two of the cleaning jobs she had. She had done cleaning for a white woman named Mrs. Hughes for some time. After the MFDP convention, Mrs. Hughes told her, "If you have any other place, I don't need you because my daughter can do the work." At another house, Mrs. Allen was told they had forgotten she was coming and done the work themselves. The fact that they didn't just fire her outright but instead pretended it was about something else suggests that even whites who opposed civil rights recognized that things were changing and they couldn't be as openly racist as before. Still, Mrs. Allen lost her jobs.[19]

This was the summer that brought civil rights workers to Marks. In June, over a thousand volunteers, mostly white college students, arrived in Mississippi to organize the MFDP and help Black people register to vote. They conducted Freedom School classes in Black history and literature for young people and literacy classes for the older generation. After state civil rights workers met Mrs. Allen, Reverend Carter, and Mr. Franklin at the convention, they decided Marks was a promising place to organize. James Jones, a Black student who directed COFO's Clarksdale project, contacted Reverend Allen's Quitman County League, which agreed to welcome civil rights workers to Marks.

The first group arrived in Marks on August 5, 1964. William Franklin picked up the story. "I told ever one of them civil rights workers when they landed here, 'What you all are doing, you ain't going to get it done the way y'all want it, except get your head whupped. I'm for it—what I understand of it.' 'Course I ain't never seen it before, just heard of it. They drove up here in about seven cars. The sheriffs told them they couldn't stay here. But they got out and started running in cafes, the colored and the white man together, and fights got started.

"I was driving . . . out of the cotton patch into Marks when the civil rights workers come pouring into town. The police come the time the civil rights workers hit the ground. The civil rights workers went into a restaurant, and the man told them to get out. Then one of the civil rights lawyers come along to see what happened, and the police jumped on him and busted his head. They left here a-crying."

It happened in front of Mrs. Allen's house, she told me. "The old sheriff jumped on them right outside of my house and hit one of them on the head, and two of them come in here to make a call. A lot of people wouldn't let them use their phones." They were too afraid of what the whites might do to them if they cooperated.

City Marshal Bob McArthur, who had clubbed the lawyer, took him to jail and left him there without treatment.[20] But neither violence nor jail stopped the movement. After all, mistreatment wasn't anything new.[21] And even in jail COFO workers won adherents. J. D. Powells told me about his experience with them. "I was in jail when the civil rights lawyer was brought in. When I was arrested, the deputy told me, 'I can't stand you at all.'

"I said, 'Why?'

"He said, 'First of all, you Black. Second, you a n——.'

"My first arrest—eighteen years old. The arrest was for assault. My wife and I rassled over a gun, and it went off. I hit her in the leg. She didn't press charges. The sheriff showed me a cattle prod and told me it was a lie detector. He said, 'N——, if you tell a lie, it's going to knock the hell out of you.' I said, 'That's a cattle prod.' I know one guy the sheriff made climb the wall with it.

"I was in jail ninety days. When the civil rights workers came to town, I saw the civil rights lawyer the sheriff locked up and hit. The deputy told me not to talk to him. And that's when I decided to get involved in the civil rights movement."

By August 9, several civil rights workers had found places to stay in Marks with local people. It wasn't easy. One couple who took in civil rights workers, Rev. Jeff Jones and his wife Mary, lived across the street from Reverend Malone, who also had civil rights workers staying with him. Mary Jones later told journalist Howell Raines that she took in seven Black and four white workers because no one else would. Most of the others were frightened because whites had threatened to burn down the homes of anyone who housed them. Mrs. Jones took a more philosophical approach. "They was here to help us," she explained. "And since they was there to help us, I was there to help them." As she told her neighbors, "Dyin' is all right. Ain't but one thing about dyin'. That's make sho' you right cause you gon' die anyway." She was warned repeatedly not to get involved with "communists," and her white employer asked her repeatedly whether she was providing housing for the civil rights workers. Mary refused to say. The white woman explained to Mary that she was worried about "this intermarriage." Mary did not hold back. "I said, 'Well, ain't no need in worryin' about that because if you wanna worry about that you oughta been talkin' to your grandaddy.'"[22]

The project director for Marks was Doris Newman. She was Black, as almost all COFO project directors were, even that summer when white participation was at a maximum. She organized the first civil rights mass meeting on August 10. It was held on the first floor of the Black Masonic Hall, which was also Reverend Carter's church on Sundays. An overflow crowd of Black people came. The civil rights workers introduced themselves to the people and showed a film about the movement, which aroused a lot of interest, because there were no movie theaters in Quitman County. The civil rights workers got all the adults at the meeting to fill out Freedom Registration Forms to participate in the MFDP primary.

The meeting was very powerful. Every meeting was. There was a lot of singing. COFO workers reached back into Black tradition to encourage participation, so they taught Freedom Songs, which were usually old spirituals, well known by the people, with new civil rights words added. For example:

> I woke up this morning with my mind
> stayed on Jesus

became

> I woke up this morning with my mind
> stayed on freedom.

And

> Ain't gonna let nobody turn me around
> Gonna keep on walking, keep on talking
> marching up to Canaan Land

became

> Ain't gonna let no jailhouse turn me around
> Gonna keep on walking . . .
> marching up to Freedom Land.

New verses could be added in any new situation. These lines from a spiritual:

> If you miss me from moaning
> And you can't find me nowhere
> Come on up to bright Glory
> And I'll be moaning up there

became

> If you miss me from the cotton fields
> And you can't find me nowhere
> Come on over to the courthouse
> And I'll be voting right there.

The songs were very popular with the young people. Of course, not all the word changes had to do with civil rights. Children in Marks sang:

> If you miss me from your kitchen, Mama,
> And you can't find me nowhere
> Come on over to the snow cone stand
> And I'll be hanging 'round there.

Although the Freedom Songs were lively and defiant, every mass meeting opened with the solemn singing of a hymn. One favorite was:

I love the Lord, He heard my cry
And pitied every groan
Long as I live, while troubles rise
I'll hasten to His throne.

Each syllable would be dragged out, up and down the scale, in "long meter," as local people called it, without the sharp rhythm of most of these songs. With the slow surge of their deep voices, that one stanza might take minutes. More than once at mass meetings someone would cry out, "I won't hold back!" or "Get the Spirit!" and start dancing in the aisle. As people in Marks said often, the Israelites were slaves in Egypt 430 years, and God set them free. Now it looked like God was going to do the same thing after 430 years of Black people being in America.

Every mass meeting ended with the people holding hands and singing:

We shall overcome
We shall overcome
We shall overcome some day.
Deep in my heart
I do believe
We shall overcome some day.

This had also come from a religious song, "I Shall Overcome."

The people needed the power of those songs for courage. The night of that first mass meeting in Marks, cars full of deputy sheriffs and police and other whites came to the Black Masonic Hall to take the license plate numbers of people at the meeting. Civil rights workers who had come over from Clarksdale to take part in the meeting were harassed. COFO worker Lew Sitzer described his treatment. Bob McArthur, the city marshal, swore at him and arrested him for suspicion because there had been a large number of bank robberies and car thefts in Marks. He threatened Sitzer with a blackjack and stopped at two gas stations to tell people there, "I want you to see what a communist civil rights worker bastard looks like." McArthur then brought Lew back to town, after threatening him and the other civil rights workers. Hank Kassler, a lawyer following up on the arrests was himself arrested and hit; only when learning of his occupation did McArthur let him go. As he left he saw about thirty white men standing on the corner watching and pointing to him. A highway patrolman had to escort him out of town. The other workers, including Sitzer, were stranded in Marks. Trying to leave, they encountered a cluster of cars on the side of the road, and had to beat a hasty retreat.[23]

On August 14, the *Quitman County Democrat* carried the names and license numbers of Black people who had attended the mass meeting. The next day, Sheriff Clint Turner went by the homes of two Black women who had been at the meeting and told them to go to the courthouse to see County Attorney Caldwell. One of the women, S. C. Rose Kendricks, was keeping civil rights workers in her house. Ernestine Evans, the other woman, was the mother of J. D. Powells, who had joined the movement after talking to the civil rights lawyer in jail.

Mrs. Kendricks described the meeting to COFO lawyer Henry Aronson. "[Mr. Caldwell] asked me whether the Freedom Riders were staying with me, and I said yes, believing he referred to the civil rights workers. He asked how many there were, and I said two now. He asked how many were there before, and I said four. He asked if they were white or colored, and I said two were white and two were colored. He asked if I knew what these people were here for, and I said yes. He also asked me if I knew a number of others, including Reverend Jones, Reverend Ingram, Mr. Love, and some other people whose names I do not remember."[24] Reverend Jones was the NAACP member in whose home eleven civil rights workers were staying. Reverend Ingram and Mr. Love were in the old Voters' League and not associated with COFO.

Like Mary Jones, Mrs. Kendricks was threatened. Mr. Caldwell told her that although she had remarried, she didn't have a legal divorce from her first husband and warned that she would "go to the penitentiary for ten years" if she continued her involvement. "He read this from some book he had with him. He went on to say, 'Those Freedom Riders got you into this, let them get you out of this.' He said I should have a meeting with the Freedom Riders and tell them to get out of town. He also said to me, in a way that sounded like a threat, didn't I know those Freedom Riders wouldn't be here in September? Then he told me that he was not going to put me in jail right then but that I was to come back to him at 2:00 p.m. Monday, and that I was under no circumstances to bring anybody with me." Caldwell also warned her that as long as people helped the COFO workers, they would be "taken to court for every violation of law they had made in their lives."[25]

Just about everyone who was involved received these kinds of threats. But Ernestine Evans wasn't worried. "I lived through all these old bad white people. I believe I could live through anything. I once got down to 60 pounds when I had my babies, and the doctors told me to jump in the river. And I lived.

"When we first had civil rights meetings, they sent us a notice to come to the county attorney's office like we had committed a crime. They fastened the door like they was going to lock it, and they threatened us about going to the civil rights meetings. They said, 'We ain't gonna allow no mess like that here.' They called in everybody I knowed that went."

And there were consequences. "After that, my husband got fired. My son J. D. got put in jail several times. I was getting medicine from the drug store. I was getting credit. I was paying my bill, and then they wouldn't let me have any more. And I got fired from chopping cotton. I took a bus driving test to haul cotton pickers, and they wouldn't let me pass it. They haven't let me have no kind of job in this county since then. So we went up to Chicago looking for a job, but there was fighting up there, so we come back."

Such harassment was more typical than outright violence. Like much of the Delta, Marks didn't have a Klan. Instead, these towns had Citizens' Councils composed of planters and white business and civic leaders. While the poorer whites of the Klan engaged in terrorism against the civil rights movement, the more affluent Citizens' Councils would coordinate programs of systematic firings and arrests. Individual whites might use violence against Blacks in Marks, but the town's Citizens' Council members could stay within the law because they were the law.

Whites continued to harass civil rights workers and the local people who put them up, but the meetings grew larger anyway. On August 17, the second mass meeting took place. This time it was held in a larger building, Eudora Methodist Church. About four hundred people, a fourth of the Black population of Marks, attended. Doris Newman counted six cars driven by police and other whites. They took down license numbers of attendees.[26] Leaders at the meeting tried to organize clubs to work on access to Social Security, jobs, and welfare. The clubs did not survive long. The problems they represented did.

The next day forty-five people attended a voter education class the civil rights workers taught at the Masonic Hall. The six who seemed most likely to pass the constitutional interpretation test went to the courthouse on August 19 to attempt to register to vote. That same day Mrs. Kendricks was arrested for bigamy. She was released on a $300 bond put up by Mr. Aronson.

All this took amazing courage because it had become all too clear that the whites' threats were real. Black people involved in the movement or who had civil rights workers staying with them had to get used to new risks to their jobs, their families, and their safety. Reverend Allen, like many of the ministers of smaller churches, was also a laborer. His employer was also his landlord, which exposed him to a double risk. "I got acquainted with the executive heads of those civil rights workers who come here in 1964," he told me. "I kept five or six of them here. Good God, I don't know how many was here. I got all kinds of phone calls threatening to put me in the river. I couldn't get a car insured here. They went to my boss man and tried to buy my house from him so they could throw me out, but he had enough God in him where he told them no. He's one that really likes colored people.

"The civil rights workers wasn't strange to me. I could enjoy them, white and Black. You take that woman down the street with a grocery, Mrs. Shaw, I don't know what she didn't do for the civil rights workers—fed them, given them money.

"All the white people told me I didn't have good sense. I had an old white man tell me I ought to go to some old 'n——' and have him learn me how to talk to white folks. I said I didn't need to learn how to talk to nobody. As for white folks, I wasn't scared of nary one. I'll work on his place, but if he misuse me, I'll move off his place, I don't care what."

Reverend Malone had a similar story of intimidation and an outsized courage that let him stand up to threatening whites. "I owned 40 acres, but I sold it after this integration thing started up. The reason was I was afraid to go out to work. My life was threatened. They met me on the road and threatened me.

"I had four civil rights workers here in my house, all men. They wasn't a bit of trouble. They was doing all they could for us. Mr. Bob Young, a white man, he come up to my door and said, 'I want to see you.' I said, 'You looking at me.' He aksed me did I have any white boys with me. I said, 'Yes, sir, I do.' He said didn't I know this wasn't no integrated country? I said it wasn't for white women and colored men, but it was for white men and colored women. I said he could go along the street in the day and see colored so light you'd think they was white.

"He aksed me did I know why that happened. He said it was because out on the plantations the planters mixed the poor whites among the colored and some of the white mens acted like a dog. I said, 'Why didn't none of the colored mens act like a dog?' It was because he would kill them, that's why.

"He told me I woulda been killed if it don't be for Mr. Cox, the planter I rode for. Mr. Cox likeded me."

On the other hand, Alec Dean reported getting no threats. "I had a gang of civil rights workers stay with me—about fourteen. It was four white girls stayed here. When they left here, I was out of $450. I was giving them pocket money, Black and white. I tried to make things pleasant for them all. The money I had was for me and my family too.

"The civil rights workers were fine people, all of them fine. You know, the white people did seem strange to me at first. I gets along with everybody. Everybody gets along with me because I treats them all right. I got white friends, and then I got some dark friends. I ain't never had no white people say nothing to me about it. I had a few colored say my boss man would fire me, but nobody never said nothing about it."

There were some decent white people in Marks. And that was important because many of the civil rights workers were white, and it was important that Black people were able to trust them. That was the vision of COFO and SNCC too—Black and white together. Black people had to take the lead, but the civil rights movement was really also in white people's interest. Mrs. Weathersby told me, "You know, when the white civil rights workers come along, I had a lot of faith in them. You know why? Because all along, we had some white friends, but they had to live under the code. They was afraid to speak openly. But I always believed there was going to be white people come and show they was on our side, and they did. Some of them was really into this thing for themselves too. They was into it for themselves and us too. But the Black man shouldn't lean on them too much. Blacks should stand up for themselves and be a man. It's hard to be left alone and stand up for yourself.

"Even our educated people, the schoolteachers and so forth, they didn't know what to do about this. This was a thing that hadn't never been before. And when you all taught us, we had to teach them. They hadn't been taught nothing but the white man's world, and we had to teach them the real thing. Now, when I first started working with the movement, I didn't know what to do. I knowed what I wanted, but I didn't know how to do it. And I wanted to do it right."

I asked her what started her with the movement. "I seen there was something needed," she explained. "And if anything could change conditions, I wanted to work with it. 'Cause we was suffering so bad. When I first started working with the movement, my father and mother was still alive. They was scared half to death for me all the time. They was for the movement, but they was worried about me, so I kind of slowed down. Then when they both passed, I got back into it.

"I tried to register to vote in '64. My eyes was bad, and I couldn't see the constitution. And you know they would scare the life out of you because they treat you so bad. I could understand the constitution, but I couldn't see to read it. I registered after they done away with the constitution test in 1965. Ain't that something? They fought us and treated us like animals to keep us from registering, and now they come around and beg you for your vote."

Atlantic City

The last week of August 1964, the MFDP sent a delegation to the National Democratic Convention in Atlantic City, New Jersey. The eighty Black and four white delegates (including a former Klansman) argued that they should be the legitimate delegation rather than the all-white regular Mississippi delegation.[27] The MFDP lawyers prepared a brief stating that the MFDP and Black Mississippians in general had been illegally excluded from the Mississippi Democratic Party. The brief noted that the MFDP was pledged to campaign for the Democratic candidate for president, Lyndon Johnson. Most of the regular Democratic leaders in Mississippi had refused to campaign for Johnson, and some were openly working for the Republican, Barry Goldwater.

The COFO project workers from Marks and Reverend Carter's daughter Florean went to the convention. They demonstrated on the boardwalk in front of the convention hall with civil rights workers and people from all over Mississippi.

Even though the MFDP brief was correct, the Democratic Party refused to replace the all-white delegation. Instead they offered the MFDP members two "at large" seats at the convention. The MFDP refused. Their anger and frustration were palpable.[28]

This is where I first encountered these Mississippi activists. I had been working in the New York SNCC office, and we all went to Atlantic City to demonstrate for the MFDP. There I met Stokely Carmichael, who was the COFO project director in Mississippi's Second Congressional District, where Marks was. He told me I could come and work there. I hitched to Holly Springs, Mississippi, when the convention was over. I spent two nights in jail on the way, once in North Carolina and once in Tennessee.

I was arrested in North Carolina because it was raining hard and I knocked on the door of a house. A white teenage girl let me in. I said I wanted to get out of the rain and asked if I could have something to eat. She gave me a jelly sandwich. Then I went to a restaurant to get out of the chilly damp weather. The girl's mother was there, talking frantically about the man who had come in while her daughter was alone. I said, "I'm the one." The policeman took me to the town jail. After an hour or so a deputy sheriff took me to the county jail. Later two deputies took me to the Georgia line and let me go.

The next day I was in western Tennessee. The weather was much milder, and I wasn't getting any rides, so I curled up under a tree and went to sleep. I didn't know I was near a roadside bar that had been burglarized not long before. The owner got the sheriff's deputies to wake me up and take me to the county jail. The next day they drove me to the county line and let me go. I had already spent two nights in jail before I even started organizing in the South. At that time I had never heard of Marks. I intended to go to Clarksdale.

CHAPTER 3

"If You Want Some Fighting, We're Here to Give It to You" 1964–1965

After the National Democratic Convention turned down the MFDP delegation, most of the COFO summer volunteers went back to their various colleges. More and more, the people of Marks had to take over leadership of the movement. They did so with the aid of several organizations, not only COFO and the MFDP but also the NAACP and a new union (the Mississippi Freedom Labor Union). For school integration and voting rights, they got some help from the Justice Department. But local people did most of the day-to-day organizing. For example, Clara Collins, whose parents had been in the NAACP, was secretary of the Quitman County MFDP. Much of what I write is possible because of the notes Clara made at each meeting. She also traveled to other places where the movement was active and brought information back for the people in Marks.

The voting rights project remained the centerpiece of movement work. But it was clear that more than voting rights was at stake. People wanted to challenge economic exploitation, the routine violence and humiliation of segregation, and white resistance to school integration. All the struggles were related. Young people who became active in voting rights efforts then demanded the right to enroll in the white school or marched into segregated businesses. Adults lost their jobs because of civil rights activities, which then drew them into other forms of organizing. It was all being fought at the same time.

Each project took a long time and was very dangerous. Even after laws and court decisions mandated equality, the local white community resisted it at every step. We had to struggle to make anything happen and then make sure people knew about it. There was a lot of violence. We also faced resistance in the Black community from those who were afraid to participate.

Integrating Schools

In August 1964, after the Clarksdale Freedom Summer project had brought the movement to Marks, some families discussed trying to integrate the schools. In September, four Black youths tried to enroll in the white high school: Irene and Martha Anne Green, their cousin Betty Brown, and Leon Phipps.[1] Leon and his brother James had spent most of their time that summer at the Black Masonic Hall with the civil rights workers. Their father, Percy, had recently lost his job, presumably for civil rights movement activity. He had worked at a cottonseed mill owned by the Selfs. This mill was the largest employer in Marks.

Percy Phipps told me what had happened. "At the end of August 1964, I was laid off from my job at the Self's [Cottonseed] Oil Mill. That evening when I came home, my wife told me that Frank Brown, a Negro, had come by the house with a bottle of whiskey and refused to dispose of it when my wife asked him to. Then my wife and my son James said the sheriff, Clint Turner, and Chief Deputy Sanford Faust entered the house and charged me with possession of illegal liquor. They left a warrant for my arrest. I left for Chicago with my family except for Leon and James that same day. I have returned to Marks and am now living in hiding." The boys stayed with their grandmother in Marks.

Willie Thompson, Betty Brown's stepfather, worked at the same mill. He too had been involved in civil rights–related activities. "The first the civil rights come to us, the first we knowed about it, there was some little childrens got killed in Alabama in 1963," he explained. He was referring to the church bombing in Birmingham, where four girls getting ready for Sunday choir were killed. "My sister had grandchildren in that Sunday school where it happened." But even before that, he'd been active. "I been voting a long time. I paid poll tax several times. It was back when Roosevelt or Truman was president. The whites didn't bother here near as bad as they did some other places. But it was very few Blacks voting."

I asked him why he wanted to try to integrate the schools. "That was to give an equal opportunity," he responded. "[SNCC worker] Dave Bradshaw was here at the time, Richard Moore also. They told us it was the time to integrate the school. We met—there was twelve or thirteen of us, but when time come, didn't but three families go: my brother-in-law Chester Green's daughters Martha Anne and Irene, my daughter Betty, and one of the Phipps boys. They turned us all down September 9.

"I lost my job at the oil mill four months later, and so did my brother-in-law about the same day. They wouldn't give me no reason, but the superintendent told me, 'Willie, you is one of the best operators we got, but Mr. Self told me to do it, and, if I don't, he'll get rid of me same as you.'

"I asked him [the superintendent], 'Why you fire me?'

"He said, 'Who say we fired you?'

"I said, 'Well, you put me off and put another man in my place. So I can't call that laying off, that's firing.' I had worked at that place in all fifteen years. They put one of the truck drivers in my place. He didn't like the job and didn't know the job.

"My brother-in-law went to Chicago for about two years when he lost his job. He didn't get nary job immediately when he come back, but he finally got one over to the mill after so long. He got laid off there again because the mill is about done gone. I tried all around finding a job after I got fired. Nobody would hire me. I went to Florida to pick oranges. I drawed my disability from my work. They fired my wife from working as a maid in the white elementary school building after they fired me.[2] She went to New York to work."

I wondered why he didn't move to Chicago to find work. "I didn't have kin in Chicago," he explained, "just a brother who stayed some little out of town. And it cost something to stay there while you look for a job." Many Black people from Marks and elsewhere relied on extended family for help in hard times and moved in what scholars have called chains of migration, following family and friends when searching for new opportunities.

I asked him whether, after all that trouble, there had been enough changes in Marks to have made that effort worthwhile. Willie's teenage daughter Jeanie Ruth nodded her head vigorously and answered, "Yes."

"Oh, I don't know about that," her father replied.

"Oh, come on, Daddy," she pressed. "It's been tremendous changes."

Mr. Thompson thought a minute. "It upset me sometimes. The people here in the community at these meetings had told me they would help me out if I'd send my children over to integrate the white school. Then they didn't help. Lots of colored people said, 'I wouldn't have done that if I was you.'" Still, he acknowledged, "The whites have stopped most of this 'buking and 'busing they used to do."

Here a friend of Jeanie Ruth's piped up. "I don't remember the names of any of the civil rights workers. There were so many of them. My mother wouldn't let me go near them."

"The main thing about that integration," Willie continued, "The colored people got as hard a line as the white folk about letting you have anything. In these meetings, they'd all agree that they was going to do something, but they ended up doing nothing to help you if you integrated and lost your job. It was really hard on me. But finally I seed my way out and I got this far."

Organizing

I was at the COFO project in Holly Springs when the integration attempt was made in Marks. I had wanted to go to Clarksdale, but all the cars COFO had were either broken down or going to Georgia to work on Rev. C. B. King's congressional campaign. And no civil rights worker would have hitched from Holly Springs, near the Tennessee line, to Clarksdale, well down in the Delta. It was too dangerous. Many places in Mississippi were experiencing more violent incidents than Marks. The events I'm narrating have to be put in the context of constant arrests, beatings, and shootings going on around the state.

Two civil rights workers, Pete Brett and Steve Sokoloff, drove me to Clarksdale. There I met up with Dave Bradshaw and Richard Moore. They said they were leaving Marks in a few days and there wouldn't be any civil rights workers there. They also said it was kind of a rough place, which made me anxious to go there, because Clarksdale seemed pretty tame, and several civil rights workers were already there. I went to the mass meeting in Marks with Dave and Richard the night of September 14.

After the meeting, we spent the night with Rev. G. W. Ward and his wife Sarah, with whom Dave and Richard had been staying. The next morning, before heading back north, they took me to COFO's office and library in the Black Masonic Hall. Some of the books there were Black history and literature, but many were leftover third-rate stuff donated by people up north. Reverend Carter, who was one of the few Black plumbers in Mississippi as well as a minister and small farmer, had installed a sink, shower, and toilet in a little room there. This was a big convenience for me, because Reverend Ward and everyone on his street were without baths or indoor toilets, even though they lived in the city limits. (Part of the Black area, like the Cotton Street neighborhood, was even worse off. It was designated outside city limits so Marks didn't have to provide running water or pave the streets. I wore out a pair of tennis shoes a month in the mud of Cotton Street.)[3]

The night I arrived, something happened that would cause a lot of trouble for the movement in Marks. A teenage couple went into the bathroom Reverend Carter had built and had sexual relations. The pipes connecting to the toilet and shower broke under the strain. The shower was useless, and the toilet wouldn't flush. Still, for some time after that, children kept coming in and using the toilet, which filled up with a constant stink and clouds of flies. Reverend Carter was upset, and for months he demanded that COFO pay him for the damage.[4]

The day after the toilet incident, nineteen-year-old Allan Goodner, the new project director, came to Marks. He had been in the first restaurant sit-ins in Nashville in 1960 and been beaten by police. We continued the voting rights program COFO had started.

All fall, Allan and I went house to house asking people to fill out registration forms for the MFDP's Freedom Vote election. Going around with the forms was a good way to get to know people, and signing one was like a minimal commitment to the civil rights movement. "I done joined up," those who filled out the forms would say. But it was cotton picking time. Most of the cotton in the Delta was still picked by hand. Even in fields where picking machines were used, people were sent in after them to scrap—picking the cotton the machines had left. Every morning at five, people would stand along the streets waiting for the beat-up old trucks and former school buses to take them to the field. For the rest of the day, the Black section of Marks was almost deserted. There were only the very old and the disabled for Allan and me to talk to, or those so well off that they had little interest in the civil rights movement. Reverend Ward, who was sixty-four, and his wife, fifty-four, were both out picking cotton. The kids we wanted to have in a Freedom School, to discuss Black history and the movement, were all "gone to the field." Usually the only time Allan and I found people at their houses was around sundown when they came in. We had to be quick about it, because people went to bed around 8:30 p.m. so they could be up by 5:00 a.m. The only days people stayed home were when it was too rainy to pick.

Picking was a social occasion as well as hard work. One old woman I knew lived with her daughter, a teacher. That meant they had a more comfortable income than the great majority of the Black people in Marks. Yet the old woman went out to the field every day. All her friends were there. If she wanted to talk with them, she had to be out picking cotton.

As Reverend Ward explained resentfully, people often "worked under the gun" while picking cotton. That meant that a white man, the planter or one of his employees, sat in a pickup with a rifle near the pickers. One member of the Self family told me that if he ever caught me on his plantation he would shoot me, and no jury would find him guilty.[5] Still, I sometimes got rides to visit shacks on plantations, including his. I probably visited over half the Black homes in Marks that fall, and probably more than half the adults filled out Freedom Vote registration forms.

Allan and I didn't have a car to visit the rest of the county. On Sundays Reverend Ward would take us to churches in the countryside—"in the rural" as people said in the Delta—where he pastored or was invited to preach. He was famous in the area for his eloquence and knowledge of the Bible, but he struggled to get enough money for gas. Some Sundays he might travel around a hundred miles and visit four churches. He was happiest when we came to one of the few churches that had a piano; he was also famous for his powerful singing and piano playing. Thanks to our travels with him, many Black people in other communities, such as Lambert and Falcon, filled out Freedom Vote registration forms.

Our Monday night mass meetings were smaller and shorter during the harvest season. People were too tired after ten hours picking cotton. They got $2.50 for every hundred pounds and usually picked two or three hundred pounds a day. Still, even though the times I could see people were limited, I got to know many of them. I would go around with J. D. Powells, who knew all the Black people in Marks and was related to a large portion of them. He said, "If you use too many big college words to people, I'll break it down where they can understand." But often he just repeated exactly what I said. The problem was that many Black people had been totally turned off to whites. They had to hear a Black voice say something before they would seriously listen to it. But after people got familiar with me, they would talk to me more easily. They began to tell me about their lives.

James Taper, an illiterate fourteen-year-old, told me about how a deputy stuck him with a cattle prod, the way J. D. had been threatened, and the kind of stuff we were in Mississippi to end. I took down his statement in case the Jackson COFO office wanted to bring a suit: "The night of September 6, 1964, I was arrested by Deputy Jesse Zimmerman at Rucker's store. Another boy had been throwing rocks at dogs in front of Rucker's store. Deputy Zimmerman said I had been throwing rocks. I had not been. He took us to jail and locked us up. Next morning Deputy Sanford came to us and said, 'You are the n——s I want.' He took us to his office. He tried to get me to say I threw rocks. I wouldn't say I threw rocks, so he said he would get out his lying machine and, if it hurt me, I was lying. He got a round box out of his desk. He took a machine out of the box. It looked like a flashlight with a cord at one end. The machine had two points at one end and he stuck them in my second and fourth fingers, and it made me cry and shake all over. He told us to come back Thursday and let us out."

People started showing me all kinds of papers, the documents the modern world had showered down on them from lawyers, welfare, county government, insurance companies, car dealers, and loan agencies. They wanted me to read the documents to them and explain in clear words what they meant, even if I couldn't give much advice.

They also had me help fill out forms. One day Jessie Franklin came into the Masonic Hall with workers' compensation forms. He had been shoveling dirt to build a levee when he slipped and injured his spine and was unable to work. I filled out the form for him as a matter of course and never realized what would come of it. When his $5,000 compensation check came, Mr. Franklin used the money to bail people out of jail who were there on civil rights charges, and for a long time he paid for gas so civil rights workers could visit Black people in remote areas of the county.

I asked him about that. "I found out that the state wasn't doing nothing for me, and nothing from nothing leaves nothing. So I been active in this situation ever since," he told me. "I used to carry the civil rights workers around to plantations to talk to people. I know practically all these people around through here from Shelby in Bolivar County all through around to Quitman County. So I introduced the civil rights workers to all the fellows I know. That was in '64 and '65. Only but one thing I know: the people stopped marching here too quick. 'Cause when you quit that marching, they think they can run over you any way they please."

The Fight for Voting Rights

People may have trusted me a little more than before, but the system hadn't changed. Despite COFO's efforts, Black citizens continued to be barred from registering to vote. Mrs. Mittia Anne Smith, inspired by the Summer Project, told me her experience: "Around the beginning of September 1964, I went to register to vote at the Quitman County Courthouse. Mrs. Marie Evanson [Eavenson], the registrar, didn't read me a section of the Mississippi constitution to interpret. She did not even tell me what to do with the second page of the registration form which consisted entirely of lines with no words. Then I was told that I had not been accepted as a voter because the form was incomplete."[6]

Nevertheless, we pressed on. The MFDP wanted its candidates on the official state ballot. Around the state, civil rights workers tried to find enough of the few Black voters to fill out nominating petitions for the MFDP candidates. In Marks, several Black youths helped us gather signatures. Then I took the nominating petitions to the county courthouse to be certified. I wrote down what happened for the MFDP to use as evidence in any future lawsuit:

> I am 22 years old. The morning of October 1, 1964, I went to the Quitman County Courthouse with Charles Ware, J. D. Powells and Sam Jackson, all minors. We were taking . . . a petition to have Mrs. Fannie Lou Hamer on the ballot as candidate for congresswoman to have it certified that the petitioners were on the list of registered voters.
>
> Mrs. Evanson, the registrar, said she was busy, and a man that J. D. Powells identified to me as James Walker, attorney for the local Citizens' Council, told me to check the names on the petition with the voters' list myself.
>
> I did so, then I needed a witness to the certification of the petition, so I returned to the Masonic Hall . . . and found D. C. Weaver, age 25. I took him with me to the courthouse. We went to the office again, and Mrs. Evanson told me she had to make a telephone call. So we went out in the hall to wait. A white man who D. C. Weaver identified to me later

as Hoke Stone, District Attorney, came out and said, "Hey, you!" Several Negro boys in the hall, D. C. Weaver and myself started forward. "I mean you," he said, pointing to D. C. Weaver. Then D. C. Weaver started forward. I did too, but Mr. Stone indicated he just wanted to talk to Mr. Weaver. "Are you trying to register to vote?" he asked Mr. Weaver.

"We are witnesses to this nominating petition," I said.

"Well, Mrs. Evanson is too busy to see you today," Mr. Stone said. "Take it to a notary public. A notary can fix you up." He told D. C. Weaver and me to go to the Graeber Lumber Company and find the notary public there. We went and the notary public there told me, "I won't notarize this unless I see all these folks here on the petition for myself."

I believe this can be fairly described as a run-around.

I took my statement and the nominating petition to Rev. A. L. Saddler, the only Black notary public in Marks. Reverend Saddler was the head of the Delta Burial Home, probably the largest Black-owned business in Quitman County at the time. He told me he would not notarize an affidavit not prepared by a lawyer.[7]

There was something I didn't know at the time about Reverend Saddler's reluctance to help me. When he had applied for the renewal of his notary license in 1961, his application was passed to the State Sovereignty Commission. The commission was concerned about Reverend Saddler because his secretary's daughter had loaned her car to her brother to attend a meeting of the Baha'i Faith, and the Baha'i believed in the universal brotherhood of all races.[8]

Sheriff Darby had told the Sovereignty Commission that Saddler was a "jackleg Negro preacher" who might have been at the Baha'i meeting himself ("jackleg" meaning without formal training or position, in this case a minister who supported himself in other ways). Commission investigator Tom Scarbrough said several people had told him that Jean K. Wright, the Black teacher who had loaned her car, and her mother, Reverend Saddler's secretary, were "smart aleck Negroes and troublemakers." Sheriff Darby told the Commission, "All of the . . . Negroes connected with the Delta Burial Association are NAACP active members."[9]

Circuit Clerk J. B. Eavenson told the commission that Reverend Saddler was a "very prominent Negro citizen" who voted in most elections, though he did not know if he had connections to the civil rights movement. However, County Attorney Caldwell agreed with Sheriff Darby that Reverend Saddler was a member of the NAACP. Mr. Caldwell said Reverend Saddler "would like very much to be a 'big shot' among the Negroes but has not been able to be one yet."[10]

Quitman County's white leadership suspected that African Americans like Reverend Saddler and his secretary, who had a prosperous business and white-collar jobs, must be subversive to the racial order—they had to be in the NAACP. Actually, Reverend Saddler was not a member. The white county leaders did not know that Reverend Townsend and Reverend Malone were the local NAACP leaders.

Reverend Saddler hired a lawyer to protect his notary public license. The lawyer told the Sovereignty Commission, "[Reverend Saddler] is a very good Negro and has taken no interest in the integration movement so far as I know. His reappointment as Notary Public will meet with the approval of the business people of this community."[11] So Reverend Saddler would not notarize my statement on October 1, 1964, to protect his license.

The next night, we were holding a mass meeting about the MFDP campaign. I saw nineteen-year-old Clondike Abbott come into the church with bandages around his right arm. He had been helping get signatures on the MFDP nominating petition. He told me that on his way to the meeting, three white youths drove up to him. One was the son of a local official. Another was the son of the manager of one of the Self plantations. They asked Clondike, "N——, where's you going?"

Clondike didn't answer. They got out of the car and beat him with a blackjack and stick. One of them jabbed him in the arm with a knife. Then they drove off, leaving Clondike lying on the ground. He got up and went to the COFO office at the Masonic Hall. Allan Goodner, the project director, was there. He bandaged Clondike's arm, and Clondike continued to the meeting. He spoke to the people about what happened. Then he went back to the Masonic Hall, and J. D. Powells and some others took him to a clinic. The nurse refused to treat him. He returned to the Masonic Hall and developed a fever. J. D. took him back to the clinic, and the nurse changed the bandages Allan had put on him.[12]

Meanwhile, as the meeting broke up, whites with guns were standing across the street. One Black youth was shot at from a moving car. Then the police came to the Masonic Hall where some local Black teens had come to see Clondike. A deputy took their names and said he'd be back the next day to arrest them. Clondike spent the night on a couch at the hall, and some of the young people stayed with him. At 2:00

a.m. some whites tried to break in, and the Black youths blocked the door with furniture and ran up to the second floor. Some Black people who lived nearby came over to see what was happening, and the whites drove away. Next morning Clondike was taken to a hospital in Greenville, seventy miles away, and treated there.

The harassment of the MFDP campaign continued. Leon Phipps, one of those who had tried unsuccessfully to integrate the school, was hanging Mrs. Hamer's congressional campaign posters on telephone poles. A white man came out of a store and told Leon, "N——, you know better than to have anything like that." He tore up Leon's remaining posters while other white men tore down the posters Leon had put up.

It wasn't just the faces of Black candidates on posters that outraged the whites. Most of white Mississippi strongly supported Goldwater for president while Blacks put Johnson stickers on their cars and Johnson posters on their walls as symbols of defiance. Although Johnson had refused to support the MFDP at the National Democratic Convention, the MFDP endorsed him. I had stacks of posters saying, "FREEDOM MEANS VOTE FOR LYNDON B. JOHNSON" and plenty of Johnson stickers. They were eagerly grabbed at mass meetings even though, more than once, those with Johnson stickers on their cars were harassed by whites.

On October 4, a deputy called Leon out of a cafe, pointed a pistol at him, and asked if he was "one of the n—— that tried to integrate the white school." Then the deputy said, "N——, get out of town, else *I'll* kill you." He offered to pay Leon to leave town.[13]

The next day the sheriff picked up Clondike to make him take back the story about the beating and stabbing. His mother was not allowed to visit him in jail.[14] Later a deputy told her Clondike had stabbed someone two weeks before. Clondike was released and told to report back to the sheriff the next morning. But that night the deputies came and took him back to jail. They told him, "Damn n——s at COFO can't help you." They said he would be fined $1,000 and sent to prison for a year. Finally, they released him. But the names of the white youths who had beaten and stabbed Clondike were spreading. Clondike refused to take back his statement that they had attacked him, even though the deputies told him he could clear himself if he changed his story.

On October 7, Clondike was arrested and charged with a knife fight that his older brother had been in. Clondike had been nowhere near the fight. The same day, J. D. Powells was arrested on the same assault charge involving his wife for which he had already served ninety days.

The next day, Allan Goodner was playing the card game Hearts with James Pete and Ernest Harris at the Masonic Hall. There were a couple of quarters on the table that Allan was going to use to buy bread and bologna. Two deputies came in without a warrant, saw the cards and money on the table, and arrested the three for gambling.[15]

At the courthouse Allan told the authorities he was from Detroit although he was actually from Nashville. Probably he did not want to involve his family in his troubles. According to a lawsuit Allan brought, the arrest was really for reporting the attack on Clondike. Chief Deputy Faust allegedly replied, "You n——s are trying to lay it on the white boys. You know damn well you n——s beat up that boy."[16]

Allan was fined $100. James Pete and Ernest Harris were fined twenty-five dollars. Allan complained he had no lawyer present and was treated more severely than the others. When civil rights lawyer Lawrence Apney arrived, County Attorney Caldwell told him Allan was treated differently because he was older and was the COFO project director. Mr. Caldwell said, "With these kind of fellows doing what they are, I'll get them for anything I can."[17]

When ACLU lawyer Aryeh Neier visited the prisoners, he found Clondike had been beaten in jail, although not seriously.[18] Authorities told J. D.'s mother, Mrs. Evans, that if her son took up with COFO again, he would be sent to prison. One deputy said, "Your son has joined COFO. You and your husband attend every meeting. Your nephew [Leon Phipps] tried to integrate the school and J. D. is going to have to pay for all this."[19]

Two Black farmers tried to put up their land for property bonds to get everyone out. The officials wouldn't accept the bonds. They demanded $1,200 cash. On October 13, the National Lawyers Guild sent us a $1,250 check to pay their bonds. As soon as they got out of jail, all but Allan were arrested again.

J. D. Powells told me the story. "We got out, and next morning there come the sheriff and arrested me. Charged me with destroying county property—destroying a mattress. They charged all of us but Allan Goodner. They knew he could bring in lawyers from the outside. Two civil rights lawyers come to defend us and got us all out."[20] Such harassment continued. "One time," he told me, "the deputy found me in a parked car and charged me with driving without a license. I had to spend twenty days in jail."

We finally got the FBI to investigate. Many Blacks in Marks thought civil rights workers were representatives of the federal government and assumed the FBI would give us maximum help. After the FBI agent came, the news got around fast that he refused to shake Leon Phipps's hand, called J. D.'s mother by her first name like any local white person would, and was on friendly terms with Sheriff Turner.[21] Black people in Marks decided the FBI agent was not to be trusted any more than any other white cop.

James Bond of the Georgia SNCC staff (and Julian Bond's brother) invited Clondike's mother Mrs. Lillie Mae Common, Mrs. Evans, and me to a program on Pacifica Radio about what was going on. We talked about the threats, the firings, the arrests, and the apparent indifference of the FBI. It was played on KPFA in San Francisco. When Mr. Caldwell found out, he wrote the station insisting we had lied.

While Allan was still in jail, twenty-year-old Stanford Brown came to work in Marks. He was originally from Lambert, three miles south of Marks. He told me his mother had tried to put him in the white school in the 1950s. After that the whites were so hostile to her that she took Stanford to Chicago. After high school he joined an NAACP youth group. He told me with amusement how the Chicago NAACP youth in suits and ties invited a group of SNCC staffers to come talk about their work in the Deep South. The NAACP group was astonished to see the SNCC workers in old overalls. Their stories made Stanford decide to return to Quitman County to help his people.

Brown's arrival wasn't unusual. During the two years I spent in Mississippi, out-of-state people, both Black and white, showed up at civil rights offices to work. In theory, they were first supposed to go through orientation sessions as I had in Oxford, Ohio, in 1964, or at least be approved by the main COFO office in Jackson. But often they just showed up.

We didn't have much to provide. As we reported to SNCC in October 1964, the office had "no money, no food, very little office supplies (like no carbon paper), no car, three busted typewriters, . . . no bathroom. . . . No desks at all, a few chairs, one mended sofa (rest sleep on floor). . . . No one knows where the project money is. Goodner might know; he's in jail."[22]

The intense strain we were under because of things like this series of arrests made us glad to see anyone who could help. At the same time, the strain often caused us to become quarrelsome with these same people. That was my relationship with Stanford Brown. At first, he was a real help to my morale because I had felt alone. After a while, I found myself getting in long, pointless arguments with him. On the surface it was because Stanford had strong Black nationalist views, but I really think it was because of the strain we were under. But any disagreements I had with Stanford were small compared to the quarrels Allan had with him when he got out of jail. Allan was sick from the bad food in the jail—what there was of it. He was in such a bad mood that he found himself quarreling with Stanford over matters that would have been trivial under normal circumstances.

Then, on October 18, the Jackson office sent two white students from Stanford University to help us publicize the upcoming MFDP vote. David Harris and Frank Morse were two of two hundred volunteers who had come to Mississippi. They had a car, a fantastic luxury because it meant we could get to Black people in every community in the county. This got us out of petty quarrels for a while.

David told me he hadn't intended to end up in Marks. "When we got to SNCC headquarters in Jackson, they asked us what kind of place we wanted to go to. We said we wanted to go to McComb. They said the McComb project was full up. We said we wanted someplace else that was rough, so they suggested Marks.

"When we drove into town, we asked directions from an old white man, and he just stared at us. We went to a meeting at a church that night. What I remember is after the meeting going to a Black café and having fried bologna sandwiches. I had never heard of that before.

"The next day I was down in Lambert with Frank Morse and J. D. Powells and Allan Goodner going from door to door talking to people about the Freedom Vote. The others went into the post office and left me to watch the car. Two white men drove up in a pickup and stuck a shotgun in my face. One said, 'Freedom Rider, I'm giving you just five minutes to get out of town.'

"I just couldn't believe it. I just stood there. Then the man pointed to his watch and said, 'N—— lover, I said you had five minutes.' I tried to decide what to do as a matter of principle—should I stay or not? Then the other three came out of the post office and it was obvious what they wanted to do. They grabbed me, and we got in the car and drove off."[23]

That day I was back in the COFO office in Marks at the phone. Though we sometimes forgot, somebody was supposed to be by the phone twenty-four hours a day. This was especially important when civil rights workers were traveling around. We had to phone the Jackson office when the car left and when it came back. The next two days Allan stayed at the phone, and Stanford Brown and I went around the county with David and Frank.

We visited Black people in Quitman and in neighboring Panola and Tallahatchie Counties. One incident that stuck in my mind was in the all-Black community of Falcon, where we met a 105-year-old man who had been born enslaved. He filled out a registration form for the Freedom Vote. When we met him, he was on the roof of his shack repairing leaks. He came down and showed us a photostat from the 1880 census to show us his age. He was a short, strongly built man who looked about seventy. As far as we could tell, the only physical defect his age had brought was that he was hard of hearing. He roared so loud when he talked that we had to stand away from the porch to converse with him.

We stopped in Vance, which was not much more than some shacks around a cotton gin. Many communities were on land belonging to big plantations. I was helping an illiterate woman fill out a Freedom Vote registration form when a white man drove up in a pickup. Carrying a knife, he went over to the others, who were at another shack, and told them, "Get out of town, and never come back." We left in a hurry.[24]

That night, October 21, we were back in the Masonic Hall. Frank Morse decided to mail a letter to his girlfriend. While he was driving around alone (something we were supposed to avoid at night) looking for a mailbox, four white youths in a pickup forced his car off the road. They told him, "We want to talk with you about civil rights." Three of them got in the car with Frank, while the fourth followed in the pickup. They went out to a country road. Then they pulled him out of the car and one of them told him, "If you want some fighting, we're here to give it to you. We don't want any trouble. We're just here to help you."

Then one of them hit Frank. He went into a crouched posture with hands covering his head, which civil rights workers were taught as part of nonviolence training. Two of them started kicking him in the head and groin. When he tried to get up, they knocked him down again. Then two of them sat on him while the other two urinated on his face and shirt. They left Frank and drove off. He couldn't get up for about ten minutes.[25] When he got back to the Masonic Hall, we were upstairs in the COFO office. Frank came staggering up the stairs with his face bruised and dripping and his shirt sopping wet. He fell on the floor and let out a roar of outrage. It was a while before he would tell us what happened.

Frank was large. He had been a marine and a football player. It was a huge effort for him to be nonviolent. As soon as he was able to get on his feet, he wanted to look for those guys and beat them up. It was all Allan, J. D., David, and I could do to hold him back. David phoned Sheriff Clint Turner, who said, "So somebody got whupped, huh? What do you expect me to do about it?" Then David called the Jackson COFO office, and they called Lee White, counsel for civil rights at the White House. He said the FBI would investigate. The next day the FBI agent came around. He seemed just as indifferent and unsympathetic as before. The local doctors, all white, wouldn't look at Frank, so he went to a doctor in Clarksdale. The next day David and Frank left.

A few days later two more white students, Joel Robinson and Don Epstein, showed up to help. On Election Day they would travel around the county with mock ballots and a ballot box for people to take part in the Freedom Vote. The day after they got to Marks, October 27, I was arrested.[26]

Jail

The Black schools were just opening that day, having been closed all fall so the children could pick cotton. I went to the white high school with Leon Phipps. We were accompanying three other Black teenagers, Charles Ware, James Kent, and Welchie McIntyre, who were attempting to register. The principal and the school superintendent refused to talk with us.

Two hours later I was standing in the alley behind the Masonic Hall on Third Street in Marks, when Chief Deputy Faust and Deputy Zimmerman drove up and said I was wanted for questioning. They told me to get in the car. I asked if they had a warrant for my arrest. They said yes and then asked my name, which they wrote in a blank space on a piece of paper. I believed the procedure irregular but got in the car, because I had been told that Chief Deputy Faust had beaten resisters or used a cattle prod on them. They told me I would be tried that afternoon.

Allan Goodner saw me being arrested and called the Jackson COFO office. When the COFO office called the jail, the authorities denied I was in custody.[27] COFO sent a lawyer the next day, Karl Shapiro of the National Lawyers Guild. He gave me legal advice and told me I would be tried the following day.

On October 29, I was brought into the sheriff's office, where I saw Sheriff Turner, Chief Deputy Faust, County Attorney Caldwell, and Justice of the Peace Billy Turner conversing with a few other people about farming. I was told this was my trial. Everyone present, both spectators and judge, asked me questions in a hostile manner about my political beliefs and associations. I said I would not accept that as my trial. I went back to jail.

The next day I was called out again for trial. I called the COFO office to have someone come to observe. Immediately after my phone call the trial was held, in County Attorney Caldwell's office, without any spectators. Superintendent of Schools L. V. Craig was a witness against me. I was sentenced for trespassing and treated to a lively speech by Mr. Caldwell. He told me I was an "invader" and accused me of having cooked up the accounts of Clondike and Frank Morse. All I could say was that I believed he knew more about who was responsible for these incidents than I did.[28]

Actually, I did have a spectator at my trial: Tom Scarbrough of the Mississippi Sovereignty Commission, who wrote later that I had a "very foul odor" and had apparently not bathed since I reached Mississippi.[29] He was right. The shower that I and other civil rights workers were supposed to use at the Masonic Hall had been wrecked by the teenage couple having sex. I lived with Reverend Ward, who had no bathtub or shower. He lived a block from an open ditch that carried raw sewage. Once a Black woman in Marks let me use her tub. She was upset when she heard the roar of water pouring into the tub as I turned the faucet on full blast, the way I was used to doing in the well-off white world I grew up in. Black families in Marks lucky enough to have bathtubs had to worry about the water bill if they turned on the water the way I had. The proper way to take a bath in Marks was to draw a thin film of water on the bottom of the tub.

At the trial, Mr. Caldwell told me local whites referred to me as "Stinky." He said I had had my right to a speedy trial; what more could I want? I told him I wanted to have had a lawyer. Then I was taken to the jail and locked in a cell for white prisoners. Within two days I had four cellmates with me, all poor whites who lived out on the plantations among Black people. Two of them were middle-aged brothers. Deputy Faust carried one of them into the cell in the middle of the night. He had this man under his arm like a Christmas package. The top of the man's head had bloody places all over it. The next morning the deputy told him, "I about wore out a blackjack on you last night." This man, small and frail, was in his fifties but looked seventy. His younger brother summed things up: "We just don't have no hope here in Mississippi."

My other two cellmates were nephews of the first two. One was in his twenties. He was there on a drunk charge, but he was worried because he had been in the state prison and feared he might have to go back. He told me when he first got out of prison he was living near one of the largest plantations in Mississippi, owned by a major political figure. The politician tried to pressure my cellmate into driving a tractor on his plantation for two dollars a day. "If you don't, I'll have you back in prison so fast your head will swim," the politician told him. My cellmate moved hurriedly to the large town of Greenwood and then up to Quitman County. He sounded a lot like Black farm workers talking about running away from the plantation.

The other cellmate, whom I'll call Billy, was fifteen. He had been working in a planter's yard. When he went to get paid, the planter was very drunk and wouldn't pay him. He just hollered at Billy, "Oh, just take the tractor out there in the driveway and go." Billy drove off on the tractor. Then the planter sobered up and called the highway patrol on him.

All my cellmates used the word "n——" freely. It was the only word they usually heard white people—and many Black people—use. But none of them had strong feelings against African Americans. On the plantations they frequently visited the shacks of Black sharecroppers and ate dinner with them. They used some expressions I had only heard among Black people. Billy had joined the Mississippi National Guard at fourteen. He served six months active duty in the army under a Black sergeant whom he liked. He said he didn't mind integration at all.

I said I thought the civil rights movement wasn't just for Black people, it was for white people like them who were getting messed around by the cops. I had a couple of crumpled up blank Freedom Vote registration forms in my pocket, and Billy and his brother filled them out.

After eight days, I got out of jail on a $300 appeal bond. Half the money came from my grandmother and the other half from the Marin

County, California, chapter of the ACLU. After the skimpy, half-frozen meals in jail, I was hungry. Mrs. Evans, J. D.'s mother, cooked me a plate of hog lungs and greens.

Many things had happened outside while I was in jail. First, we were told we could no longer have mass meetings at Eudora Methodist Church. Over fifty Black churches had been burned down in Mississippi for allowing civil rights meetings. In fact, Shelton Grove Church, just outside of Marks, was broken into and destroyed in November 1964.[30] The insurance company said they would cancel the church's policy if we had more meetings there, so COFO moved the meetings to the Masonic Hall.

Statewide, the Freedom Vote took place. About sixty-seven thousand Black Mississippians voted, fewer than had voted in the 1963 mock election for Aaron Henry for governor. But more people in Quitman County took part in 1964 than in 1963. Mrs. Hamer got on the official ballot for Congress. On Election Day, she received about twenty-five hundred votes from the Black people in the Delta who were registered voters. Jamie Whitten, the incumbent, won. [31] And Lyndon Johnson was elected president. To many Black people that was proof that the leading local whites didn't have as much power as they said they did. One Black woman told me how her white employer told her that soon Goldwater would be president, as if she didn't have a TV, as if she never watched the news. She told the white woman, "Mm-hm, Miss Anne, you watch your TV and I'll watch mine, and we'll see who goin' win."

In Clarksdale a Black woman thought up a song about Goldwater's defeat that spread quickly. It expresses well the glee of the Black people of the Delta at seeing their big shot white people left in the lurch.

CHORUS: Oh, Goldwater! Oh, Goldwater!
Oh, Goldwater! Done got over Goldwater at last.

Goldwater went around from track to track
Done got over Goldwater at last
Now he's a-dragging a cotton sack
Done got over Goldwater at last (CHORUS)

Goldwater went around a-buying votes
Done got over Goldwater at last

Now he's wearing a cotton sack coat
Done got over Goldwater at last (CHORUS)

When the peoples all heard that Johnson was the winner
Done got over Goldwater at last
They all went jumping from corner to corner
Done got over Goldwater at last (CHORUS)

Everyday Realities

By this time the Black schools had started. Since Mississippi had no compulsory schooling laws, however, many children and teenagers were still picking cotton. But there were enough kids around to hold Freedom School after regular school. They would come to the Masonic Hall after their classes. They were grade school age, thirteen and under. I tried talking about Black history some with them and about the movement, but it was difficult to find much of this that would interest all of them. Several were almost or completely illiterate. I tried teaching them how to read a little, but mostly we played games and talked with each other about our lives.[32]

They told me about picking cotton. It was hard work to reach your fingers in the bolls and pull out the fluff, they said, because the bolls had sharp places that would cut your fingers. It was easier to snap—to just break the boll off and throw it in the sack. But you didn't snap unless the planter was in a hurry to make the crop.

When you were out picking cotton, you had to wear two pairs of jeans or wrap burlap around your legs. The fields were soaked with insecticides and defoliants. You wanted to insulate your legs to keep the stuff off as much as possible. The youngsters showed me "camel backs," big, lumpy sores where chemicals got on them. One twelve-year-old boy who looked eight had such a large, painful sore on his knee that he could barely walk. I wrote a complaint to the U.S. Department of Agriculture and got no reply.

Some things I could do for individual children. One liked to paint pictures. Among the used books we had was one of Van Gogh reproductions he wanted to copy from. I brought it by his house one hot day. His mother was at her job mopping floors, and he was tending his little brother who was lying asleep covered with flies. As much as the older brother tried to chase the flies off with a fan, they settled back on his little brother's face. That image has stayed with me ever since.

The kids mostly told me about school. It seemed they were constantly being punished by their teachers because they could not absorb information that was usually irrelevant and often untrue. For example, here is what a Mississippi state history textbook said about the people of the Delta: "Deltans are rich; they live well. . . . Deltans have access to money, and they do not hesitate to spend it. Social life in the Delta tends to be gay; Deltans lack few of the good things of life. The cultural element is not forgotten, either. Delta folk spend considerable money getting educated. They dance and frolic, but they also read books and write them." The textbook also mentioned that Delta people now needed less "Negro-power" to run the plantations.[33]

The impression I got was that many Black teachers were still trying to prove that they had made it to a higher level than the rest of the Black community. They did this by picking on the poorer children. There were spankings and speeches by the teachers to the effect of "I made it, why can't you?" The children who had it worst were from families on plantations or from the very poor neighborhood just outside the city limits. When they first came to school many of them had never seen an indoor toilet. They were too intimidated by their new surroundings to ask what to do, or they forgot. Every year some first-graders got spanked for using the playground or a corner of the classroom. It had happened to some of the kids I tried to have Freedom School with.

A lot of these children had only worn-out secondhand clothes going ragged at the edges. Some of the other students—and some of the teachers—would make fun of the way they looked. So their parents would keep them at home, or out picking cotton, until they could afford to have nice enough clothes to go to school in. This caused a permanent headache for the civil rights movement. For several years the NAACP in Clarksdale had been getting shipments of clothes from people up North. After the summer volunteers went back and told about the needs of Mississippi, even more people sent clothes to COFO offices. The demand for these clothes was tremendous. People would come from miles around. In a small place like Marks, civil rights leaders were expected to go to larger towns like Clarksdale and bring back clothes. "All that fuss about them rags," Mr. Franklin used to say. "They ain't going after the important thing, and that's the freedom."

The clothes turned people against each other. Reverend Carter would get clothes in Clarksdale and keep them in Reverend Wilder's storehouse. Both men were constantly accused of giving more clothing to their favorites. They were always trying new ways of distributing the clothes to make sure everyone got a fair share, but there was never enough. No one was satisfied. There were always rumors that someone who didn't need the clothes had gotten them and sold them to people out on the plantations. As I walked down the street, people continually called to me to talk to them. A lot of the time it was about these clothing rumors. It gave me a headache, especially when we had to worry about people in jail or people who had lost their jobs for supporting the movement.

The more the clothing rumors spread against Reverend Carter, the more he spoke passionately on his favorite theme at mass meetings: that we ought to pay him for his damaged bathroom. The last straw for Reverend Carter came when the Black entertainer Dick Gregory sent thousands of Christmas turkeys to Mississippi. In Marks, the turkeys were a disaster. There just weren't enough turkeys for all the hungry people. Rumors about sales of gift turkeys reached a high pitch. When Reverend Carter was giving out the turkeys, some people fought over them and pulled them back and forth. Reverend Carter had to pull a pistol out. People who came late got only half a turkey for their families. Some who came too late got none.

The turkey affair left a lot of bad feeling. About the only person who came out of it well was Reverend Ward. I went with him when he gave most of his turkey to a woman and her children out on a plantation. Reverend Carter was in a worse mood than ever. He told Allan and me that we had to leave the Masonic Hall, which was also his church. He told us not to take any of our stuff with us. He probably hoped he could sell some of it to pay for the damage to his bathroom. But Allan and I loaded the books and the documents into Mr. Franklin's truck, and he stored them in his house. When Reverend Carter found out, he called the sheriff to have us arrested for breaking and entering the Masonic Hall. We hid out for two days with local people. Then Allan called Stokely Carmichael, who oversaw the district's COFO projects, and Stokely got the Jackson office to pay for the damages to Reverend Carter's bathroom. Reverend Carter then dropped charges against us.

Right after that, Allan went to Jackson. His health had been poor ever since he had gotten out of jail that last time. Stanford Brown left for Jackson too. I moved in with the Franklins because that was where all the office materials were.[34] The sheriff came by and harangued Mr. Franklin because he was helping the civil rights movement. Mr. Franklin told me, "After I saw the business that something had to be done, I jumped in it with my crazy self and took over. The sheriff told me that I was gone crazy doing it. He begged me not to do it. He told me, 'Franklin, that stuff ain't nothing but that old Commickism. I wish you wouldn't get in it.' I told him, 'Man, I lived under y'all's rule all my life, and I guess I can live under what these people got.'"

The Franklins had two grown daughters up north, Elnora and Lenora. The oldest at home was Mae Ella, who was sixteen. Then came Presley, fourteen, Melvin, twelve, Hull, ten, Ruby Lee, seven, and Jimmie Lee, four. Mr. Franklin got jobs tearing down deserted shacks out on the plantations and bringing the lumber into town to build new shacks. He and his brother Jessie also hauled firewood or government commodity food for people who couldn't pick it up themselves. Mrs. Franklin had been on the jobs committee the civil rights workers had set up. She and the other Black committeewomen asked repeatedly for work at a small textile mill that had just been set up in nearby Lambert. So far, the only Black women who had gotten jobs there were a couple of scrubwomen, while white women were being hired from forty miles away.

Although Mr. and Mrs. Franklin had difficulty reading, their children were among the best students in the Black school. They were able to take good advantage of the books we had brought from the Masonic Hall, and so did other young people in the Cotton Street neighborhood. Like a lot else in the movement, the books produced some strange contrasts. For example, Junior Phipps, cousin of Leon Phipps, was reading H. G. Wells's *Outline of Science* while his parents, Armistead and Ora Phipps, insisted to me that the world was not round. "Man that made it say it got four corners," they said. Yet Junior got his urge to learn from his parents. Mr. and Mrs. Phipps went regularly to Bible study classes, and they were constantly asking Mr. Franklin and me questions about the news they saw on TV. They did so much for the movement, they could believe the world was any shape they pleased, as far as I cared.

Still No Right to Vote

Three more civil rights workers came to Marks. The first was Harry Swann, a young Black man from Biloxi. We had met in December 1964 when I traveled there with Reverend and Mrs. Ward and Reverend Allen for a conference on the MFDP's congressional challenge. At the first session of Congress in January 1965, representatives sympathetic to the MFDP intended to challenge the right of the five Mississippi congressmen to take their seats, on the grounds that they had been elected by fraud. They had a huge brief of all the intimidation of would-be voters, the constitutional interpretation test, and run-arounds of Black voters that civil rights workers had been documenting for years.

While we were at the conference, we met Harry. He looked almost white. He had worked on shrimp boats until the movement came to southern Mississippi in 1961. He had been through the most dangerous times. He had a deep dent on the side of his head from a policeman's club. Now he felt the whites around Biloxi were so hostile to him, and he wanted to work for the movement in a place where he was less well known. This was the way a lot of local people started as full-time civil rights workers. Their hometown would get too hot for them, and they would work in civil rights offices elsewhere. Leon and James Phipps had left Marks because their lives were threatened, and they worked in other COFO projects.

Harry wanted to come to Marks, and I said it was all right with me. We shared some cold, hungry days that winter. I started getting a ten-dollar weekly subsidy that COFO arranged from the City-wide Sunday School Alliance of Springfield, Ohio.[35] Much of this money went for rides to reach people in the county. The money was for gas and for emergency funds, since any Black person who carried civil rights workers ran the risk of arrest or being run off the road. Once we were left in Lambert for a few hours. We spent a good deal of it hiding from some whites who fired a shotgun at us from their pickup. At last we were able to connect with our ride and get back to Marks.

That was when the new project director, R. T. Smith, came from Clarksdale. He brought a white civil rights worker, John Siegel, from Pennsylvania. Harry and I were so glad to see them. Civil rights workers were always happy for reinforcements or even visits from other civil rights workers.[36]

We were able to continue having mass meetings at the Masonic Hall, even though we couldn't use it as an office any more. Reverend Carter continued having disputes with people at the meetings about clothes. Then Harry had an outburst at Reverend Carter full of words not said in mixed company in Marks. Using a local euphemism, he called Reverend Carter a monkeyflier. After the beatings cops had given Harry, he often had fits of anger during which he seemed almost in a trance before he would snap back to normal. Reverend Carter threatened to have Harry arrested, so R. T., John, and I took up a collection to buy Harry a bus ticket to Memphis. From there he hitchhiked to the North.

That January there was heavy rain. As always happened in wet weather, much of the neighborhood flooded from the open sewer that cut across the Black section of Marks where I was staying.[37] You had to cross on planks to get to some people's houses. In warm weather, the stink was terrible. The houses along it swarmed with roaches, even in the refrigerators. Many children in the area were sickly. Now that the rain had come, the sewer flooded Mr. Franklin's back yard. It surrounded his brother Jessie's house, up to the porch. The place where a drainage ditch could be dug to keep the area from flooding belonged to the Self family. They had set a price on the land too high for the Marks city council to buy. They also tried to keep a family member or employee on the city council. When we wanted to go see Mr. Jessie or any of the other people who lived in the flooded area, we had to pole a shallow wooden boat. Once John and I were poling the boat to Mr. Jessie's house, and I fell in. This is what the right to vote meant—freedom from being flooded by sewage.

R. T., John, and I planned a Freedom Day for early February. We wanted as many people as possible to try to register to vote. We squeezed out handbills about Freedom Day from a battered mimeograph machine we got from the Batesville COFO project. We invited Lula Belle Johnson, the MFDP vice president, who spoke to a crowded mass meeting. Mrs. Johnson had lost her maid's job for being in the movement. She had learned to read and write since joining the MFDP. People in Marks could identify with her, and they cheered loudly as she spoke. "Tell your preacher to lead you in civil rights," Mrs. Johnson said. "If he say he don't go in for politics, you tell him that every one of them preachers got George Washington in their pockets and that the very man that started politics!"

The next afternoon, twenty-four people went to the courthouse with Mrs. Johnson, some local preachers, R. T., John, and me to try to register.[38] Mae Ella Franklin got a group of Black high school students to go too. The students made signs that they carried under their coats, ready to picket the courthouse if the cops turned us away. "I want to tell you one thing about these young Negroes around here," Reverend Allen told me proudly several years later. "They don't pay these white folks no attention. When they was working for freedom back here a few years ago, these young Negroes wasn't afraid. These old ones that grew up under the gun was still shy. Some of the preachers was bought out by the whites.

"We took a bunch of people to the courthouse to register. Four or five of us ministers was leading it, and the white men with guns was there. They took me to one side—they recognized me—and said, 'Preacher, why did you bring so many of these young n——s here?'

"I said, 'I didn't go around and get them. They caught the truck and got on, and I sure didn't compel them to get on.' At that time they wasn't used to being registered, and you had to have some grit in your craw to go up there, and I had a truckload of them. Look like it scared them to death when them Negroes began to fall out of that truck and go to register."

Of the twenty-four who went to register that day, only eight were able to finish the test by the time the courthouse closed. One passed. From this experience we estimated that if every Black person of voting age in Quitman County tried to register, it would take over a year for them all to take the test. Obviously, as long as the test was required, Black people would have no political power.

CHAPTER 4

"We Was Glad That We Had to Stand Up for Ourselves"
1965–1966

While we were having Freedom Day in Marks that February 1965, there were demonstrations for voting rights in Marion and Selma, Alabama. On February 18, during one of these nonviolent protests, an Alabama state trooper shot twenty-six-year-old Jimmie Lee Jackson twice in the stomach. Eight days later, Jimmie Lee died. He was shot for what Mae Ella, J. D. Powells, Clondike Abbott, and other Black young people around Marks had been doing. It galvanized civil rights efforts across the entire region.[1]

Jail (Again)

Mae Ella told me, "Joe, what we need here is a little integration." She called a meeting of young people at Allen Chapel Methodist Church the night of February 28. John Siegel and I were there but said very little. Mae Ella and the other teenagers decided to try to eat at Bob Young's restaurant at the edge of the Black community, where less-well-off whites ate. They considered Mr. Young one of the whites most hostile to civil rights. He had threatened Reverend Malone for keeping civil rights workers in his house.

R. T. Smith, the project director, didn't come with us. He was out on bond on another charge and didn't want to burden the Jackson COFO office. So, the morning of March 1, John and I went to Bob Young's cafe with Mae Ella and the other high school students. Mr. Young came charging out the door with a hammer. As they had planned, the teenagers marched downtown and started clapping rhythms and singing Freedom Songs. We went up and down Main Street. For the Black young people it was a tremendous release.[2]

Shortly after we returned to the Black part of town, John and I were arrested. Chief Deputy Faust, who knew Mr. Young's attitude, asked me, "Did you want to get killed?" When we got to the jail, we found R. T. had been arrested too. R. T. was in a small cell crowded with Black prisoners. John and I were in a cell with two white prisoners on their way to state prison for theft. They had been in prison before and were not looking forward to it, so they had a lot of bitterness to take out on John and me. They were extremely hostile. One night when we were almost asleep, one of them burned my finger with a cigarette. Then they told us to get out of our bunks. We squatted on the floor in the nonviolent crouch with our hands on top of our heads. I whispered "Be calm!" to John, as much for my sake as his. The convicts kicked us until they saw we wouldn't resist. One of them said disgustedly, "Whoever heard of a fighting Yankee?" referring to John, who was from Pennsylvania. But they were angrier at me because I was a southerner, and they felt I was going against my own kind. The next night they kept waking us up, making us clean the cell bars with toilet paper or mop the floor. After a while, though, they became bored with that and wanted to play dominoes with us. Time drags in jail, even if you are only there for about ten days, as I was.

The day came when they were supposed to set our trial date. All the Black prisoners had to have their heads shaved for court. When R. T. refused, a Black trusty threatened to beat him up, so he let the trusty shave his head. When we got to the courtroom, two civil rights lawyers were there. We told them what the white prisoners were doing to John and me. Our lawyers requested that we be put in R. T.'s cell, but County Attorney Caldwell refused. He said that, according to Mississippi law, Black and white prisoners had to be segregated.

The next day William Franklin and some others came with food for us. Mr. Franklin was arrested because he had a Lyndon Johnson sticker on the windshield of his truck where the inspection sticker was supposed to be, and the inspection sticker was too low. His daughter Mae Ella came with other high school students and demonstrated in front of the jail to protest our arrests and the conditions we endured. The sheriff threatened the students with blackjacks, and they retreated. Several returned later and were detained, threatened with reform school, and held until released to their parents.[3] Mr. Franklin's brother Jessie bonded Mr. Franklin out of jail later that day, but Mae Ella was expelled from school.

That week, over one thousand people in Mississippi went to jail for demonstrating in sympathy with the Selma protests. The Jackson COFO office had its hands full, but after six days they were able to pay R. T.'s bond. The next day John's family got him out on bond. James Phipps, Leon's brother, came back from Jackson to help. He and John got on the phone to newspapers in Oklahoma, my home state, to describe conditions in the jail. Louie Hamilton, an Oklahoman who had just gotten out of prison, and Jeanie Pickering, an old friend of mine, raised $500 to get me out of jail. I was released March 10. My health was bad from the jail food, so I went back to Oklahoma to see my family.

Louie and Jeanie's money to release me was brought by Frank Garner, a reporter for the *Daily Oklahoman*. Before I left with him, I shook hands with Chief Deputy Sanford Faust and gave him my sympathies because his daughter had just died in a car wreck. Mr. Caldwell and Sheriff Turner wished me well in Oklahoma and advised me to stay there. Caldwell told Frank that I was "emotionally upset" and added, "Seriously, Joe, . . . you need to be under a doctor's care. You need help." Both men told me they very much hoped that I would not return.

We were talking with Mr. Caldwell when an elderly Black man from Lambert came into the courthouse. Mr. Caldwell introduced the reporter and told the Black man, "Tell him how your people down in Lambert don't support this civil rights stuff."

The old man said, "No, sir, I can't say that. It's a bunch of folks down there that's for it." Mr. Caldwell got a look of shock on his face that I will always remember. As exhausted and demoralized as I was, I was very grateful to that old man.

When Frank Garner took me to the Franklins' house, ten or fifteen people were there to say good-bye and told me they hoped I would come back. Mr. Garner took a picture of Jessie Franklin shaking my hand. Then we flew to Oklahoma City.[4]

William Franklin called the Civil Rights Division of the Justice Department. They sent representatives to Marks who got after the sheriff and county attorney for leaving John and me in the cell with the hostile white prisoners. They also inspected the abominable jail food and made the sheriff promise to improve it. They got all charges dropped against R. T., John, Mr. Franklin, Mae Ella, and me.

Planters Push Back

In April, Delta planters decided to get rid of as many sharecroppers and day laborers as possible. They knew the Voting Rights Act was going to pass because of the Selma demonstrations and the killings there. They didn't want to see themselves outvoted. They started using chemical weed killers as much as possible so they wouldn't have to hire so many people to chop weeds. They lowered the wages of those Black workers they still needed from $3 for a ten-hour day to $2 or $1.75.

Near Greenville, some African Americans who had learned about labor unions in a COFO Freedom School started a strike and organized the Mississippi Freedom Labor Union (MFLU). They were thrown off their plantation and moved onto the land of a Black small farmer. They set up a tent city and started a handcraft co-op to sell crafts up north to make enough money to build regular houses.[5]

The wage cuts affected the entire Delta. The Franklins and some others drove down to the tent city to see what was happening. Many of them joined the MFLU and went on strike. One of the leaders of the MFLU in Quitman County was Willie Brown, a sharecropper near Lambert. Mr. Brown had already had experience with unions, having led a strike at the Campbell Soup Company in Chicago in the 1930s.

Everyone who joined the MFLU signed a paper that summed up the hopes of the Black people of the Delta:

> I am a member of the Mississippi Freedom Labor Union.
>
> I believe that everybody should get at least $1.25 an hour for their work.
>
> I believe that children under 16 should not have to work.
>
> I believe that poor people should not have to work for more than 8 hours unless they get time and a half for overtime.
>
> I believe that people over 60 should not have to work.
>
> I believe that people who are sick should not have to work and should receive free medical care.
>
> I believe that all people who can not get full-time jobs should get full compensation from the Government.
>
> I believe that all work should carry social security and accident insurance.
>
> I believe that all people should be treated equally in hiring, wages and working conditions, whatever their race or color. I pledge to work

together with other members of the MISSISSIPPI FREEDOM LABOR UNION to win these rights.

I believe that we should use strikes, picketing, boycotts, collective bargaining and non-violent direct action to make the people we work for meet our demands.[6]

Because of an unusually wet spring, the chemical weed killers did not mix with the soil effectively. Many cotton fields were overgrown with weeds. Soon the planters were driving up and down the road begging people to come back to work at three dollars or even four dollars a day. Still, this did not stop the planters from trying to get as many Black people as possible to leave before they could start voting. They made things hard, Lula Belle Weathersby told me later. "When we was on the farm, we never paid when we needed to go to the doctor. The boss man wrote a scrip for us. And we never paid the light bill. He paid for us. But when the civil rights thing come along, he got mad at us and stopped paying for us. Some of us was really worried, but after a while we was glad that we had to stand up for ourselves.

"Then he told us we couldn't raise a stalk of corn to feed our hogs, and that just froze us plumb out. We couldn't buy food for them. We had to sell them. That was when he cut off paying our light bill and our doctor bill. He wanted to see us suffer.

"Then they brought in all these tractors and got rid of all their hands but a few tractor drivers. This farm where we lived used to have forty families and now [1975] there ain't but two. They got these chemicals to kill the grass in the fields to replace the choppers. 'Course the chemical lose its strength when it rain too much," she chuckled. But the process of pushing Black people off the land continued.

"When the farming cut down from machinery replacing the labor, that made many a man have to go to other parts of the world to find a job and send money to his family back home. And that caused so many families to break up, so many separations and divorces. See, these was young people, but when you leave a young woman alone, something might happen and it did.

"They tore down our houses, and we started piling up in these little towns. We used to be out there on the farms raising our own food. But then he started drawing up on what we could raise. Then we had to pile into town and we had to live on commercial food. 'Course I raise a little garden here, but not nearly what I could out there. So now there's a shortage of this and that 'cause we depend on that commercially grown food." Many who were thrown off their plantations relied on donated food trucked to the Delta from Chicago. Barbara Mitchell, a white Mississippian, began those donations during the hard winter of 1965–66, and they continued—with my brother participating—for almost a year.

Reorganization

Our organizing continued through this time, but there were changes in how we did things. Two carloads of people had traveled from Marks to Alabama for the Selma-to-Montgomery voting rights march. Reverend Malone drove one car, and Mr. Franklin drove the other with his brother Jessie, R. T., and John. When they got back to Marks, John went home to Pennsylvania. R. T., Reverend Allen, and Reverend Malone were now holding meetings in Allen Chapel, which had a young new minister who strongly supported the movement. There were not many people coming to meetings, but more of them were from Lambert. All the weeks we had gone from door to door in Lambert talking to people were finally showing results.

Still, R. T. had no workable typewriter or mimeograph machine, and he had to go several blocks to find a phone. Few Black families in Marks had telephones. When I was in Oklahoma, I made an appeal in the student newspaper for funds for Mississippi. This is what civil rights workers usually did, but nobody gave me anything. All I could do was send R. T. some of my own money.

Later that spring, COFO dissolved. The NAACP had pulled out of COFO in December 1964 because the MFDP was challenging the Mississippi congressmen's right to sit in Congress, arguing that they had been elected by fraud and terrorism.[7] The NAACP believed that since President Johnson didn't support the MFDP, the challenge was "politically unrealistic." Then in April 1965, John Shaw, a popular young civil rights worker in McComb, was killed in Vietnam. The McComb chapter of the MFDP passed a strong resolution against the Vietnam War. James Phipps told me later that many northern liberals wrote the MFDP saying they wouldn't send any more contributions because of the McComb resolution.

Many people were still in favor of the war. On my twenty-third birthday, February 8, 1965, John Siegel and I heard over the radio that a massive bombing of North Vietnam had started. I was very alarmed, thinking it might lead to war with the Soviet Union. At that point John was a Johnson liberal, very much for the war. (I got a letter from him a year later saying that he had turned against the war.) Mr. Franklin was always strongly against the war although his brilliant son Presley was for the war, at least at first. It was a very radicalizing experience for me. I think people remember the war as Nixon's war and the Democrats as antiwar, but at the beginning, most liberals were for the war. If you opposed it, you became a leftist by default. I thought of myself as a socialist, but I was comfortable working with a liberal Democratic administration until 1965. That May, when I went back to the University of Oklahoma to take summer courses, I joined SDS demonstrations against the war. I also joined one in Washington, D.C., on my way back to Marks.

COFO turned over all its offices and staff to the MFDP. In Marks, NAACP members continued to work as steadily with the MFDP as ever. The only change they noticed was that the NAACP leaders in Clarksdale started treating them in a distant way.

After the Selma demonstrations, R. T. Smith quit as project director and went back to Clarksdale. James Pete, one of our local activists, briefly became director. "When Reverend Malone started everything, it was a secret more or less, like the Masons," James Pete told me later. "I didn't understand it so I didn't get involved in it then. I lived with my great-grandmother. She was blind and ninety-five years old. Her father was a Black soldier in the Civil War. My mother stayed two doors down. I used to trim trees with Mr. Alec Dean. I got involved in the Aaron Henry Freedom Vote campaign in 1963. In 1965, I was the youngest project director in the state—age seventeen. I went to jail once in the civil rights movement. I had a lot of voters I got registered. A lot of the older peoples couldn't even read they name. That were one of my projects."

In late summer, Jessie Franklin went to Clarksdale and met Rev. L. C. Coleman, a revival preacher without a church. He was supporting himself sweeping the beauty parlor of Mrs. Vera Mae Pigee, a prominent member of the NAACP there. He was about fifty. He asked Mr. Jessie to take him to Marks to help with the movement. He became the new project director, and James Pete was assistant director.

The Voting Rights Act became law on August 6, 1965, just as James Pete and Reverend Coleman began. The act abolished the constitutional interpretation test. William and Jessie Franklin took about five hundred

Black adults to register to vote in August, and James Pete took others. "In 1965 I got into the act with the Voter Registration Act and won it," William Franklin explained. "Eight or ten government people come here a gang of times. I had them booked for the church, and they come to the church and talked and stayed until we won. All I knowed is they was out of Washington, D.C." They were Justice Department officials, there to investigate the oppression and harassment he had written to them about.[8] "I had to go to federal court and give an account of what they did when we was registering. They tried to make it slow. They registered us four days and shut up the courthouse the off days. Letters was found in front of my place that said, 'How would you like for your wife to be hung from that telephone pole?' 'How would you like your children to be killed?'

"I'll tell you how the government got worked into me. I was over at Preacher Allen's, and they was going around talking to the preachers. And they ask me what church I belongs to and what I has," meaning what his grievances were. "And then two more come while I was in the field. And they left word for me to hold a meeting at Allen Chapel Church. And I left word with Ruth Figgs and the little old preacher that run Allen Chapel. And we called a meeting at Allen Chapel, and them government people talked, them old justice of the peace.

"At that time the Negro was scared to take any more whites in their houses. For a while there wasn't nobody from outside here. Then attorney Mel Leventhal come tearing up here with this old senator." Mr. Franklin was probably referring to a member of the Senate's Subcommittee on Civil Rights. Mel Leventhal, then an NYU law student, worked for the NAACP Legal Defense and Educational Fund (LDF).

"Mel Leventhal met me at a meeting at a lady's house. He got acquainted with me. He said, 'Look, you can get all the help you need. I'll be with you every day I can.' I said, 'All right, I'll take you.' We had conversation and became more friends and more friends. I carried him around, and he told me what all's to be done in Quitman County, and a gang of them—Ruth Figgs and Mrs. [Dorothy] Stanford and all—they promised to go along with it, and they appointed me leader. Then after I said I would take over, them old senators said they would help me. They was driving over from Oxford every evening, and I didn't know if I could win, and they said, 'Oh, Mr. Franklin, you can.' And that's when we got them running scared. One night the park was filled with white folks with guns, thinking we was coming over. Marian Wright, Mel Leventhal, John Doar, outstanding lawyers. I never will forget them. They helped me win a lot of cases." Mr. Franklin showed tremendous courage in bringing a number of lawsuits, mostly involving school integration.

Schools

Integration of the schools had proven even more explosive to many local whites than voting. Mae Ella Franklin had attended the Black high school's summer session, the one held early so Black children could pick cotton in the fall. But she had been continually harassed by the Black principal and teachers, who knew of her civil rights activities. One teacher beat her so severely she required medical attention. As she told it,

> That summer by the business math room in the agriculture classes workshop room, they were building a two-bale cotton trailer. My business math teacher would go and get one of the one-by-four planks they were sawing off the trailer and use it to whip boys and girls both—girls just as hard as the boys. For seven weeks just about every Monday and Friday evening he would whip us, about our lessons and any other thing he was mad at. So I told him I would rather go home than get a whipping, and he said if I go home I should just stay there. That Friday I walked away from the school and Monday stayed home and went to the doctor.
>
> I came back to school that Tuesday. I was still sick. I made it through my fourth period class, and then I went to the principal to ask may I go home, and he said have I reported to Mr. _____ to get my whipping, and I said, "No, sir." He said don't set foot in that school no more until I get my whipping. Then I said, "I can't take no more 'cause of what the doctor say. The first time it cost $7 and the second time $4 and what do you think that is? Eleven dollars. Then $3.60 for pills."
>
> I went back that Monday morning, and I wasn't well then. The principal caught me in my second period class and asked me had I been to Mr. _____ for my whipping, and I said, "No, sir. . . . And it ain't no whipping—it's a beating." . . . He told me if I didn't take no whipping to take my books and go home.
>
> And now I'm a school dropout. . . . I won't go back because I guarantee you, one of that man's whippings, it's going to bust the blisters on you.[9]

Mae Ella was expelled. Her parents tried to get her enrolled in the white school, but L. V. Craig, the school superintendent, told them she could not enter yet because she had already attended the summer session in the Black school. She could not enroll in the white school until the second semester. The Franklins and I talked with Henry Aronson of the LDF, but there was nothing he could do about it quickly enough.

Her father brought Mae Ella's problem to the movement leaders. "So then, we had a meeting about integrating the schools in Jackson at the Heidelberg Hotel," Mr. Franklin recalled. "They called me to make a speech. I said we didn't have no guards, we didn't have no polices, we didn't have no doctors or lawyers. Then the Kennedy boy made a speech"—he meant Attorney General Robert Kennedy—"and told us we had to do it in the open where the public could give an account of it, to tell the police which way you doing. And the colored started crying, and I said, 'What you going to do about the Ku Klux Klan? If we do it like that and show the public, the Ku Klux Klan is going to blow up the schoolhouses and blow the Negroes up.'"

By the fall of 1965, I had returned to Marks. I got another beat-up old mimeograph machine that could be coaxed to produce a few copies and put out two issues of a newsletter, which we sold for a nickel each to get money to cover the expense of driving around the county. We called it the *Quitman County Freedom Democrat*, as opposed to the white people's *Quitman County Democrat*. We put in this announcement about school integration:

> The Quitman County school superintendent, L. V. Craig has sent in a plan to integrate the schools in the county to the federal government. . . . The federal government has not yet said that the plan . . . is all right. As soon as they agree to the plan, the *Quitman County Democrat* will print the plan.
>
> The Negroes will probably start going to the white school in September 1966. They will probably be grade school children and at first the white school may not take very many of them.

We had to be the ones to get this kind of information out to the Black community, because the white-controlled media would say nothing about these things.

But the white people hadn't given up their resistance. In October, Quitman County's state representative James Walker got a bill passed in the Mississippi legislature requiring people with children from out of state living with them to pay $37 monthly tuition per child to attend school or pay $150 to adopt the child. This deliberately targeted the many Black families keeping the children of relatives up north who didn't have enough living space or income to support them. It passed just before the Black schools opened. The law was the equivalent of the evictions by the planters—an effort to minimize the number of Black children who would be in integrated schools. The Black woman who had taken care of Jimmy Walker as a child was upset that he would find such a way to hurt her and others like her after what she had done for him.

Although they hadn't been able to help Mr. Franklin's daughter, the LDF got the federal court to order that people didn't have to pay the tuition until the court decided whether the law was constitutional. We told people at mass meetings they didn't have to pay. We went around the county telling them. We printed the information in our newsletter. Still, there were people we couldn't reach. Narsis Taylor, the mother-in-law of Willie Brown, the Freedom Labor Union leader, paid tuition for her grandchildren from Chicago who were staying with her. When the federal court finally ruled the law unconstitutional, Mrs. Taylor didn't get any of her money back.[10]

The Voting Rights Struggle Continues

We also used the newsletter to keep the community informed about their new gains under the Voting Rights Act. We put this notice in about voter registration: "What they want you to fill out at the courthouse is just information. It is not supposed to be a test. Mr. Martin at the courthouse is supposed to help you out. He has to sign your name in the book even if you can't read or write. If your boss gives you any trouble about registering to vote, tell the MFDP office at once."

By now only about seventy-five people were coming to mass meetings. We had been getting over a hundred, but there was a certain amount of exhaustion and frustration at things not getting done quickly enough. Also, many were tired of the endless quarrels between Reverend Coleman and the others, especially Ruth Figgs, about everything from clothing distribution to what order to do things in. Both Reverend Coleman and Mrs. Figgs were strong personalities.

Still, there was plenty of energy for the work. Three local women took me around the county: Mary Jones, wife of county MFDP chairman Rev. Jeff Jones; S. C. Rose Kendricks; and Clondike's mother, Lillie Mae Common. Mrs. Jones would sell MFDP membership cards—"mule cards" they were called because of the Democratic donkey on them. Then Mrs. Kendricks would explain about the Freedom Labor Union's distribution of old clothes. Mrs. Common would explain voter registration procedures. I said nothing unless I was asked something about the statewide MFDP or somebody had a legal or financial document they wanted me to explain.

Meanwhile, Congress was getting ready to hear the MFDP's challenge to the right of the five Mississippi congressmen to their seats. MFDP supporters went to Washington, D.C., to demand the removal of the elected congressmen. Reverend Coleman and several young people from Marks went to Washington on the MFDP's bus. As the NAACP had predicted, President Johnson was completely opposed to it, and the challenge failed.[11] Reverend Coleman and many other demonstrators wept. Even after all that had happened, the people of Marks still held hope that America would live up to its professed ideals.

When the demonstrators returned, they brought a new volunteer with them. He was a young white carpenter named Darrell Fountain. He had just gotten out of the army and was hanging around Washington, where he had met the demonstrating Mississippians. He had asked them what it was about, and they explained it. He decided he liked them and that they were in the right, so he joined them.

Darrell came back on the bus with the demonstrators. He stayed with Mr. and Mrs. Buck in Lambert, whose teenage son had gone to the demonstration. Darrell was the only white civil rights worker to ever stay in Lambert. He was very popular with the young Black people there. But after a couple of weeks, local whites had made so many threats on his life that he had to leave. The Black people in Lambert gave him some money, and Mr. Buck drove him to Memphis around daybreak. Mr. Buck told me he hated to see Darrell go.

In December, the MFDP organized a statewide campaign to get African Americans elected to the Agricultural Stabilization and Conservation Service (ASCS) committees. These committees allotted the number of acres each farmer could plant. The rest had to lie fallow to replenish the soil. In theory, sharecroppers could farm the allotments as well as planters, but there were no Black ASCS committee members in Mississippi, so the allocations always favored whites. One advantage of this election was that people didn't have to be registered voters to take part. On the plantations, most Black people were not yet registered. If they could serve on an ASCS committee, sharecroppers could begin to get a fair proportion of the allotments.

In several Mississippi counties, Black people got elected to those committees. In Quitman, the story was less happy. Two sharecroppers ran. One of them was Willie Brown, the local union activist. James Pete described the election in his report to the Jackson MFDP office: "Negro Mr. Willie Brown ran for the ASCS election. He didn't win. Willie Brown's name didn't appear on the ballot. Also Negro Mr. Eddie B. Mitchell received two ballots." Shortly after this, Mr. Brown was evicted from the plantation where he lived.[12]

White retaliation went further. Pete's report to the Jackson office for January 1966 described the mass eviction campaign the planters were carrying out in Quitman County. On one of the Self family plantations "approximately 20 families has been kick off. Also, down below Lambert, Miss. approximately 15 families been kick off."

Pete also mentioned that the Quitman MFDP had registered at least twenty complaints about irregularities by the county in registering Black voters. Between August 1965 and year's end, he noted, about six hundred African Americans there had registered to vote, about 20 percent of the eligible Black population. But almost all of these were in the towns, not on plantations. In Marks and Lambert about half the Black population had registered.[13]

Pete had also tried to speak with the welfare supervisor and the head of the school board so he could help local people with those issues. But, he noted, these officials refused to give him any information because he didn't remove his hat.

It was about this time that I went back to Oklahoma to see a dentist. My gums were yellow and swollen and aching. I had lived for a long time in a place without dentists, toothbrushes, and bathroom sinks (or bathrooms, for that matter). I had other health problems as well. We were living on government surplus commodity food—"commodesty" as they called it in Marks—which came in winter when there was no picking or chopping cotton. So many people needed it that the best items were rare, like beef with juice, which we had only very occasionally. I didn't know the commodity program offered fruit juice and dried fruit until I came back to Oklahoma. In Mississippi every day we had a plate of beans, white rice, "biscuit bread" made of white flour, and maybe cornbread. All this was cooked in the fat from the hog that the Franklins, like many Cotton Street families, killed in December when the moon was in the right phase. At that time no one had freezers, so most of the meat was salted down on the back porch, and the salt pork was put in the beans and greens for months. Much of the rest of the hog became sausage. (Every house had strings of red peppers for this.) Occasionally we might have some neck bones to flavor the food and gnaw meat from.

We were not the only ones to eat this way. One of the volunteers, David Harris, wrote about conditions for the family he stayed with. For breakfast the day before, he reported, they had

> Biscuits with fatback (fatback is a hunk of lard)
> For Lunch: Nothin
> For Dinner: Turnip Greens
> A "prosperous" family eats two meals a day
> (and uses bacon instead of fatback for breakfast).[14]

Because everything was cooked in pork fat, I didn't lose much weight on the winter diet, but I felt dizzy a lot. I had a low resistance to infection, so any cut I got never really healed. The Franklins had bad colds all winter. However, they were better off than others. David's host family, he wrote, was inflicted with a case of goiters due to malnutrition. Some had children with rickets, caused by lack of vitamin D, and some children were intellectually compromised from malnutrition. Margaret Franklin, Jessie's wife, was thirty-five, but she had lost every tooth, after eleven pregnancies and a poor diet, so she looked about seventy.

While I was gone, another white civil rights worker, Alex Shimkin, came to Marks. Alex had been in a demonstration in Natchez where four hundred people were arrested. There wasn't enough room in the local jail, so they were taken to the Mississippi State Penitentiary at Parchman. There they were made to stand at attention naked in the November night. When Alex shifted position, a guard knocked his upper front teeth out. One of the demonstrators was having a nervous breakdown by the time the MFDP lawyers bailed them out.

School Integration Takes Its First Steps

It wasn't safe for Alex to stay in Natchez, so the Jackson MFDP office sent him to Marks. Just after he arrived, the children of the Franklin brothers finally entered the white school. In a letter to a friend, Alex described a February 1966 trip to Edwards, Mississippi, for a conference on school integration:

> The weather has been splendid and wet alternately, either raining like the Flood or sunny and warm. There is a lot of water on the ground. We have been having a good time. Yesterday we went to Issaquena County [Mississippi] with a big truck loaded with mattresses and rode on top. The experience of jolting on the mattresses over the hills to the south was slightly like riding a pogo stick (by pogo stick to Paradise?). While life for the people is bad, we workers enjoy ourselves a good part of the time, and of course, Mississippi Negroes are pretty resourceful at enjoying themselves, however poor they may be. I have a nice place to stay and lots to eat (relatively) so I am not complaining.
>
> School integration has been relatively peaceful on the whole. The kids get called n——s by (some of) their classmates, but they got lots of Valentines. They are pretty ragged, but my mother got together some decent clothes for them. They are all pretty bright, despite coming from homes with no indoor plumbing, wood stoves and no refrigerators etc. They have piles of books (one legacy of the Movement) however.[15]

Mr. Franklin and Alex called meetings of people who might be interested in school integration in the coming fall. Mrs. Weathersby, who had moved from the plantation to Lambert, explained to me why she decided to take part. "Mr. Franklin and Alex Shimkin was having big meetings in '66 calling the community together two and three times a week to integrate the school. They wasn't trying to force nothing. I was wanting to do it all the time but I didn't know what steps I should take.

"See, what was the trouble, when there was so much money appropriated for education every year, the biggest of it went to the white side. I figured if my boy went there, he would get a better quality education. That was the main reason. But also I wanted the Blacks and the whites to grow up together and get used to each other. Like some of my schoolmates, when I see them we still like brothers and sisters. I figured if we could get the Black and the white together we could blot out some of that hatred.

"Yes, so many times I have wondered about white people. But Joe, you know I'm not prejudiced. I believe a man is a man and a woman is a woman. I brought my child up to love. I never hated white folks. I just didn't like the way they was doing me."

CHAPTER 5

"Trying to Take It from the Power Structure" 1966

About this time, President Johnson's War on Poverty program came to Mississippi in a big way.[1] Under this legislation, a Community Action Program (CAP) directed federal subsidies through the Office of Economic Opportunity (OEO) to local community groups working on welfare issues. Around the state, local white political machines and civil rights workers fought for control of those funds.[2] The machines set up local CAP boards with their own people, to control money that was supposed to better the condition of the poor people they had dominated for so long. Ira Grupper, a white SNCC worker, described a board in southeastern Mississippi in a letter to me dated May 13, 1966:

> We just lost a battle: the tri-county CAP set up here has been funded at last. Several Klansmen, two millionaires, the Black bourgeoisie, a few poor are on the advisory board. Many local folks sent letters of protest to the . . . OEO . . . in Wash. D.C. and Atlanta protesting the lack of participation by the poor, but evidently, even though funds were withheld for a while, it didn't do much good.
>
> If your CAP has already been funded, there ain't much you can do from without. You have to pressure from within.

In Quitman County, the new poverty funds were under the control of a five-county CAP called Mid-State Opportunities (MSO), headed by a white former game warden from Tallahatchie County named Rex

McRainey. Although part of the Democratic machine, McRainey was a moderate—by Mississippi standards.

Of course, MSO wanted to control all welfare funding, to keep money in the white community or at least out of "radical" Black hands. But the movement was already involved with one antipoverty program, Head Start. With the help of child development experts, the MFDP had created the Child Development Group of Mississippi (CDGM) in the summer of 1965. They planned to give jobs to poor mothers as teachers' aides, especially those who had lost their jobs for participating in the civil rights movement. The heads of CDGM were Jesse Harris and Hunter Morey, well-known civil rights workers. Child psychologists worked with CDGM to train the mothers to work with preschool children.[3]

This was the major sticking point between the CDGM and the MSO, which argued that Head Start jobs should go to Black teachers because they were better qualified. Alex Shimkin and other movement people believed poor mothers had important skills from their life experience and could do the job well with some training. They argued that Black teachers in the impoverished Delta could not be as effective with these children because they formed a "caste" that held themselves above the mass of Black people in poverty, although there were notable exceptions like Mrs. Clara Rucker in Marks and Mrs. Oma McNiece in Falcon. While Black teachers would not have been considered well off by most white Americans, in Mississippi they were far better off than most Black people.

Arguably too, these jobs would help poor Black women more than the Black teachers. Not only did these undereducated women gain valuable job training, the jobs helped to support people who had been fired or thrown off plantations for civil rights activity. Most teachers, understandably, had not been active given their highly vulnerable jobs.

War on Poverty legislation called for "maximum feasible participation by the poor" in decision making. In most places, including Quitman County, however, such participation antagonized local power structures and was quickly scaled back to be less than "maximum." The CDGM wanted to maximize poor people's participation in Head Start, while the MSO would have created a new elite of better-off Blacks and "moderate" whites. (And it just so happened that those advocating "maximum" participation tended to be closer to Bobby Kennedy, President Johnson's main potential rival for the presidency in 1968.)

Another sticking point between the two organizations was that several of the CDGM staff, like Hunter Morey, had been SNCC staffers. Early in 1966, SNCC had come out against the Vietnam War, so the Johnson administration did not want to create jobs for SNCC people. Instead they turned to Black people who had not been activists. That included most of the teachers. I think the struggle over Head Start in Quitman County is a case study of what happened to the poverty program as it became part of an administration that was fighting a war in Vietnam.

These differences between the CDGM and MSO are why so much of the struggle over antipoverty programs in Quitman County (and Mississippi) was over control of Head Start. Also, we were not prepared to directly confront other welfare issues until the summer of 1966 when I was able to attend a workshop on welfare given by the NAACP's Legal Defense Fund (LDF).

So at first we concentrated on Head Start.

Head Start

Although Black people in Quitman County were enthusiastic about preschool programs, few were aware of the CDGM at first. I was gone between December 1965 and February 1966, and Alex didn't arrive there until late January. And from the civil rights leadership's point of view, Quitman was a low-priority area.

James Wilson Sr. of Marks finally heard about CDGM from Amzie Moore, a SNCC leader in Bolivar County. But to develop a program for Quitman, they needed someone with literacy skills and political connections. Most Black people with those skills and connections supported CAP. Mr. Wilson became that person. He rarely attended civil rights meetings. But J. D. Powells was his son's half-brother, so he knew what was going on. Although he had been reluctant to participate at first, he was now eager to act.

Mr. Wilson was an influential man in the Black community. He held an important position as the head of the Delta Burial Society, which guaranteed even its poorest members an adequate burial. He knew all the traditional Black leaders in the county, including Claude Martin, the biggest Black landowner. These were people in the non–civil rights movement Voters' League (which the MFDP called "the 'Tom' Negro org"), and they wanted to be sure they would keep the same leadership position in the new world—the one to be created by the civil rights movement and Johnson's Great Society—that they had always had.[4] They had the ear of people like McRainey, part of a new "moderate" white leadership the Johnson administration was trying to cultivate in the South. Mr. Wilson was going against some of those people when he set up a local CDGM program, but he was able to make sure that they didn't go against us. I didn't fully realize his importance until I heard years later about what had gone on behind the scenes at that time.

A note in Mr. Wilson's personal papers describes the reaction when he told the Black community about the CDGM: "Mothers and their children they come together, decided in their mind Head Start program will be their program. They called a meeting and organized theirselves in January 1966. In February they organized the [CDGM] Centers."[5] Alex Shimkin then went around the county organizing CDGM Head Start programs in Black churches. It is a measure of how far out of the loop Quitman County was that Alex knew little about the already-existing CAP and the complications that would cause.

Black people in rural communities who had never had anything to do with the civil rights movement before enthusiastically volunteered to help in the CDGM programs, using their own funds, to show the federal government they could run them. But the poverty program offices were biased toward McRainey's MSO. They had already caught a lot of hostility from southern members of Congress for funding CDGM Head Starts elsewhere in Mississippi.

Because the CDGM was already getting static from the Johnson administration, Mr. Wilson created the Quitman County Associated Community Corporation to administer the program locally. In the midst of its power struggles, CDGM was reluctant to fight for any new projects, however sympathetic the organization's leadership might feel. It certainly had no clout to compel the OEO to give funds to Mr. Wilson's organization.[6]

Further complicating matters, even if the pay was low CDGM was the first regular job some of these former SNCC workers had ever had. If they pressed too hard on behalf of the Quitman programs, they risked their own living as well as those of the many poor Black people who desperately needed the CDGM jobs. They had learned a certain amount of caution. Movement people used the word "co-optation" to describe activists made cautious by the need for government funding.[7]

Mr. Wilson persuaded Rev. William McCloud, who had been pastor of Allen Chapel for just two months, to chair the Head Start Committee. Reverend McCloud had worked with the civil rights movement in Yazoo City and Canton, Mississippi. The committee also had to include a white person because the federal government required these organizations to be biracial. But no local whites were willing to participate. He finally found a white man from California who owned a secondhand clothing store in the Black section of Marks. The first volunteer Head Start center opened in Allen Chapel on March 28, 1966.

Alex wrote a report to the OEO in May requesting funding for Marks's center. In it he chronicled the program's history and argued that these small projects played a central role in the struggle "to help the great mass of plantation Negroes gain *their* rights."

> While Marks has not known the systematic terror of McComb or Natchez, it has been the scene of enough racial violence to make this factor important. Despite, therefore, the presence of these two Negroes on the CAP Board, the Negro community as a whole, and certainly . . . the poverty Negro community, has little sense of being represented.
>
> The organization of the CDGM program is such that it is *the Negro people's* program in their eyes. The schools are not Negro institutions, after all; they are controlled by all-white school boards and white superintendents. The only institutions over which Negroes feel they have real control are their churches. The fact that CDGM holds its Headstarts, in many instances, in the churches and in other cases in Negro-owned buildings gives the community a feeling that the program belongs to them.
>
> When we began, we had no idea of what would be required to get the program funded. We did learn how the community committees should be organized, and proceeded to organize these committees in every community in the county. . . .
>
> Quitman County was not, of course, included in the original [CDGM] proposal [for federal funding]. We were told that we might come in on the second grant, and assumed the central staff was handling the paperwork.

In the meantime, Alex explained, the people of Marks decided to move forward. "We began the operation of 8 centers on a volunteer basis, with about 400 children in regular attendance. Up until this time, we had received little or no assistance from the central staff of CDGM, other than to suggest the formation of community committees and the provision of large numbers of application forms. This last was a mistake in that it gave the strong impression to people that there were relatively few obstacles in their path. Indeed . . . most of us believed it was relatively simple." Unfortunately, it was not. The letter continued: "Early in March, 1966, I talked with R. Hunter Morey . . . of CDGM Central Staff, who stated that before we could get money from the Federal government we had to apply to the CAP board and (presumably) be turned down. Therefore we wrote . . . to Mr. Rex McRainey. . . . The proposal left here on the 10th of April and was not completed by the central staff until the 22nd. On the 25th it was delivered to McRainey."

Mr. McRainey refused every opportunity to meet. Frustrated, Alex concluded his letter:

> The basic impetus for this program has come from the people of the county. Assistance from CDGM central staff has been minimal and tardy. Undoubtedly, they had no desire to become embroiled in a factional fight with Mid-State [MSO] until virtually dragged in.
>
> There is no doubt at all that the persons involved are quite capable of operating a CDGM program. . . . The community committees have been set up; petitions collected; and the schools operated with enthusiasm for over five weeks without a cent of outside money. Yet, decisions by persons whom they did not elect can apparently prevent the Negro people of Quitman County from getting a program they want.[8]

I don't think Alex understood how fully the OEO, like the rest of the Johnson administration, was committed to preventing any further expansion of the CDGM. But he was to some degree aware that by escalating the Vietnam War the administration was taking a turn to the right. That meant support was moving away from civil rights activists and toward so-called moderates less likely to oppose the war. SNCC had already stated its opposition to the war by the time Alex wrote. He understood how unlikely he was to persuade the OEO. And he didn't.[9]

I got back to Marks on March 9. Alex had just begun helping set up the centers. Because of the poor diet and constant work, he had lost a lot of weight and was exhausted. He wrote George Williams of the Jackson MFDP office requesting a leave of absence. "I would like to work to help candidates opposing a pro-war Congresswoman in Detroit, a lady who also voted against the [MFDP] challenge. Since I came . . . in June

[1965], I have left only twice, once for my army physical exam, and once for about two weeks at Christmas. . . . Also I could do some fundraising for Mississippi."[10] Alex's plans were characteristic of civil rights workers. I participated in the antiwar movement while I was in Oklahoma waiting to see the dentist and made a speech to raise funds for Marks.

A few days after I got back, Alex received Williams's approval and went north for a couple of weeks. I was left to carry out the plans he had drawn up, going to meetings of poverty program bureaucrats, visiting the county's still-volunteer Head Start centers to explain the latest developments, and at the same time sustaining our ongoing campaigns for voter registration and expanding access to welfare and Social Security.

We held mass meetings around the county to support CDGM, and the meetings in Marks were very loud and enthusiastic. Women volunteered in the centers, and men offered to paint and repair them, hoping to be taken on as janitors when funding came. Many had been thrown off the land they had been working because of civil rights activity. Bernice Gates and her husband, for example, had been evicted from one of the Self plantations for going to civil rights meetings and registering to vote.[11] The Gates family was very active in the volunteer Head Start work. Sarah Ann Brown, another volunteer, was the wife of Willie Brown, a leader in the Freedom Labor Union local. The Browns were put off a plantation near Lambert because Mr. Brown had run for the Agricultural Stabilization and Conservation Service Committee.[12]

Mrs. Gates told me how the program began. "The volunteer Head Start program started out in '66 under our director who was a colored man, which is Reverend McCloud. We volunteered and set up centers and fed those children with food from our homes free, for a year and nine months. When the government money come, they pushed out those peoples what had volunteered and give the jobs to those peoples what didn't do nothing.

"You talk about making a job—that *was* a job, and we made it. And we didn't get nothing for it. We bought a deep freeze for the center, we bought tables, we bought pencils. My husband, he hauled children to the centers free. Reverend McCloud said we'd just work it up. The fact of the matter is we was trying to take it from the power structure. We wanted to take it from McRainey and hold it up our own self. After we met in Jackson he agreed to sign it over to us, and we got back some money, but we never got back what we put into it.

"I learned a little too much. While we was volunteering, folks would say, 'Oh this is a dumb thing, y'all crazy.' And us dumb, crazy people worked up the best thing Quitman County ever had. And wouldn't none of the educated people here meet with us to help us with it. When we got furnished by the government, they hired some of them that volunteered, but not all of them. They said you had to finish the ninth grade to work there. I went as far as the eighth grade."

At a meeting in Jackson that summer, it was decided that a significant number of poor mothers already volunteering in the centers would get jobs. If they hadn't done that, many parents would have boycotted. But others would be let go and replaced by teachers. Some of the poor men working as janitors in the center received paying jobs. Most of the administrative jobs went to Black people already connected to the MSO. They were generally better off, like Claude Martin. Later, as money for Head Start was cut because of the Vietnam War, the poor mothers were the first to go.

I asked Mrs. Gates how many children the early volunteer program served. "At the church where I worked there was eighty-six. There was supposed to be over four hundred in the whole county. I enjoyed the work, but to work so long and not get the money—but I enjoyed working with the children."

Sarah Ann Brown told me she set up the Lambert Head Start center. "I was the first one come here to Marks and got the racket of it and carried the news back to Lambert. I found a room in my church for them to have the center in and help clean it up. We worked there near a year without a penny of money carrying the food from our houses, asking people for food. I'd stick my head in the stores and ask for food, and they'd give it to me. Lots of times people would be scared to go with me, but finally I'd carry the committee to the store to ask for food for the center.

"One season I was working there, and then they put me out. I was a fourth-grade scholar, but I had enough education to do what I was doing. I don't regret my work at all. I enjoyed the work, and I enjoyed helping getting it in here. The Lord answered my prayer to get something done here, and I hope it last as long as it needed. They called it Child Development, and it sure did develop a lot of children. The children all look so much better, healthier than they used to because of it. But putting me and the others out of a job after just one season, that was wrong. It was because I was working for the civil rights movement."[13]

The struggle over Head Start continued. Negotiations about who should be hired were constant. But CAP knew they would never be able to open Head Starts unless the Black people in poverty agreed to the program. The OEO sent representatives to make the poor people agree to the demands of CAP and the Black teachers. They used a lot of fancy words, and one even waved a Bible. All I could do was explain to people in plain English what he was asking them to do.

Reverend McCloud was unhappy with me about that. He was very popular with the Black people in poverty for taking up their cause, but at the same time he was pastor of Allen Chapel Church, whose membership included many Black teachers and their families. He was under pressure from both directions.

All this controversy created some momentum in the spring of 1966. There was a sudden increase in the number of Black parents who went to PTA meetings. They had heated words with the Black teachers, insisting poor women be hired as aides or they wouldn't send their children. I went with hundreds of Black people to the courthouse one night. It was possibly the largest gathering of Black people in the history of Marks. They questioned CAP director McRainey much more sharply than they would have ever dared question a white man before. In the end, the compromise largely favored CAP but did provide some participation by poor women. We had gone against the Johnson administration so we won only a little. But what we did win was thanks to the boldness of those Black parents.

Other signs of change: two children from a poor white family attended the volunteer Head Start center in Lambert for a while. And the mayor of Marks, Howard Langford, came by the Franklins' house to ask for our support for a youth center he wanted the poverty program to fund.

What I enjoyed most was borrowing a guitar and going to the Head Start centers to play songs for the children. The centers had been operating throughout all these negotiations and struggles, and many children were eating who might have gone hungry. When I saw them learning the alphabet or playing traditional ring games, it was obvious they were happy. Many of these children learned about indoor toilets in the center and were spared humiliation in the first grade. Their life was much better than that of the child I had once seen covered with flies waiting for his mother to return from work. The women at the centers treated the children with great affection but firmness.

Fighting for a Fair Share

We had less success with other federal agencies. Now that a few Black people around Mississippi were on ASCS committees, they could get the Department of Agriculture to investigate some of the abuses Black people faced on plantations. But it was thirty years too late, since planters had already pushed out most of their sharecroppers and now hired only a few wage workers.

On March 4, 1966, Assistant Secretary of Agriculture William Seabron wrote civil rights offices in Mississippi asking if anyone there knew of sharecroppers not getting the cotton subsidy checks they were supposed to get. As Alec Dean pointed out to me, sharecroppers had never gotten these payments from the time they began during the New Deal. Planters had had a variety of rackets for taking the payments. The planter who routinely snatched the check from Mr. Franklin's hand said that Mr. Franklin owed that money to him. The planters wanted the money, and, just as important, they didn't want the sharecroppers to have an independent source of funds. And only now, as sharecropping was coming to an end, was the government trying to do anything about it.

When Alex got back from up north, he responded to Mr. Seabron in a letter dated April 14, 1966. He described Vance, a rural community where eighteen of the thirty-four plantations had no sharecroppers left whatever:

> I am writing in reference to your letter dated March 4, 1966. While, as I speak only English, French, Mandarin, and Gullah, I don't exactly understand the Cotton Program, it appears that a group of sharecroppers have not received the payments to which they are entitled. First of all, sharecropping has virtually disappeared from the Delta in the last few years. However, the A. L. King plantation at Vance has about ten families cropping. The person for whom I am inquiring is Mr. Thomas Young. . . . The other sharecroppers are [nine names]. Last year Mr. Young made 21 bales of cotton. This year he went down to the county agent's office with his landlord . . . and the other croppers. They were instructed to sign "a blue paper" which they did. . . . Mr. Young attempted to question his landlord . . . but was not enlightened as to what they were doing. . . . He does not remember signing any papers last year; nor did he receive any payments. Is he entitled to a diversion payment? What was the "blue paper"? Will he receive a diversion payment? If so, when?

> Both Mr. Young and I would appreciate information on this matter. Needless to say, I expect that this inquiry will be kept strictly confidential. By way of illustration, Mr. Young is the only registered voter on the King place.[14]

Mr. Young moved off the plantation and into Lambert. He told me later that in 1967 he finally received some cotton fund money.

We did make progress on another front that spring. Mr. Franklin and I were invited to a statewide meeting on school integration, held by the federal Department of Health, Education, and Welfare in Jackson. There were Black parents, civil rights workers, and members of lily-white school boards from all over the state. School superintendent Craig, who had once had me jailed for trespassing on school grounds, was there. He stared at me and backed away. After the morning session, someone told the Black participants they didn't have to walk to the Black section to find a restaurant any more. Now they could eat in the hotel dining room. And they all did.

But the school integration effort hit another snag. Quitman County, like most of the South, had finally integrated, but had done so under a "freedom of choice" plan. This meant that all parents were to fill out a form designating which school they wished their children to attend.[15]

All the white parents chose the "white" school, and almost all the Black parents chose the "colored" school out of fear of being fired or harassed by the police. As a result, only a few Black students had enrolled in the white school. A group of white kids ganged up on one of them, twelve-year-old Hull Franklin, in the school gym. When they wouldn't let go of him, he bit one of them on the arm. Then one of the white boys stuck him twice in the face with a sharp pencil. The deep cuts got infected, and Hull's face swelled up. The white teachers and principal appeared indifferent.

I phoned Mel Leventhal of the LDF. He drove to Marks and talked with us about how to avoid such incidents in the future. Mel said as long as most Black families continued to choose the Black school, the handful of Black pupils in the white school would be in danger of being ganged up on. The LDF hoped to get "freedom of choice" replaced by court orders merging the students and teachers of both races in the same schools, rather than putting responsibility on individual parents. Our job was to gather as much information as possible about harassment of Black pupils in school, indifference by the school staff to their problems, and discrimination in extracurricular activities, to use as evidence in a court case.

As spring weather got hotter and the programs we were involved with ground slowly on, we often felt burned out, tired and frustrated. There were days when all we did was read Alex's *Lord of the Rings* or his Chinese language textbooks. All civil rights workers knew some of the feelings Alex describes in a letter to a friend in May 1966. This was shortly after Lurleen Wallace, Governor George Wallace's wife, won the primary for governor of Alabama. George Wallace was beloved by many whites for resisting integration; when he was unable to run again, his wife ran in his stead, a public illustration of continued resistance to civil rights.

> Well, it is dreadfully hot now and the streets are full of children and people sit on their porches and stoops. So anyway, here I am back in Marks (where else?).... I think the county is fairly well organized now, but I am too listless to describe much. I am getting very weary and apathetic. Nobody I write to answers my letters.... Nothing seems to mean much anymore. I wish I hadn't left school, ROTC, etc. because it would be easier on me later on. I love the people in the Movement, and I believe it is right, but it is hard to work up any enthusiasm when one is dragging around wretchedly in the heat.... The war in Vietnam is wrong. They don't want us there, but there doesn't seem to be anything we can do about it. It is part of the order of things, ordered by fate and immutable.
>
> I have no interests, no relaxations. I just work and lie about in a stupor. Jackson is good fun, but a long way away—although Jackson is now civilized. All the principal places are integrated, the Child Development Group of Mississippi (our Head Start) operates... in downtown Jackson, but... little has changed in white folks' attitude as shown by Mrs. Wallace's victory.[16]

March Against Fear

Meanwhile, we were also preparing for the Democratic primary on June 7.[17] For most Black Mississippians this was their first chance to vote in a regular election. For all of them this was their first chance to vote for Black candidates. The MFDP was running Rev. Clifton

Whitley for the Senate against James Eastland, who had been in office since 1940. In the Second Congressional District where Marks was, the MFDP was running Ralthus Hayes against incumbent Jamie Whitten.

Like civil rights workers around the state, we distributed sample ballots, and we put a ballot box in Allen Chapel where people could practice. Our main problem was that the last name of Clifton Whitley, the MFDP Senate candidate, sounded like the name of Congressman Whitten, who we were urging people to vote against. This caused a lot of confusion, and we had to explain until we were exhausted.

On June 4, James Meredith, who had integrated the University of Mississippi in 1962, started walking with a handful of others from Memphis to Jackson on a "March Against Fear." He said he hoped to give Black Mississippians confidence to break "the all-pervasive, overriding fear that dominates the day-to-day life of the Negro in the United States—especially in the South and particularly in Mississippi" so they would register and vote.[18]

On Monday, June 6, Mel Leventhal met with Black parents planning to integrate the school. Mel and I had just left the meeting when Reverend Coleman ran up and told us a white man had shot James Meredith outside Hernando, Mississippi. Meredith was rushed by ambulance to a Memphis hospital. Fortunately, his injuries were not life-threatening.[19] After visiting with Meredith in his hospital room, Martin Luther King Jr. and Stokely Carmichael called on Black people to continue the March Against Fear from the place Meredith had been shot.

The next day was the primary. Some white students from the University of North Carolina brought a van to help transport people to the polls. In Quitman County, the MFDP candidates got about 250 votes even though 600 Black people were registered. Statewide, Reverend Whitley received 31,258 votes to Eastland's 216,943. Ralthus Hayes got 4,590 votes from the Second District, to Jamie Whitten's 39,855. Still, Black voters cast just over 12 percent of the ballots, the highest percentage since 1890.[20]

The Memphis *Commercial Appeal* suggested the MFDP candidates' poor showing was largely because the NAACP "had been openly cool toward FDP-backed candidates."[21] This was possibly true in Clarksdale where Dr. Henry lived and in other places with strong NAACP chapters. The NAACP didn't help get Black voters to the polls there because the national NAACP was close to the Johnson administration and many MFDP leaders opposed his war in Vietnam. The NAACP believed Black people needed the support of the administration, so in larger cities the association distanced itself from SNCC and the MFDP.

In a small place like Marks, however, there was no division. NAACP leaders worked hard to get people to the polls to vote for MFDP candidates. All the people involved in the civil rights movement there were involved in the same thing. The people in the NAACP and the MFDP were the same people. Instead, I think a major problem was the confusion in the candidates' names. An NAACP member told me that even he got the names mixed up and didn't know on election morning whom to advise people to vote for.

That same day Alex went to join the March Against Fear. The next day Reverend Coleman and I joined the march for a few miles. I got a ride back to Marks with Stokely Carmichael. Two days after the primary, a carload of Black people from Marks joined. One was Armistead Phipps, a fifty-eight-year-old father of six, who joined the group at the last minute. His wife had begged him not to go because he had a heart condition. While marching from Senatobia to Como in the ninety-five-degree heat, he collapsed. He was taken to a car where he died. Two days before, he had voted for the first time in his life.

On June 10, the marchers held a memorial service for Mr. Phipps at North Panola High School in Batesville. A speaker at that service said Mr. Phipps was a "hero just as much as the boys who are dying in Vietnam." Another proposed, "He should be buried in Arlington Cemetery in Washington, D.C."[22] I found that ironic since Mr. Phipps had strongly opposed the Vietnam war.

Mr. Franklin told me he believed Mr. Phipps had probably known he was going to die soon and wanted to die in the right place, urging his people forward. Alex Shimkin said much the same thing. "He was a decent Christian man. I feel honestly that if he'd known he was about to die he would have done it this way."[23] As Dr. King put it, "He was determined to die free."[24] Mr. Franklin told me he had a dream the night before Mr. Phipps died. In the dream Mr. Phipps came to tell Mr. Franklin what a fine march it was.

On June 12, Mr. Phipps's funeral took place. Because of the large crowd—well over three hundred people, including both Marks people and marchers—it had to be held in one of the larger Black Baptist churches, although Mr. Phipps had belonged to the Church of Christ.

Many believed also that the funeral was moved from his church to fool whites looking to make trouble. That was how intense the fear was.

Mrs. Phipps told me that during the service a helicopter flew overhead: "Some people left there running because they was scared in that time. I was scared, more scared than I ever have been in my life. Any time you talk about helping the people, helping humanity, they gonna kill you."[25]

As was the custom, at the funeral there was a cardboard model of a clock beside the pulpit, with the hands pointing to the hour of Mr. Phipps's death. A speaker announced the date Mr. Phipps was born, the age he first professed his faith in Christ, the date of his marriage, and how many children he had. Then Dr. King came in with his bodyguards from the Deacons for Defense and Justice, a Black self-defense group.

Most of these men were deacons in Black churches in the Deep South, and many were high-ranking Masons. A number had been decorated for bravery in World War II or Korea. They were dignified middle-aged men with pistols bulging from their coat pockets. While King himself was a pacifist, he accepted aid from those willing to use weapons in his defense. As Charles Sims, one of the Deacons, put it, King would not enter the Delta unless the Deacons protected him. "I had to carry him with my gun and my mens," Sims told journalist Howell Raines. "He can let his men trail along at the tail end, but in front and behind it was gon' be me. And that was the only way he'd go. So when the chips were down, I won't say the man woulda picked up a gun, but I'll say this, he didn't run one away."[26]

Dr. King preached the funeral sermon with his usual free-flowing eloquence. He spoke about the civil rights movement and Mr. Phipps's participation in it, not only by marching but also by voting. "This was a man who loved freedom and was willing to suffer and sacrifice for freedom."[27]

On the way out of the church I met Richard Arvedon. He was eighteen. He had met Stanford Brown on the march, and Stanford, who had worked in Marks, suggested Richard go there. After talking for a while, Richard had agreed. He told me he had discussed it with Stokely Carmichael, who thought it was a good idea. This was when the media claimed Stokely opposed participation by whites, because he talked about Black Power and how important it was for Black people to control the movement.[28] But Richard, who was white, said Stokely told him there was still a need in places like Marks, and there was no Black person to fill that need, so Richard might as well come to Marks.

The clearest evidence I had about Stokely's attitude toward white workers is what he said when he had given Reverend Coleman and me a ride back to Marks from the march four days before: "I've been coming through the Delta for five years now, and things haven't changed a bit. I'm going to talk about the white man like he's a dog because he's acted like a dog and he knows he could act better. I'm going to say it all in terms of Black and white." But he was friendly with me.

As Richard said to me many years later, "The more I reflect on that apparent contradiction, the more I believe that the answer might be that the astonishing poverty of Marks had already led you and Mr. Franklin to articulate and organize around a radical economic analysis. Economic empowerment was in fact compatible with Stokely's call for Black Power. So, while it might have been more convenient for Stokely had you and I been Black, we were doing the basic organizing work that Stokely saw should be done and if not us, then, at that moment, who else?

"I remember you and I were walking on Cotton Street, and I was moaning about why was I in Marks, why was I dirty and hungry when I didn't have to be. You listened to me carry on for a while and then answered me in no uncertain terms. 'You're here because you're a radical organizer. It's who you are.' It was a defining moment in my life." I agree with Richard. It was hard not to be radicalized by the unrelenting and violent white opposition to any step toward Black and poor people gaining their voice. When I first went to Marks in 1964 for COFO, it was for civil rights and integration. By 1966 that had changed.

Stokely's own views also shifted over time, as he navigated the highly competitive shark tank of growing Black nationalism. These activists had cut themselves loose from white liberalism because of the war. Now they wanted to cut themselves loose from whites in general—in this specific case, white leftists. In 1968 Stokely was still insisting, "Socialism is not an ideology fitted for Black people. Period. Period."[29] I think that was an oblique criticism of the Black Panthers, who along with their socialist ideology maintained a working relationship with white leftists.

Five years after Richard and I spoke with him, which at that time could seem like five centuries, Stokely was giving a talk at the University of Oklahoma. I was there. He called capitalism "a very backward system" and said Black people needed "a crystal-clear ideology." That ideology, he insisted, was "socialism." It was easy to see that at times by "socialist" he meant Black and by "capitalist" he meant white, and that this is how a lot of the Black audience members understood what he was saying. But he was using the word "socialist" to describe himself because this was how many Africans he was working with, like Kwame Nkrumah (who had died recently) and the government of Guinea, which had given him shelter, saw things.[30]

Soon after Richard arrived in Marks, we went down to Grenada and joined the march again. This was June 14, 1966. In just those first two weeks of the march, 2,250 Black Mississippians registered to vote. The next day we marched from Grenada to Holcomb.

The day after that, Alex and I got a ride back to Marks with Larry Caroline, a friend of his from Ann Arbor, Michigan. It was very hot, and, after all those events and all the work of the primary, I was exhausted. Two women came running up to me shouting about the latest rumors of scandal in the distribution of old clothes. By the time they left, I was just about to go to pieces. Alex suggested I go back with Larry to Ann Arbor and rest for a few days. Larry and I left that night. I spent five days there, amazed at luxuries like an unlimited supply of food, running water, and indoor toilets everywhere. Above all, there was the luxurious feeling I didn't have to be any place at a certain time.

On June 22 I started back for Marks, hitchhiking part of the way and taking a bus the rest. When I got back, the Franklins and I heard on TV that two thousand marchers had been tear-gassed in Canton by the Mississippi Highway Patrol. The troopers had refused to allow the marchers to pitch tents for the night on the grounds of an all-Black elementary school. Many marchers remained in the schoolyard while leaders negotiated with the troopers. Some marchers didn't even know there was any problem. The tear gas came very suddenly, followed by kicking and clubbing by the state troopers.[31]

The next day, June 24, I got a ride to Canton. Alex and Richard were both very sick. Not only had they been gassed, they'd also been clubbed by members of the Mississippi Highway Patrol. Stanford Brown had also received a heavy gassing. He didn't know what was happening. He just started running, blinded by the gas, trying to get away. He couldn't see which way he was going, so he ran toward the troopers. He might have been shot if Stokely hadn't grabbed him and held him back. It must have been difficult, because Stanford was much larger and stronger than Stokely. We were all angry to hear President Johnson say that the troopers' action was justified.[32]

Despite the injuries and the tear gas, we continued marching for the next two days to Jackson. Mr. Franklin and his wife and children drove from Marks and joined the march for the final day, July 2. Then Alex, Richard, Stanford, and I went back to Marks.

The situation in Marks, and in the entire Deep South, seemed to be getting worse. White violence had been increasing and provoking Black anger. We began with the hopeful moment of an election; now it seemed the MFDP failure was only one of many disappointments. Too many white officials were resisting every attempt Black people made to gain equality.[33] This frustrated SNCC folks, who had begun chanting "Black Power!" during the Meredith march, much to the dismay of Dr. King. This growing anger didn't affect Richard or me in Marks, but tensions were certainly rising.

Segregation Forever?

Still, we kept trying. Federal enforcement of the Civil Rights Act of 1964 had already compelled some white establishments in Marks to rethink their attitudes about segregation. One afternoon Jessie Franklin took me to eat at the Marks Hotel dining room. It was the first time in the history of Marks that a Black person had been served in a "white" restaurant. I had the chicken-fried steak.

However, some white businesspeople in Marks refused to accept the law and maintained segregation. Bob Young was one. As Richard recounted, "Jessie Franklin brought up in a mass meeting that a lot of fear remained from the time in 1965 when a group of high school students led by his niece, Mae Ella Franklin, had attempted to integrate Bob Young's cafe. Young had used a hammer to chase those students from his doorway. That attempt to integrate the cafe had ended with the arrest and vicious incarceration of Joe Bateman, John Siegel and R. T. Smith.

"The cafe remained whites only. People believed that now, a year later, it was time to try again. The irony was that none of us cared about eating at the cafe, yet we were willing to put our bodies on the line simply to assert our lawful right to be Young's customers.

"We knew that hamburgers cost twenty-five cents and Cokes were a dime. So we took up a collection. With everyone pitching in we were able to raise enough for seven of us to go. It ended up being Jessie Franklin, Clara Collins, Olivia W., Rev. L. C. Coleman, a young girl whose name I do not recall, Joe Bateman, and myself.

"This time we made it through the doorway with no problem. But before we could find seats, Young blocked our way and started hollering something to the effect that the law might force him to serve us, but it did not require him to serve 'white trash,' all the while pointing at Joe. In those days, with my deep tan and close-cropped hair, no one in Marks was quite sure whether I was Black or white. On this particular day Young obviously believed I was Black. Our group quietly talked it over and decided that rather than letting ourselves be drawn into an argument over the scope of the Public Accommodation [Civil Rights] Act, Joe would leave, and the rest of us would stay to integrate the cafe.

"When we were quickly shown to a booth, we were puzzled. Would it be this easy? I was seated across from Reverend Coleman, and I recall that his entire body was shivering. I knew that L. C. had been around, and if he was this frightened then I believed we were in a lot of trouble. But the waitress did approach and even offered us menus. We declined the menus and told her all we wanted was a burger and a Coke each. The waitress kept going on about how we should really have a look at the menus and at that point it dawned on us that something was really wrong. We asked to see the menus and were shocked that they had obviously been specially doctored for us: hamburgers at two dollars and fifty cents, Cokes for a dollar, and all the other fare priced equally outrageously.

"Their tactic worked. We had steeled ourselves to face the business end of a hammer or even a shotgun, but with only thirty-five cents apiece we were flummoxed. I stood up and said that we wanted to cancel our orders. Bob Young yelled out that it was too late; the cook had already put the burgers on the grill, and we would either pay for them or we would be arrested.

"The deputy was waiting for us as we exited. He arrested us on charges of intent to commit fraud and contributing to the delinquency of a minor, since one girl with us was not of age. We were all crowded into the deputy's car. While driving us to the jail the deputy told us he knew 'things were going to change.' He was treating us with courtesy and hoped we would 'remember that later.'

"At the jail we were lined up outside while the jailer inspected us. He asked me if I was 'white or n——.' Above all I desperately hoped to avoid the fates of Joe Bateman and John Siegel the year before. I did not want to be placed in the white section of the jail. But I also hoped to prevent the imminence of jail from demoralizing our group, so I was looking for a wisecrack. I asked the jailer what day it was. He said it was Thursday. I said, 'If it's Thursday I must be a n——.' I recall Clara Collins doubled over in her effort to not laugh out loud.

"My ploy initially worked as I was placed in a tiny cell with Jessie, Reverend Coleman, and other prisoners in the Black section. Later I was moved to a larger cell by myself in the white section. I used a nickel of the thirty-five cents in my pocket to have a young Black trusty bring me a bottle of Coke. I drank the Coke and put the empty bottle in my pocket. If they were going to come for me later that night I at least now had a weapon with which to fight back. I spent a sleepless, anxious night, but no one bothered or even approached me.

"The next morning a deputy escorted me to the office of County Attorney Caldwell. Caldwell told me I was in serious trouble and was looking at time in the state prison farm at Parchman, but if I was willing to leave Marks all charges would be dropped. What stood out in my mind about the notorious Parchman prison farm was that the civil rights workers I knew who had been incarcerated there never spoke of their time in the institution. So I knew conditions there were bad.[34] At first I thought Caldwell was talking about dropping charges against all six of us if I agreed to leave town, and I figured I should at least talk that offer over with the group. But when I asked to be allowed to speak with the prisoners in our group, Caldwell made clear that the offer applied only to me. I told him I was not interested.

"Later that day our whole group was walked over to the courthouse. Joe Bateman had been in contact with the office in Jackson, and we had a lawyer appear for us. He was a corporation counsel for the city of New York and was spending his summer helping the movement. We were his first case. Joe had also turned out a good portion of the population of Cotton Street, whose presence in the courtroom seemed to me to be the strongest argument on our behalf. We had been arrested in the hope of tamping down activism among the people of Cotton Street. Instead, most of Cotton Street had now taken the unprecedented step of showing up at the courthouse as a group. Caldwell and his cronies appeared nervous.

"Our lawyer argued that 'intent to commit fraud' was not a crime in Mississippi. (According to state statutes, only fraud itself was a crime.) The judge, Billy Turner, said he could not understand a word our lawyer said. Caldwell told the judge not to worry about it since they were going to find us guilty anyway. I recall our attorney being literally dumbfounded and my having to tell him, 'This is Mississippi.'

"We were found guilty, but I had a fifty-dollar check my uncle had sent to help with Mr. Franklin's work on the Freedom House Community Center he was building behind his house. We were holding the check until we could get to Clarksdale to cash it. Our lawyer was able to barter the check for the release of our whole group on appeal bond."

Richard reflected a moment. "To me the real significance of the 1966 Bob Young affair was the contrast between how our arrest was handled and what happened in 1965 when Mae Ella Franklin and the other high school students had tried to integrate the same cafe. In 1965 the incarceration of Joe, John, and R. T. was brutal and lengthy. In 1966 we were only held for a night, and no one bothered us. In 1965 when Mr. Franklin tried to bring food to the jail, he was arrested. In 1966 many folks from Cotton Street crowded the courthouse for our hearing and no one was harassed. Even the deputy who arrested us more or less apologized by calling attention to his decent treatment of us. To my mind it seems that in 1965 the white leadership of Marks were still defending segregation, but by 1966 they were seeking ways to accommodate a day they had never seen before but now realized was inevitable."

"My God, It's the Revolution!"

After the incidents at Bob Young's cafe and the courthouse, there was a lot of hostility among the local whites toward the Franklins. Mae Ella was working at another cafe owned by a white woman. Later that day, after our people were released from jail, Mae Ella's employer drove her home early. She told us some drunken whites in her restaurant had threatened Mae Ella and said they would follow her home after work and shoot up her house. The white woman had gotten her pistol and brought Mae Ella home and warned us.

As white threats intensified, some people in the community began to question their commitment to nonviolence. Alex argued that Black people had to be ready to protect themselves. Reverend Coleman, Alex, and Richard had some military training. They and some local men overturned some trash cans in the middle of Cotton Street as a barricade. That night they all sat at the barricade with rifles and shotguns around a fire. I wouldn't carry a gun because I still believed in nonviolence. Reverend Coleman would run from the barricade to challenge each car as it entered Cotton Street. All the people who lived on the street had agreed to blink their car lights twice as a signal.

Reverend Coleman and Alex were up all night. Richard and I went to sleep. When we woke up we saw a fourteen-year-old girl at the barricade carrying a rifle over her shoulder, like a poster from Cuba. "My God, it's the revolution!" Richard said.

That afternoon Alex, Richard, Stanford Brown, and some local Black youths practiced shooting tin cans in a nearby cotton field where passing whites could see them. Although the threatened white attack did not come, even I began to have very strong doubts about absolute nonviolence, thinking about how the Franklin children might have been killed.

All this made Alex think deeply. He told me that when he was teargassed he hated poor and working-class whites like Mr. Young who had always bullied and terrorized Blacks. Now, as Alex read the history of the South and talked with Black people about local history, he had come to understand how poor whites had been turned against them by the wealthy and powerful. If poor whites like Mr. Young had ever seen Black people as allies, they would have joined with them to overthrow the power of rich whites like the Self family who dominated Quitman County.

Now Alex said he could feel sorry for Mr. Young even after he had Mr. Jessie, Richard, and the others arrested. Several people had told Alex they had seen the former sheriff, Gordon Darby, chase Mr. Young down the street, beating him over the head with a billy club. Now he understood Mr. Young as a man with almost no power, taking his anger and frustration out on people who had even less. Alex said he could even sympathize a little with Mr. Darby, who, after all, was just a poor white man put into office to protect the interests of the rich. He started to realize that class was as important a division as race in the South, and that if he could help Black people to understand the economic system and how it affected local politics, they could fight for themselves more effectively.

Shortly after that, Alex and Stanford left Marks. Stanford went to Port Chicago, California, where he joined an ongoing protest against shipping napalm bombs to Vietnam. Alex went to Jackson to work with the Freedom Information Service, which gathered material for the movement. He produced a series of political handbooks in simple language, for example, that explained how state, county, and local governments worked and what local and outside financial interests dominated each county.

William Franklin, circa 1967–68. Mr. Franklin had a profound influence on me. He showed me the potential of people in the most difficult circumstances. *Photo by Jim Peppler, courtesy of Alabama Department of Archives and History.*

Henrietta Franklin, circa 1967–68. Mrs. Franklin was interviewed for an NAACP Legal Defense and Educational Fund project documenting poverty. *Photo by Jim Peppler, courtesy of Alabama Department of Archives and History.*

I wore out a pair of tennis shoes a month in the mud of Cotton Street.

Photo by Frank Garner, courtesy of Oklahoma Historical Society, Gateway to Oklahoma History.

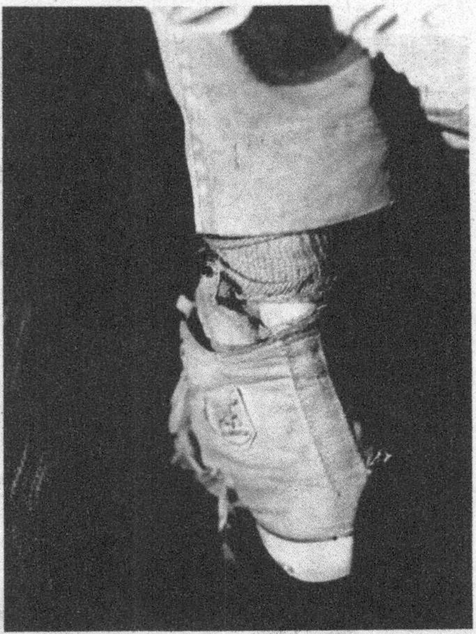

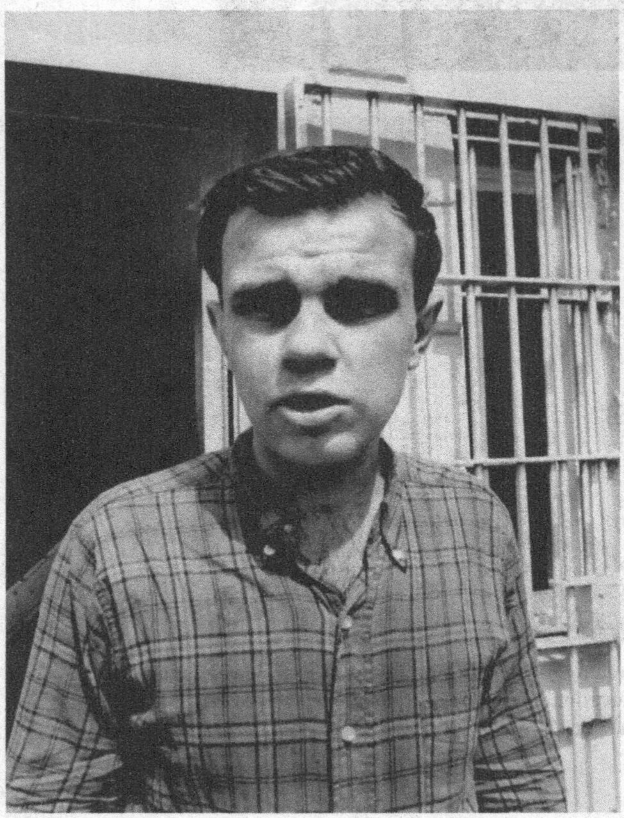

I am released from jail in Marks, March 10, 1965.

Daily Oklahoman, *courtesy of Oklahoma Historical Society, Gateway to Oklahoma History.*

Mr. Jessie Franklin and I shake hands after I am released from jail, March 10, 1965. Hull Franklin is the child wearing a cap.

Photo by Frank Garner, courtesy of Oklahoma Historical Society, Gateway to Oklahoma History.

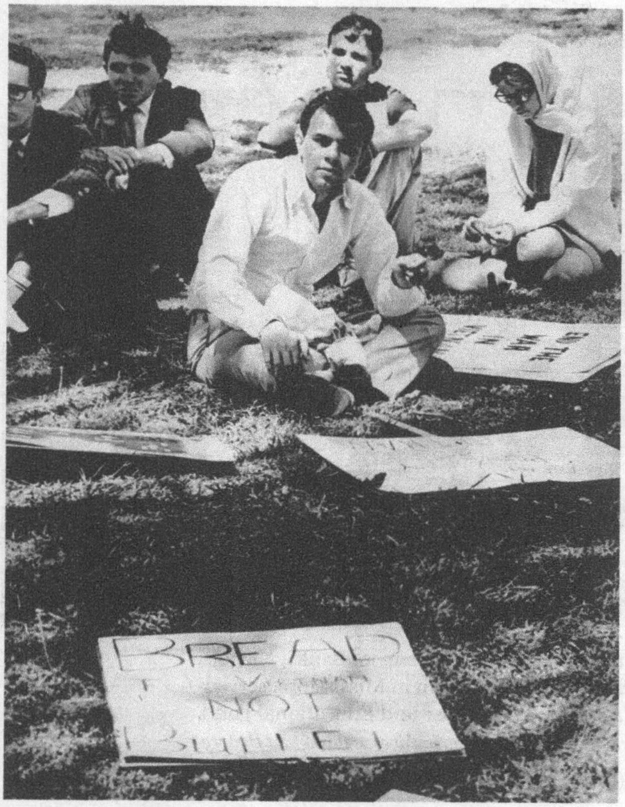

At an antiwar protest, May 1965, during my visit home to Oklahoma.

Photo by Jim Lukas, courtesy of Oklahoma Historical Society, Gateway to Oklahoma History.

Dr. Martin Luther King preaching at Amistead Phipps's funeral, June 12, 1966: "This was a man who loved freedom and was willing to suffer and sacrifice for freedom."
Associated Press/Shutterstock.

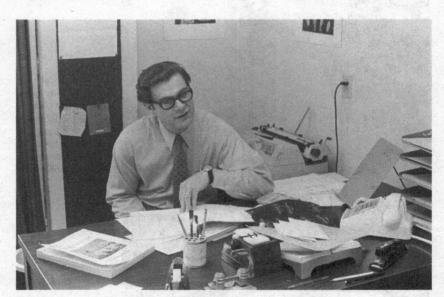

Attorney Mel Leventhal, circa 1971–74. Anderson, Banks, Nichols, and Leventhal, the first interracial law firm in Mississippi, served as attorneys for the NAACP Legal Defense and Educational Fund.
Photo by Jim Peppler, courtesy of Alabama Department of Archives and History.

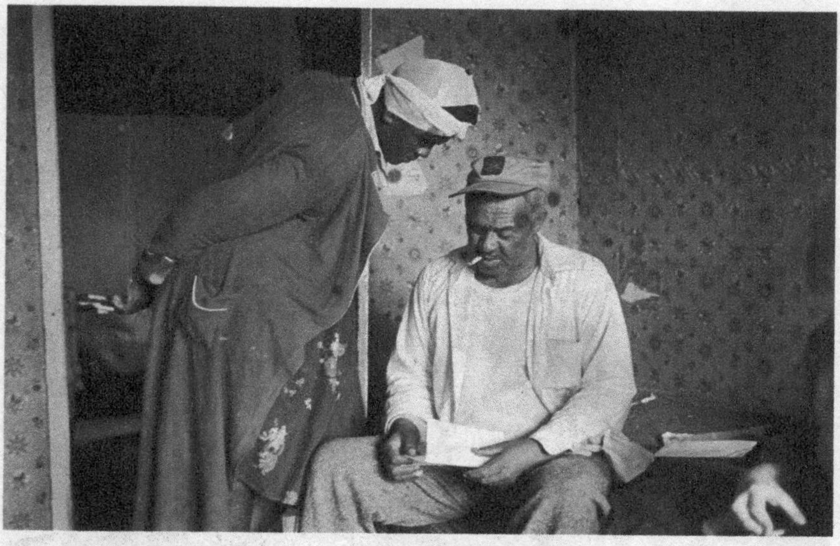

Mr. and Mrs. Franklin interviewed in their home, circa 1967–68.
Photo by Jim Peppler, courtesy of Alabama Department of Archives and History.

Organizing in nearby Falcon, Mississippi, 1968.
Associated Press.

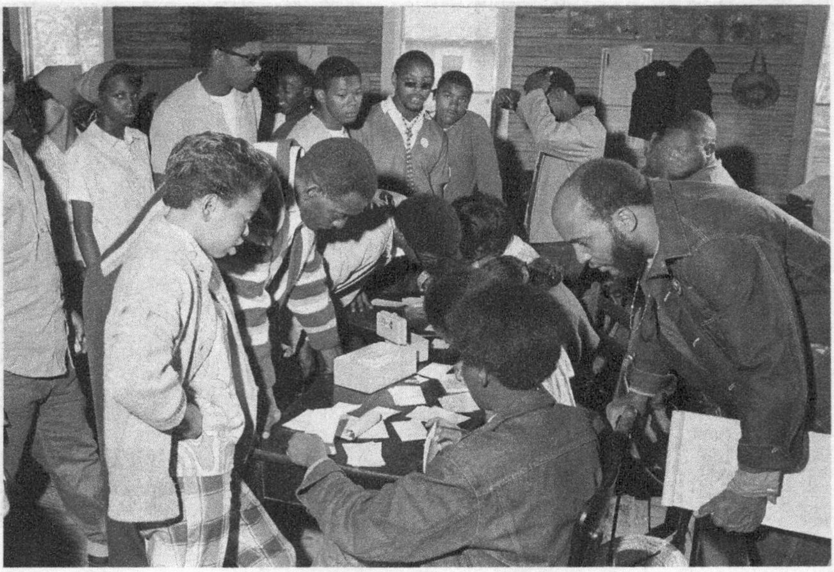

The SCLC's James Bevel (right) signing in volunteers for the Mule Train at Eudora Methodist Church in Marks, 1968.
Photo by Jack Thornell, Associated Press.

Sit-in at the Marks jail, May 1, 1968, just before highway patrolmen attacked.
Associated Press, courtesy of Oklahoma Historical Society, Gateway to Oklahoma History.

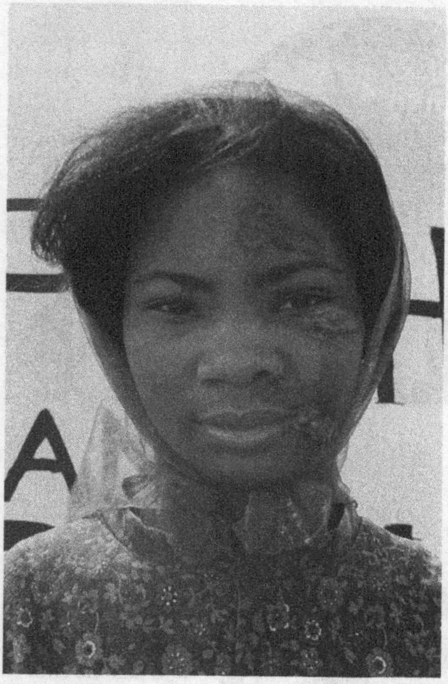

Lydia McKinnon showing the bruises from being beaten at the sit-in on May 1, 1968.
© *Roland L. Freeman.*

Jessie Franklin driving a Mule Train wagon, May 1968. Shirley Collins (left) and Ida Mae Lloyd ride the mules.
© *Roland L. Freeman.*

Rev. L. C. Coleman, May 1968. *© Roland L. Freeman.*

Jack Franklin and Debbie Ann Johnson, May 1968. *© Roland L. Freeman.*

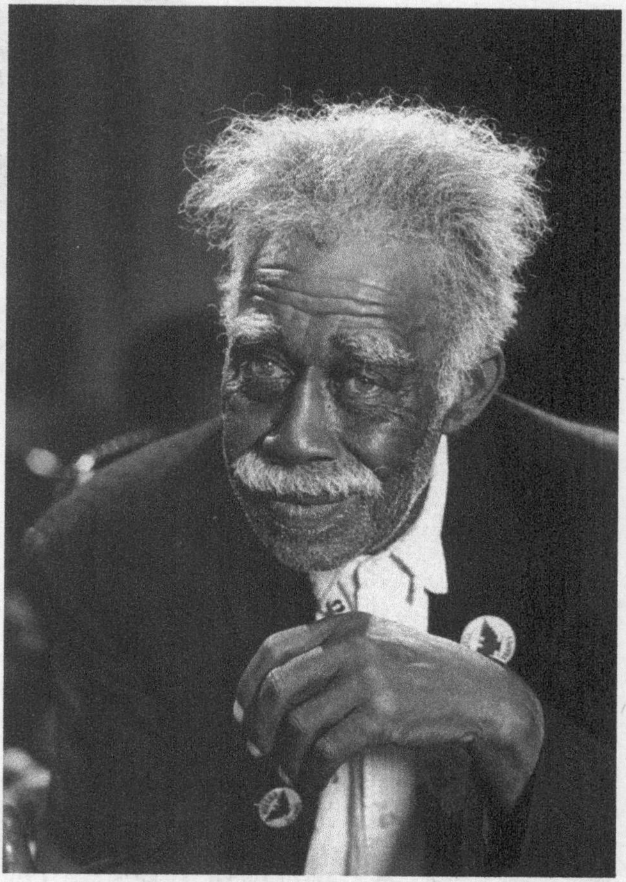

George "Cap" Nickerson testifying before Congress during the Poor People's Campaign in 1968. Mr. Nickerson came to civil rights meetings faithfully, even in the worst weather when no one else would show up. © *Roland L. Freeman.*

Lee Dora Collins, 1995. © *Roland L. Freeman.*

Ora Bea Phipps in front of her house, 2015.
Photo by Richard Arvedon.

Quitman County Development Organization CEO and Mississippi state senator Robert Jackson, 2015.
Photo by Richard Arvedon.

CHAPTER 6

"This Corner of the Great Society"

1966

Richard Arvedon wanted to reinvigorate civil rights efforts in Marks after he got out of jail. He believed the Head Start issue had been overemphasized. Now that it was obvious that only a limited number of people would be hired at the newly funded centers, he feared interest in the movement was slackening.[1]

The Reality of Poverty

Richard invited the most active local people to meet at the new COFO office and library—Richard and I had recently moved it into the community center Mr. Franklin had built. They decided to establish the Quitman County Freedom Organization (QCFO) to help guide civil rights progress in the area. The group met only twice before joining forces with the MFDP.[2] During its brief existence, however, the QCFO got crucial help to needy families. It circulated a petition to maintain the distribution of commodities (actual food) rather than switch to food stamps, as other counties had.[3] In those years, food stamps were coupons poor people had to buy. They could exchange them at the stores for food at a lower price. But many Black people in the Delta did not have cash for months at a time. Some got around this problem by having white planters pay for their stamps, and in return they would do jobs for the planter without pay. Getting food stamps for their workers was one more way planters were able to keep their control of Black people. But for those without either white folks to buy their stamps or the education to get a job up north, there was real danger of starvation. The food stamp program really hurt poor Black people.

I remember when Aaron Henry, head of the state NAACP, tried to explain to a Black audience in Marks how food stamps would work. William Franklin asked him where poor people were supposed to find the money to pay for the food stamps. Dr. Henry said they could go along the highway and look for pop bottles to exchange for cash. Mr. Franklin shook his head and laughed. It was absurd to think that empty pop bottles could bring in enough money to feed a family dependent on food stamps.

The QCFO managed to delay food stamps in the county and keep commodities going for about another year. I remember once Mrs. Franklin opened a monthly box in her house, and I saw that some cheese had been included. I was so happy that I went into a riff, "Cheese at last, cheese at last, thank God Almighty, cheese at last."

The QCFO also tried to survey poverty conditions in the county to document the problems and make sure government help went to the right people. After we set up the volunteer Head Start centers, people started writing us about their legal and financial problems with welfare. So just after the March Against Fear I went with Mel Leventhal to Tougaloo College, a Black institution just north of Jackson, for a workshop by the LDF on welfare rights. Here is a typical letter we got, from a woman near Lambert:

> July 8, 1966
>
> i would like very much to see you[.] i have some other thangs that i would like to talk to you about[.] i have no transportation and it so hard for me to get any one to help me out [illegible] peopl is so afraid but any way i am not able to hire a lawyer because we are very poor peopl and i do not want to get into any thing that I cant handle[.] about the house i wish that i did have one just one of any kind [but] no i do not own a home and I do not have a bank account not even a Bill fold[.] i am living on my daughter property and she require rent and we ant able to pay that so you see how it is[.] if i did have any thing i would not ask for any aid[.] i been working free work with the CDGM for 3 month and ant got one penny as of yet.[4]

In another letter, an illiterate woman in the country got a neighbor to write us the names of all her children and the clothing sizes they needed so they would have something to wear to school. When the family finally got a ride to Marks, I saw that all her children were in rags that were about to fall apart. All these children were working in the cotton fields whenever possible—and growing up illiterate—until they could get the money to buy clothes presentable enough that no one would make fun of them at school.

All we could do for such people was to advise them to apply for welfare and record every detail of what happened. We would go to the office with them and observe as much as we were allowed to—which usually wasn't much—and ask them immediately afterward about what happened.[5]

When people were refused, as most were, we helped them apply to the state welfare office in Jackson for a fair hearing, using every irregularity by the local office that they could remember. We also sent statements about these irregularities to Mel Leventhal in Jackson. Being challenged made Annie Dukes, the county welfare agent, alternately try to court our favor or push back against us. I remember she would drive to the Franklins' house and lecture us with barely concealed rage in the front yard. She knew that to some degree the federal government was behind us, but she (and we) were not sure just how far they would back us.

We lost most of the cases we brought. Mrs. Dukes's favorite excuse for denying welfare was "immorality." I remember two of these cases well. Jimmie Billups, a World War I veteran, lived down Cotton Street from us. He was seventy-three and getting $109 a month from the Veterans Administration and $12 from welfare. But, he said, "My wife ain't getting nothing. She have to take medicine regular. She got the sugar [diabetes]. It cost anywhere from $25 to $30 a month. We can't get enough to eat. I don't have the money." The excuse Mrs. Dukes gave for not giving his wife welfare was that she had no divorce papers from her first husband, who had disappeared in 1915. Back then everyone believed he had been lynched, so she was afraid to go to the white authorities and make an inquiry. She was illiterate and had no conception of death certificates and divorce papers. Now, fifty-one years later, she and her second husband could get no help from welfare and were being talked about as if they were having some casual affair. Laura Engle of the LDF was finally able to help this woman get welfare.

In another case a woman had fourteen children. Her husband broke under the strain of trying to support them with the little he made in the cotton fields, and he deserted them. The woman went to the welfare office. All welfare did was take a photo of the woman and her children that was published in the *Quitman County Democrat* with an insulting nickname she was known by and an appeal to readers to send her some old clothes. It was very embarrassing to the children, who were teased about it at school. The woman might have applied for a divorce, but she couldn't afford to pay a lawyer. Finally, she allowed a man with a steady job to move in with her to help support her children. This made her completely ineligible for welfare. This woman was deeply religious. She was overjoyed when we could give her a Bible out of the stock of books we had in the office. It made me angry to hear Mrs. Dukes talk about her as if she were a prostitute.

If we couldn't win most of our cases, at least we got the welfare office to treat Black clients with basic courtesy. According to custom in Mississippi, Black clients called the welfare agent "Mrs. Dukes" and "Ma'am," and she called them by their first names. We complained to the federal Health, Education, and Welfare office in Atlanta about this practice several times. Mel Leventhal advised Mr. Franklin that as long as Mrs. Dukes called him "William," he should call her "Annie." When he did this, he said, "She stared at me like her eyes about to come out of her head." But eventually she became more polite.

All these projects kept us very busy. Richard kept careful records during each meeting so he could remember the confusing details of each project he was working on. The fragments of these notes that have survived show the day-to-day problems of the movement.

> [Name] . . . lives on Eddie Meeks place—has a son 13 years [old] in Oakley Training [reform] School—has been there 13 months. . . . Being held on grounds of forgery—committed three years previous to arrest—might not have even done this. Supposed to have a nervous disorder and looks like this is why he is being held. . . . Boy was active in movement and Mrs. Smith the principle [*sic*] of the [all-Black] Crenshaw Elementary School took offense at this. . . . both his teachers and . . . the [Crenshaw] town marshal said . . . [he] needed psychiatric help.[6]

In this case we called the civil rights lawyers in Jackson. Also on Richard's list:

> [Three names] with possessions they can use on property bonds
> those who worked as volunteers in the [Quitman County Head

Start program] . . . and did not get jobs or have other legitimate grievances: [Names]

those who got jobs who people felt shouldn't have:

[Name]—considerably better off than the average Black Quitman resident

[Name] definitely should not have a job

[Name]—didn't start at the beginning

[Name]—didn't work all the time

[Name]—McCloud put her off because she was pregnant

Mrs. Mitchell from the Atlanta office of the OEO without authority made some changes [in funding procedures]. Claimed authority from Washington. Mrs. Clancy from [OEO office in] Atlanta OK'd the [Quitman County Head Start] project and fought for it the way it is.

[Name] disabled both physically and mentally—applied [for welfare] for six years unable to get anything. Going to herb doctor.

[Name] wants a car to pick him up to register [to vote] Aug 5.

[Name]—husband not registered—sick.

[Name]—been to [MFDP] meeting, might be registered. Lives on highway outside of N. S. plantation.

[Name]—will go down tomorrow [to register] by herself.

Get from Mel the names of the [Black] children going to the white school [in the coming fall].

Find out about free lunches at school for the . . . [Black] children.

[Name] will wait for husband's decision [to register to vote].

The possibility of [protest or sit in] *of Bob Young's the week of the 25th.*

[Three names] willing to go out and organize one day next week for the [Mississippi Freedom] Labor Union.[7]

I went back to Oklahoma to try to get some aid for Marks. A group of students at Oklahoma University got together a truckload of old clothes and some food and drove it to Marks. And once again, what started as help turned into a problem. When we tried to give the clothes out in an orderly fashion in Mr. Franklin's house, some of the women went into a frenzy. They grabbed at the clothes frantically and even took an old pair of Mr. Franklin's pants. That was the last Mr. Franklin would have anything to do with clothing distribution.

Richard also proposed several ambitious plans that we were never able to carry out. We were exhausted. Richard was a relative newcomer.

And things worked slowly in Marks. The things Black people were most reluctant to do were those that involved integration performed in front of whites. For example, although the city park was integrated in theory, at that time no Black people dared go there. Richard wanted a large group to hold a picnic there. It never came off, but within a few years Black people were using the park a great deal.

He also wanted a group to try to get cards at the public library. This was also integrated in theory, but in practice Black residents were too afraid to go. After the school was integrated, though, Black students had to go there to check out required books, and the matter took care of itself.[8]

But Richard wanted to do more than integrate public facilities. He went to the local MFDP meeting to present his ideas on what should be done for the movement to start advancing again. The meeting minutes, kept by the secretary, Clara Collins, describe the continued toll that disagreements and infighting were taking on our momentum.

> Aug. 9, 1966. FDP meeting were open up by Rev. W. L. Malone. [First] we went into the discussion of the welfare conference which were held in Edwards, Miss. Saturday and Sunday. Rev. Malone said we didn't meet to argue. He said that we argued so [much] once that the people were discourage to come out.
>
> Then Richard Arvedon ask how many people are from the five beats of Quitman County. He said Joe and he tried to get people from each beat for the meeting. He said he came up with a proposal on what should be done in Quitman County. He ask for each one to give a five minute suggestion on the proposal. He also said he didn't want any arguing or the going back on something that happen last year.
>
> He ask what is the actually meaning of FDP. He said we have some white people in the movement, but it is not enough to do anything. What is FDP for and what does it do?
>
> [He said] what is economic power, It the power to insist and demand for wages so you will not have to work for $3.00 and $4.00 a day. Voter Registration is the whole key to FDP. . . . Do not let the white man tell us what to do. We are going to stop all the fights, when you come to these meeting leave your fights outside. We almost got CDGM in this county. But why people stop caring about the movement. Preach Malone ask for all of the people to go [the MFDP meeting at] Lambert Saturday night.

1. Divide the county into FDP beats.
2. Each beat will have an FDP.
3. The chairman of each beat will composed the executive committee . . . and two others elected from the members.
4. The beats will meet once a week.
5. The co[unty] wide [MFDP meeting] once a month.

Proposal were accepted by the body.[9]

Then Richard and Olivia, a Black high school student who had been active in the movement, fell in love. "Let 'em," Mr. Franklin said, "Now that this thing has started, people gonna be mixing up all over the place, colored and white." But as his brother Jessie said, "It scandalize some people." This was true even in the Black community, and many feared local whites might react even worse, so Richard and Olivia went to Fort Worth. Olivia came back a few weeks later because she and Richard couldn't find a place to stay, either in Black or white neighborhoods, even if they got married.

Integrating Schools

In late August 1966, the school integration effort took another turn. The school board wrote to all the Black parents who had filled out "freedom of choice" forms to send their children to the white school. The letters asked the parents to come by the school board office. We believed the board intended to threaten them into revoking their forms. I sent the letters to Mel Leventhal. He said they would be useful in showing that "freedom of choice" was a farce so integration would require explicit court orders.

He also asked me to collect information to show how the all-Black school was inferior to the white one. I found the "colored" school never issued enough textbooks and charged a fee for some of them, so some poor Black children, like Clondike Abbott's younger brothers and sisters, had to look through the garbage dump for worn-out textbooks. Mr. Franklin had done maintenance work on both the "colored" and white schools. He said that the "colored" school looked more impressive but was poorly constructed and poorly ventilated compared with the white school. "On hot days," he said, "their children is cool as cucumbers while ours is hassling like dogs."

That September some Black parents in Marks and Lambert sent their children to the previously all-white schools, joining the Franklin children who were already there. Willie Thompson, who had lost his job after an unsuccessful attempt to send his daughter to the white school in 1964, now sent his other children. Lee Dora Collins sent all her children to the white school, including Clara, the local MFDP secretary. These families reported severe challenges and real rewards, yet no two had the same experience.

Incidents of harassment had declined from earlier years. Still, only four of the Black high school students passed that first year at the white school, including Presley and Melvin Franklin. At the integrated grade school, many Black pupils also failed. I believe they failed mostly from inadequate preparation, but this was reinforced by hostility from white kids and teachers. Yet even Black youths who dropped out like Robert Holland felt integration had its benefits. All told, sixteen Black students integrated Marks's white high school that year.

In 1975 when I visited Marks, several of these students and their parents talked with me about their experiences. Lula Belle Weathersby began. "The first day they integrated at Lambert, I brought my child and Tommy Young's children. And there was two other Black children who vas scared to get from their mama. One of them crying, scared to death. Negroes taught their children to be scared of white people. But my child—I had to look for him when school was out. He was out sliding and running around with the white children."

Willie Thompson took up the story. "All my children finally went to an integrated school. They had a little court of it [it required a legal decision] before they let them enter. It was hard for them at first. Not from the white children. Most of the segregation started out with the white teachers."

His son Willie Edgar Thompson explained. "I was in the fourth grade. We was running to the building. We had to be in the building before the bell stop ringing. And there was some white girls in front of us. And the teachers told the principal that we was chasing the white girls. And the principal told the principal at the high school, and he come and gave me ten licks. I was blue all over.

"And then it was this way on the merry-go-round. The teacher told us some had to ride and some had to stay. She told me I couldn't get off the merry-go-round. She said I was her prisoner. And somebody pushed me off and the teacher slapped me because I got off."

"He went to the colored school next year," his father interjected. "You couldn't hardly get him to go back to the white school."

Willie Edgar nodded. "I stayed in trouble at the white school. What time was that when I ran away rather than take a whipping? They said I couldn't get in without a whipping, and I stayed away."

"I went over and sot up with the white school about it," Mr. Thompson added. "I told them I would see about my children. Even if they was in the lion's den, I would see about them. Back then they wouldn't let Black and white children play together. I went to see the elementary principal about it, 'cause if they caught my son playing with white, they'd whup him. I told her there was about twenty-five to thirty children telling me their problems, and if they told me any more I'd send word to the HEW office in Atlanta. The biggest part of the trouble stopped after that."

Robert Holland was the same age as Willie Edgar. He said, "I seen how they got an integrated school now. I don't see why they didn't have one all along. If you cut me and I cut you, the same red blood come out. I had to whup a couple of white kids—we meddled with each other. I enjoyed whupping 'em. At that time Black folks had to go to they school. They wasn't coming to ours. Now they come over here.

"I met a whole lot of white dudes. They not so mean once you get acquainted with them. The white always think they more than we are. They got the authority, and we ain't got nothing."

I asked him whether he thought the education was better at the white school. "No," he responded. "The teachers was about the same. But at the time, we had one recess and they had four. Now everybody got two recesses, and the school time shorter. I quit school when I was thirteen 'cause they wouldn't let me wear no silk T-shirt to school. And all the hunkies [whites] wearing theirs. Now all of them, Black and white, can wear silk T-shirts and short pants if they want to."

Kay Collins, a year older than the boys, agreed. "Things have improved very much since the school was integrated. I think people have better relationships. No one is discriminating. We got more to do in school now."

"When we first integrated," Kay's mother Lee Dora Collins explained, "one of the teachers kicked her. Kay and a white girl was pulling on a old tire. The teacher walked up to her and kicked her behind. I wanted to see a lawyer, but the principal told us not to. That been handed down a long time. They used to the white kicking the Black."

Kay's younger sister Jeddie fared better. "Sometimes the white kids just kid around, but they don't meddle. They know too much to mess with me."

Mr. Franklin's son Presley described his experiences at somewhat greater length in an article in the *Southern Courier*, a Black newspaper in Montgomery, Alabama.

> During the first week of school . . . the Negro students took over formerly all-white Marks High School. The white students merely observed us.
>
> There were 16 of us and we had the run of the school because a rumor was making a turn around the campus. As one white student said in class, "If you hit a n——, President Johnson will put you in jail."
>
> But after the first week, the rumor died away and the white students really got to us. They made fun of our skin, hair and noses.
>
> I believe it got to me the most because I was the only Negro student in the 11th grade. I hope I don't be the only one in the 12th. . . .
>
> Two white boys gave me the most trouble. Every day for the whole school year, one of them would meet me in the hallway as I was going to my sixth period class. He would call anyone nearby to help him annoy me because he and I were nearly the same size.
>
> He would say things like "Hey, look at burr-head," and "Look at that stinking n——."
>
> One day during our chemistry class he and another white boy suddenly said, "Let's kill that n——." After a while, the teacher got tired of hearing the same statement over and over, so she made them stop.
>
> But nearly every day thereafter, the same two white boys made similar remarks such as "Let's throw phosphorus on that n——." . . .
>
> In history class one day, the history teacher's son asked if white students would be forced to go to the "n—— school" next year. A white girl replied, "You'll get some money like the n—— that come over here."
>
> The teacher asked me, "Do you get any money for coming over here?" I told her that I did not. . . .
>
> This year I am going to make it a policy to leave the classroom whenever the teachers leave—because when they were gone, the white children threw spitballs, crayons, rubber bands, and broken pencils at me.
>
> . . . We could put up with the annoyance and try to make a grade, or answer back when the white students bothered us and fail to make a grade. Of the 16 Negro students at Marks last year, only one-fourth

> passed into the next grade. The other three-fourths—the ones who defended themselves—all failed.[10]

Although sixteen Black students had entered the white school, more had been rejected. At the end of September my report to the Jackson MFDP office described the problems still confronting Black parents who wanted to send their children to white schools.

> Around 15 Negro children who applied for admission to the "white" school are still being refused admission to either the "white" or the "Negro" school. The reasons given for not admitting them are very trivial—for example in one family the . . . children are refused admission because the same parent didn't sign all the freedom of choice forms.
>
> A Negro was put off the plantation of H. H. at Sledge for trying to send his children to the "white" school. He is unwilling to have his name used under any circumstances.

At the same time, some parents were hoping to take adult education courses that had been started by the poverty program. However, such hopes seemed as elusive as public school integration. Mississippi's program was administered by whites with strong connections to the old landowning elites who still did not want African Americans on their plantations to get an education. As I wrote in that same report:

> On the Denton plantation near Belen, tenants were told they would be put off the plantation if they entered the poverty program's adult education program. "I heard it out the man's mouth," a woman there said. The man in this case is C. W. Denton, brother of . . . a Marks attorney who serves on the CAP board for Quitman, Panola, Tunica, Grenada and Tallahatchie counties.
>
> Thus ends another month in this corner of the Great Society.[11]

At this point, Alex sent me money to come to Jackson to work with him at the Freedom Information Service. When I arrived he had me research southern history, but I think he brought me there so I could relax and unwind. It was such a relief to bathe in the place where I was staying instead of walking several blocks to a house where the people were too poor to let me use more than a little water in the bottom of the tub. I drank one glass of beer when I got to Jackson and felt incredibly loosened up.

It only lasted a few days. Then Mel Leventhal came by and angrily asked me why I was wasting my time on this research stuff when there were people in Marks who needed me. He drove me back at daybreak the next morning. It turned out Reverend Malone had called Mel to get me to come back.

For the next few weeks I documented the evasions and abuses of the "freedom of choice" plan the school board engaged in. Also there was the day-to-day business of all our ongoing civil rights projects.

Behind Race Is Class

One night a young white man from one of the richest families in Marks came to see Mr. Franklin. According to him, the wealthy whites had been worried about the possibility of a riot ever since that July night the people of Cotton Street erected a barricade of overturned garbage cans and patrolled it with rifles. The leading whites had collected $5,000 and sent this young man to offer it to Mr. Franklin to use his influence to prevent a riot.

Mr. Franklin refused the money. He said he couldn't guarantee how the Black people of Marks would act. He added that people would hear about it and some would be suspicious of him and others would try to steal the money. He said he wanted to live in peace with his neighbors.

There was little or no danger of Black people in Marks rioting. But it was funny to discover what this young white man didn't know about the Black people in his own town. For example, he didn't know—and we didn't tell him—that the Black maid who worked for his family was one of the more active people in the movement. Yet his mother talked to this Black woman often about her personal problems. Nor did he know why the Black people were so angry. It is surprising to me how little most whites in Marks knew about the Black community. Perhaps their fear was triggered by news of violence elsewhere or by statements by people like Stokely Carmichael.

While they talked, Mr. Franklin and his brothers started rolling cigarettes. The young man was surprised to find they couldn't afford ready-made cigarettes. Then he looked in Mr. Franklin's refrigerator and was amazed to find there was almost nothing in it. He brought Mr. Franklin and Mr. Jessie and me to his house, since his parents were away, to raid his ice box.

While we were rummaging through it, Mr. Franklin found a jar of caviar. He asked the young man what it was. "Oh, that's good stuff," the young man said, "I like to spread it on bread." But when Mr. Franklin found out it was fish eggs, he refused to take it. In the Delta only the most desperately poor Black people would fry masses of fish eggs and eat them. We took the rest of the food and went home.

Another incident with a white person, which I hoped would be a sign of the future, happened a few nights later. As we walked out of an MFDP meeting, we found a middle-aged white man in work clothes. He said, "I'm drunk, but that don't matter. I only been to the third grade, and I can't read or write. I been kicked around all my life, and I want to know—do y'all have something for the white as well as the colored?" I tried to talk with the white man as best I could, and he shook hands with me and left, but I knew we weren't ready to answer his question yet. I have always believed that behind race is the issue of class, but it seemed an extraordinarily difficult task to promote unity between Blacks and whites in the poor and working classes. At that point we didn't have any program yet for that white man who approached me. I hoped we would someday.

By then I was ready to leave Marks, even though I was sad to leave so many close friends. The Vietnam War kept getting bigger, and I wanted to work in the antiwar movement. I figured the progress of Black people in Mississippi depended on ending the war. Already more and more young Black men were being drafted, and those who were illiterate were sent into the Job Corps to learn just enough to be drafted. For too many Black people, the war hurt them because of both their race and their class.[12] I left Marks in late October 1966, but I stayed in contact by letters and telephone calls.

CHAPTER 7

"Boy, We Got Things Rolling"
1966–1968

The fall of 1966 began quietly. Reverend Ward, Reverend Allen, and Reverend Malone, strong civil rights supporters, held revival meetings with Rev. O. W. Ingram, the leader of the Voters' League.[1] Reverend Malone had become the head of the county MFDP, but because he was so busy with revivals there were no meetings until the last week of September. At that meeting, which endorsed Richard Arvedon's proposals for reorganizing the group, only twelve people were present. It was obvious to all three ministers that to revitalize the effort it was time to heal the split that had created two rival voter groups in 1962.[2] As Reverend Allen explained, "It was two leagues, but I was sick here, and that put that league down automatically. Reverend Ingram was the leader of that other league, and when I came back I joined up in his league." So the Quitman County League and the Voters' League finally came back together. (Things have changed a lot since then. In 1975, Reverend Allen observed, "It ain't doing nothing now. The league people all go to the NAACP.")

The biggest challenge facing the newly united Quitman MFDP was the terrible economic situation. It was a cold, hard winter in the Delta. Because of mechanization, there had not been many jobs picking cotton that fall. Most Black people couldn't get on welfare, and large posters in many Mississippi welfare offices described better benefits available up north. Local officials also worked with the federal government to finally replace the commodity food program with food stamps even though most people still lacked money to buy them. In this way, the state welfare department and the Department of Agriculture cooperated with white planters to force Black workers out of the Delta before they could use their newfound voting power.

As a result, the county population fell dramatically.[3] Between 1965 and 1970, the number of Black school-age children declined by more than a quarter. Even Mr. Franklin went up to Kenosha, Wisconsin, to stay with his brother Booker and look for a job. But he found that no one in the North would hire a man his age, especially with so little education, so he came back to Marks.

"Quitman County needs more protesting, picketing, more sit-ins," Clara Collins wrote in a March 1967 report to the Jackson MFDP office. "Quitman County needs to be broken in more than what has been done. The people need to stop being afraid, they need to stand up and do more fighting for their rights."

Regaining Momentum

On April 27, 1967, Reverend Coleman and Rev. Chris Cole from a rural church near Lambert held a citizenship class at the community center in Mr. Franklin's backyard. Reverend Coleman announced that he was running for the county board of supervisors. That made him the first Black candidate for public office in the history of the county. At the same time Reverend Coleman and Reverend Cole announced a massive new voter registration drive.

A white law student named Alex Capron came to help. As of April 1967, there were 1,192 Black voters registered in Quitman County. Three months later there were 2,557—35 percent of all voters. In Beat Two, one of the five voting districts, Black voters were in the majority, as they were in several rural precincts. In the West Marks precinct, where most of the Black community lived, there were 807 Black and 826 white voters registered. But as Alex Capron noted, "It is probable that West Marks is now majority Negro." Those Black people who stayed in Quitman County were determined to be full citizens—although Reverend Coleman lost the election.[4]

Meanwhile, with Alex's help, William and Jessie Franklin started a series of lawsuits against the county and town governments regarding everything from welfare to fair pay. Most of them succeeded, and the people of Marks, Black and white, looked on in amazement. Johnny

Thompson commented, "For people with no education, them Franklins sure had a lot of power here for a while."

"Boy, we had a time when Alex Capron come here in '67 and stayed till '68," William Franklin agreed. "Anything that happened to anybody here, I got the lawyers and got them on the case. I got one boy out of Parchman Prison. Then I jumped on the commodity. Boy, we got things rolling. I got the head welfare man to tell folks how much they was allowing folks on welfare. I jumped on teachers' pay. Them teachers started getting more than they ever got in their lives. They didn't know what teacher pay was. They had been beating them out of they money.

"We gone on a man with a plantation how when the government was cutting acreage, the Negroes on the place didn't get the money. We fastened the Department of Agriculture on him. The Negroes was too scared to sign the paper against him, but we sure scared him. He come to me and Jessie and begged us not to go against him."[5]

Mel Leventhal worked closely with Mr. Franklin on several cases. "William Franklin was hands down my favorite client," Mel remembered. "In terms of courage and determination he was in all respects the equal of Fannie Lou Hamer. He also had the most colorful language of any movement person. I don't mean that he was vulgar. He would say things like 'well the federals ain't coming here,' when he meant the U.S. government."[6]

With Mel's help, on July 24, 1967, Mr. Franklin and seven other Black parents and grandparents launched a suit against the Quitman County Board of Education in the names of thirty-four children to end the "freedom of choice" plan and completely merge the student bodies. The federal court ordered a ten-day transfer period when any Black parents might enroll their children in the formerly all-white school. Mr. Franklin got permission to use the Black Masonic Hall in Lambert to explain the transfer period to interested parents on August 25. That morning, Rev. K. C. Brown, who owned the building, said it was not available for discussions of school integration. So Mr. Franklin and Alex Capron stood across the street from the hall and spoke with parents. They then arranged to use a Black church to meet later. Alex grumbled, "It's one thing if you don't want your freedom. But it's another thing to use your power over other people to keep them from getting theirs."[7]

The suit, now with the Franklins as the sole plaintiffs, was heard in federal court in Clarksdale on March 18, 1968. Leventhal remembered it well because it was his birthday. He turned twenty-five, and although he had written several motions against the school system, he had not yet been admitted to the bar. He "tagged along" to listen.[8]

Dr. C. S. Phelps, county school board chairman, defended the "freedom of choice" plan. He insisted that everyone who wished to change schools was able to do so. He testified, "The four colored schools are still totally colored [after the selection process]. The school at Crowder has only white students. Marks, Lambert, [and] Sledge have varying degrees of integration. These three schools show a slight increase in members of the Negro race. As of Tuesday, April 16, 11 [Black] students requested transfer to Marks, 10 to Sledge, 5 to Lambert. This is in addition to the ones who have previously chosen to go there."[9]

Under cross-examination by Iris Brest of the LDF about plans for a new, consolidated, primarily white high school, Dr. Phelps revealed the thinking of the white community: "The voters approved the bond issue . . . for construction of a more centrally located high school which would be open to freedom of choice. . . . The board feels strongly that the money was approved for that specific purpose and it would require a lot of discussion before we would . . . [use] the money for something the voters did not vote for [i.e., a fully integrated school]."

> Q. [Mrs. Brest]: Why do you feel that the freedom of choice issue was a crucial one to the bond issue? . . . What are the benefits that people voted for which they would not receive if you built the new high school without having freedom of choice . . . at that school?
>
> A. . . . I think it very, very unlikely that the bond issue would have been approved if voters had not been assured that there would be freedom of choice in the county-wide high school.
>
> Q. Why is that, Dr. Phelps?
>
> A. Mrs. Brest, this is Marks, Mississippi, and it would take quite a bit of time to go back and explain that feeling to you.
>
> Q. Well, is it because the people of Quitman County would not spend money for an integrated school, is that it?
>
> A. Bluntly, yes.

Although the court ruled that eight white teachers were to be placed in the all-Black school and eight Black teachers in the white school by that fall, the basic case, complete integration of the schools, dragged on.

Marks reached another milestone in late 1967 when Town Marshal Bob McArthur died. Originally white officials proposed to make former sheriff Gordon Darby the new town marshal. The Black community responded with a petition to stop Darby's appointment:

> [He] showed by his conduct as sheriff that he doesn't know how to treat people right. We Negro people are tired of this kind of treatment and his appointment might lead to disorders and disturbances and a lack of respect for the law in Marks. On the other hand, many of the Negroes here, particularly the teenagers, will respect a Negro police officer more than they will a white one and that will help maintain racial harmony in our city. We make up better than half the population of Marks and we think it is high time that we be represented on the city's police force.[10]

L. C. Pride was appointed, Marks's first Black town marshal. He succeeded the white marshal who had clubbed a civil rights lawyer.

About this time, the Quitman County Associated Community Corporation, the group James Wilson Sr. had organized in 1965 to support the CDGM, quietly removed Reverend McCloud as chair of its Head Start Committee. Reverend McCloud had been very popular as long as the women in poverty believed he was trying to employ as many of them as possible in Head Start. But he was under too much pressure from the teachers and their relatives in his church to give them the jobs, and the poor women were angry.

The Community Corporation also circulated a petition to get Head Start away from the white-controlled MSO. The petition argued:

> 1. Mid-State don't benefit poor children.
> 2. Not enough poor mothers [are employed].
> 3. Quitman County does not approve of the fund being used for utilities and the poor children needs it.[11]

The movement was regaining momentum, largely thanks to women. Women had always taken important roles in the civil rights movement in Mississippi. In Marks they were more overshadowed by the ministers, but in outlying towns like Lambert, women like Sarah Ann Brown were the central figures. In Marks, Lillie Mae Common had proposed setting up a women's organization back in 1966. On January 23, 1968, Ruth Figgs spoke to a meeting of Black Quitman County women about the National Council of Negro Women (NCNW).

"We are trying to gain some power," she said. "Women have become a part of anything now. I have learned the foundation from Washington on down. It is a National Council was spreaded across the country. One thing [locally is a] . . . housing project. What have made us be so interested is we are concerned. We are helping our children be better than we are."[12] The "Lady Council," as people called it, became part of Black life in the area, although not much was done about housing until after the Poor People's March that spring.

Marks and the Poor People's March

On February 19, three staff women from the Southern Christian Leadership Conference spoke to the NCNW's new Marks chapter about the group's proposed Poor People's Campaign and a march like the March on Washington to launch it. The campaign represented the SCLC's shift toward poverty and class issues dividing America. The march was intended to dramatize the plight of poor people, Black and white—although, as SCLC leaders often pointed out, Black people were disproportionately represented there.[13]

The SCLC had decided Marks should be the starting point for the march because things were so bad there. In March, Dr. King visited the Black section of Marks. In his last formal sermon, delivered at the National Cathedral in Washington, D.C., Dr. King described his visit.

> I was in Marks, Mississippi, the other day, which is in Whitman [Quitman] County, the poorest county in the United States. I tell you, I saw hundreds of little black boys and black girls walking the streets with no shoes to wear. I saw their mothers and their fathers trying to carry on a little Head Start program, but they had no money. The federal government hadn't funded them, but they were trying to carry on. They raised a little money here and there; trying to get a little food to feed the children; trying to teach them a little something.
>
> And I saw mothers and fathers who said to me not only were they unemployed, they didn't get any kind of income—no old-age pension, no welfare check, or anything. I said, "How do you live?" And they say, "Well, we go around—go around the neighbors and ask them for a little something. When the berry season comes, we pick berries. When the rabbit season comes, we hunt and catch a few rabbits. And that's about it."[14]

Reverend Ralph Abernathy, Dr. King's friend and colleague, described the scene at the Eudora Methodist Church preschool program in Marks. A teacher speaking with Dr. King paused to feed the children lunch. She gave each child a few crackers and then divided apples into quarters so each child could have some. The meager meal devastated Dr. King. "I saw that his eyes were full of tears," Reverend Abernathy wrote. "King had seen a vision in Marks, Mississippi, that would haunt him for the rest of his life."[15] The issue of the white local paper the *Quitman County Democrat*, which came out just after Dr. King's visit, didn't carry one word about it. Instead its main story was "Mrs. June Snead Wins Treasure Hunt."

Journalist James Batten highlighted the symbolism of Marks as launching pad for the Poor People's Campaign. King could not have selected a better location "than this obscure little town and the rural county that surrounds it," he noted.

> For one thing, the soil of the Mississippi Delta is among the richest in the world, yet nearly half the families here in Quitman County are poor—some of them desperately poor. . . .
>
> The symbolism doesn't stop there. . . . [The local landscape includes] field after field where huge tractors [are] tilling the fertile black soil. These very tractors—and other modern machinery—have squeezed unskilled farm people off the land, making their plight even more severe than before.[16]

The SCLC trained young people from Marks and other poor southern communities to be march organizers. Eighteen-year-old Johnny Thompson was one. He told me, "I went to Atlanta, Georgia, and Hosea Williams of SCLC signed me for to be the youth organizer. He had me working all over Mississippi organizing. We had plenty of young people to help. I went to Atlanta four weeks before the march started.

"We had some volunteer workers that was helping us out. Alex Capron was one of them. After that we got seven or eight from Marks that went to Atlanta. It was like a workshop. They taught us how to do everything. They taught some to be office workers and keep records and some to be field workers to go out and organize."

This effort calmed differences over nonviolence for a time. James Figgs remembers, "Being with SNCC and COFO and what have you, we felt that we had to be aggressive and . . . would not stand for anybody to take our rights . . . , but we respected and loved Dr. King and we wanted to cooperate. . . . I believe that if he had led us to that Red Sea and the water had been there we would have walked in the water with him because that's the kind of hope that he had instilled in us."[17]

SCLC also conducted literacy classes in Marks. Bertha Burres taught there.

> When the SCLC come in here to get the people registered for the Poor People Campaign, they wanted me to be their secretary. . . . What they would do, give me change enough to pay my light bill, my gas bill. . . . So I think that's what got me into politics, by working with the people in these different organizations. . . . I had my six children to take care of, so I had to do whatever work I could get. I didn't have choice!
>
> When we got the means together here, we brought in the adult basic education program. And I went through a lot of hours talking to senior citizens, older people. . . . There were some old people, "I want to be able to write. Before I leave this world I want to be able to sign my name instead of an x."
>
> What encouraged them to come was they were getting a little stipend. Although some of them were too old to carry a job, but the satisfaction of being able to write their name. . . . They'd see their name, but they really couldn't read it, they just knew it was their name. . . . But it meant a lot to them . . . to write their name.

"And to count their money," she chuckled. "Through the program a lot of them registered, a lot of people found out about assistance, a lot of people tried for that assistance when they found out that there were food stamps, welfare, Social Security."[18]

Beatrice Humphreys described her experience to me. "The SCLC had a school here at Silent Grove Missionary Baptist Church, and they give us the papers to go on the march, and Mrs. Martin Luther King sont me a diploma. I helped four or five people learn to read and write a little at the school, and Rev. L. C. Coleman was the teacher. I learned to read and write a whole lot better." It spurred her to join the upcoming Poor People's March.

On April 4, 1968, only a few weeks before the march was to begin, a white man killed Dr. King in Memphis. Mrs. Weathersby described the reaction in Marks to Peter Joseph.[19] "I'll be straight honest. My first reaction, when I *first* heard it, . . . violence kind of blurried up in my mind. I got angry, but it wasn't no time before I could think what he had taught us, and it soon passed away. I tell you, after that anger flew up and I settled down from there, it was just sobbing and tears and sorry then. We had three silent marches here coming up to his funeral. We went to the courthouse and we had a service on the courthouse steps. It was very sad that day."

The SCLC decided to go ahead with the march, to honor Dr. King's memory. Mr. Franklin was among the one hundred leaders of poverty communities that the SCLC took to Washington, D.C., in advance of the march to talk to government officials about what the poor needed. "I was called to [Secretary] Orville Freeman's office in the Department of Agriculture and I told them I wanted the [surplus] commodity [food program] to stay. I said, 'If you allow them to bring the food stamps in here, they'll raise the price of everything and we'll get cussed at. You all gonna use them food stamps as a slogan against us.' And it's happening now. They called me Preacher Franklin. Well, I was raised with the white man on my back, and I wants him off, and my children ain't going to come up like I did. But them store people run the food stamps over us. I kept asking Orville Freeman how come they was to lie to us about the food stamps, promising to give them to us free and not doing it. He got mad and run out of the room.

"People started asking old [Secretary of State] Dean Rusk why he sent their children to Vietnam, and he walked out. Then we walked in the housing secretary Robert Weaver's office. And he tried to tell us a bunch of lies about how much they was doing for us. And I told him, 'Listen, you Black like me. You know how it is with us. If you don't stop preaching for these white folks and get something done for us, you might as well get out.' And he run out of his office.

"A lot of us finally figured out that if these high officials didn't do nothing for us, we had to go back there and take over and run things for ourselves. Because things here was really serious. That Poor People's March was a great education for me. One thing that amazed me was how many poor white people was marching with us. And I told them officials, 'Now I know you all been against my Black side of the people ever since I been in the world. But how can y'all be so hard on your own color?' There was so many nations of us marching, and we all got to get out from under the same thing."

Demonstrators Attacked

While Mr. Franklin was in Washington, D.C., Town Marshal L. C. Pride (Black) and Highway Patrolman J. W. Jenkins (white) arrested Mr. and Mrs. Anderson, a Black couple, and a Black man named Johnny Neal, and allegedly beat them up. On May 1, SCLC staffer Willie Bolden convinced 300 students to leave the all-Black Industrial High School for a protest demonstration. He was arrested. Then 240 Black students and adults marched to the jail and sat down. The police removed the demonstrators bodily and arrested five SCLC staff people and a young woman from Marks. Two Black women were injured: sixteen-year-old Helen Carthan from Lambert, who was pregnant, and Lydia McKinnon of Marks, a young teacher. Miss McKinnon had been sitting on the jailhouse lawn. "The next thing I knew, someone was picking me up and taking me to the car," she told reporters. A teacher who asked not to be identified explained that "about eighteen or twenty" highway patrolmen came from the courthouse after someone "went over to them and told them to do whatever they had to do to move us."

The officers "just turned their guns upside down and started hitting the kids across the face with them," Miss McKinnon added. "They chased them all the way across town."[20]

People in Marks shared memories with me that varied a good deal in the details, but everyone remembered that multiple people were injured. Johnny Thompson recounted, "We was at first with a lot of schoolkids, and all the school come out like they was going to join the march they had there. We got to the schoolhouse and asked all the kids to come out. The principal at the school, he got kind of stirred up, but most all the kids said they was going to leave with us. So, they went on the march with us to the jailhouse yard. Everybody was just sitting down, and the police come on and jumped on us. They knocked me out. They didn't arrest me then.

"But later on that night, we had a little choir thing together going down the street, six of us on the way to the church. It was me, Rev. L. C. Coleman, Leo Martinez, Margaret Burnet, and Bertha Johnson. They had something to pick with us, so they arrested us and didn't tell us why. Then when we got to the jail, they told us we was disturbing the peace. The cops come up and told us in the jail they was going to beat us.

"After midnight they said they was going to let us out, but we said we wouldn't leave there unless they got somebody to come pick us up. They said we had to walk. But we wouldn't leave that night. We were quite sure they was going to jump us when we left. So we stayed there five days."

Elsa Mae Mitchell had been protesting outside the jail. "We went to the jailhouse yard because they had Willie Bolden in jail. The police come out, and I started away from there, but they come over and whipped me in the side. That same day somebody come up with a paper and had us sign it and said we would get something for all the police done to us. We sure did get something out of it—nothing but a whipping and a good run." That night 150 people marched from Eudora Church to the courthouse singing "We Shall Overcome" while dozens of highway patrolmen, deputies, and police looked on.

Reverend Ingram, one of the most moderate Black leaders in Marks, got six Black property owners to put up bonds to get the SCLC organizers out of jail. The four all-Black schools in Quitman County closed for two days because 121 of the 126 Black teachers refused to report for work. These teachers had always been cautious before. Lydia McKinnon explained thirty years later how her attitude had changed during the demonstration.

> I don't know what came over me. I don't think that I was courageous; it's just that for those few short moments, my life flashed before me. I had been in the segregated South all my life. White folks had the best of everything, and what we Blacks were getting was worse than second best, and we were expected to do a good job with hardly anything. So for that one crazy moment, I stood up for what I knew to be right, and with the butts of their guns and the heels of their boots they knocked me unconscious for it. My parents asked me: "What got into you—don't you know you could have been killed?" Today, looking back on it, I probably would not have done what I did, but as that young woman I was just tired of the way we were being treated.[21]

Reverend Ingram was made leader of a boycott committee that issued the following statement on May 2:

> Be it resolved by the Quitman County Voters' League, the Quitman County branch of the NAACP, the Quitman Teachers' Association, Black Community of Quitman County and all others concerned who love freedom and justice:

We on this day, announce a selective buying campaign against all *White Stores and Service Stations* in this city of Marks. No Black people . . . will purchase anything from the above named stores until the selective buying campaign is . . . lifted.

We, the Black people of Quitman County . . . are tired of being hungry, jobless and houseless; consequently we have no other alternative but to launch a massive selective buying campaign until we can not only see but feel the effects of this method used to benefit the entire Black community.

We must make it crystal clear that we will never stand for brutal, barbaric and wicked acts like those that were made upon the innocent women and children on May 1, 1968, by the law enforcement of this city, county and state.

There were old men, old women, young men, young women, boys and girls stomped, kicked and billy-clubbed by savage law-enforcement officers. The act was not only uncalled-for but also unmerciful to the point where a pregnant young lady was endangered of not only losing her baby, but her life as well. A schoolteacher was beaten unmercifully and had to be rushed away to Coahoma County Hospital and many others were treated by physicians.

The entire Black Community of Marks and Quitman County was already in a great dilemma because of the assassination of our leader, *Dr. Martin Luther King Jr.*, and over the reported beating of Mr. and Mrs. Anderson, Mr. Johnny Neal and *many, many* other acts of brutality inflicted upon the Black Community by untrained, uneducated law-enforcement officers of Quitman County, namely L. C. Pride, J. W. Jenkins and others.

We, the Black people of Quitman County are here and now presenting and addressing our grievances to all elected officers on discriminatory practices used in hiring personnel to work in their businesses . . . :

1. We demand that the sheriff of Quitman County, L. V. Harrison, hire a full time Black deputy. . . .
2. We further demand hiring Black in proportion to population in each supervisor's district [on road repair crews]. We further demand that an equal number of Black and White be hired at the Food Stamp Office and Welfare Office.
3. We further demand that all Grocery and Dry Good Stores of Marks, Mississippi hire Black as well as White. . . .

4. We . . . demand that the [school] Superintendent . . . and the Board of Education immediately hire an equal number of Black and White in the Office of Education and desegregate all schools, faculty as well as students, all school buses and all other employment pertaining to the educational system. . . .
5. We also demand that all government programs . . . operating in Quitman County . . . present a copy of [their] guidelines . . . to the leaders of the following . . . : 1. Quitman County Teachers' Association 2. NAACP 3. SCLC 4. Quitman County Voters' League.
6. We further demand that the Mayor and Board of Aldermen of Marks, Miss. immediately begin to run in West Marks sewer, water, blacktop and all other facilities that are located in [white] East Marks.
7. We request that Cotton Street and all adjacent streets be surveyed for annexation. If the survey shows approval, we further request that the residents of Cotton Street receive the same services as stated in Demand No. 6.
8. We demand that the Post Office and Citizens Bank employ Black in positions other than that of janitor.
9. We demand that the school buildings and grounds be made available for public use when not being used for school operations.[22]

I think it is significant that in this list of demands—not requests—sponsored by some of the most moderate elements in the community, the word "Black" was used for the first time in public life in Marks instead of "Negro."

On May 2, Willie Bolden, just out of jail, led a demonstration of 125 people at the courthouse. In a speech he accused L. C. Pride of "helping them"—meaning the white power structure. Officer Pride pushed his way through the crowd to Willie Bolden and shouted, "You're a damn liar!" Still it was a sign of change in Marks that a man who was arrested for leading a demonstration could lead another one as soon as he was released without being arrested again.

That same day SCLC brought thirty charter buses of marchers to Marks. They camped in a field on the edge of town. At first, before SCLC put up tents, some of the marchers had to stay in local Black homes. The white leadership of Marks responded as they had when COFO workers first arrived in 1964. James Wilson Sr. described the scene. "I had a houseful of civil rights workers. Reverend Saddler called me. He said Caldwell, the county attorney, called him. Reverend Saddler said, 'Mr. Wilson, are you participating in this civil rights movement?'

"And I said, 'I got twenty of them, some of them in every room in my house.'

"Saddler said, 'Ain't you afraid you and Franklin gonna have some trouble?'

"I said, 'These is our people. We gonna make every plan we can to help them.' I didn't worry. The white folks couldn't harm me. I was independent—a carpenter. They needed me as bad as I needed them."

Marks in the Spotlight

Network TV teams also came to Marks. Thomas Davis, a fifty-one-year-old white man, was arrested for firing a rifle at a CBS News helicopter.[23] The next day the local congressman, Jamie Whitten, denounced CBS's video coverage of Marks. He said the camera crew had gone outside the city, "ignoring its many substantial homes and businesses," and showed "a nearby Negro neighborhood" as the main city. He also claimed the camera crew asked the Black residents to remove their cars and avoided filming the TV antennas on the houses. Congressman Whitten said the coverage would have a "very bad effect on the reputation of the city" and called for a law permitting a community to prevent news media from releasing unfavorable stories about it.

CBS denied these accusations. The "nearby Negro neighborhood" they filmed was the Cotton Street area. And no number of cars or TV antennas would keep that neighborhood from looking awful, especially because the open sewer had overflowed again and left foul pools around many of the houses. The CBS crew must have been impressed by the smell, even if there was no way they could put it on TV. Willie Thomas told me, "They was taking a picture of the water around my place. My landlord thought they was going to put him out of business. He come by after they left and said, 'Give me my house.' I had to move out up to a little house with just a kitchen and a room to sleep in for about five or six month." Living with Mr. Thomas in that two-room shack were his wife and six children.[24]

The *Memphis Commercial Appeal*'s Gregory Jaynes interviewed Annie Morgan, a seventy-two-year-old Black woman who lived with her blind aunt Lula DeWalt in another two-room shack. Mrs. Morgan and her husband had been sharecroppers until her husband's death earlier that year. "She's my baby, you know," Mrs. Morgan said, speaking of her aunt. "She's getting so old now she don't understand things."

"Baby, those [SCLC workers] are wonderful people," Mrs. Morgan told her aunt.

"They came over and gave us a sandwich yesterday. It was bologna and they called it 'round steak.'

"They're trying to help people like us, . . . poor people. . . .

"They gonna go to Washington and tell the President what bad shape we're in down here. They gonna tell him how much money it costs for your medicine when you have one of your spells."

Mrs. DeWalt got $50 a month from welfare. Her niece received $25 a month from Social Security. Rent was $25 a month. "And the medicine eats up the rest," Mrs. Morgan added. Her wood stove "don't put out much heat when the wind blows under the house at night.

"Yes sir, I sure would like to go to Washington with those folks, 'cause it looks like what they're doing is a wonderful thing [but] I got to stay here till the Lord takes my baby," Mrs. Morgan told Mr. Jaynes, "'cause you know the Lord wouldn't bless me if I went off to Washington and leave her. I don't want the Lord to take her. I'd be alone if he did."

"Yes'm," said Mrs. DeWalt.[25]

Jaynes also interviewed Claude Martin, an African American who owned four hundred acres, leased five hundred more, and had seven Black families living on his land. He had assets of $250,000 in 1967, when the median annual Black family income in Quitman County was $1,700.

> My daddy farmed, sharecropped a little. He died . . . and I went to Ohio to live with my sister. You know I had four years of schooling down here, and when I got to Ohio, they put me back in the first reader. That's how bad schooling was in this state.
>
> I came back here when I was eighteen. . . . in 1930. I hired to a farmer, name of Jack Yeager for 75 cents a day. Wasn't three or four years till I was making $1.50 a day— . . . the highest paid farm worker in the county. . . .
>
> I worked for Mr. Yeager till he died in '46. That's when his widow told me about what she and the man had decided. . . . Mrs. Yeager told

> me she was going to sell me 161 acres at $60 an acre. That was a lot of money, but I sure took that offer. Yes, sir. I rented the land the first three years and paid a third of the price. Three years later I paid it all off.

Mr. Martin didn't have much faith in the Poor People's March.

> Don't look to me like they're going to accomplish much. Seems like a lot of the young ones want something for nothing. That ain't how to do it. You got to work and be eager, show the man you want to do something more, take everything you can honest ways, but use your head....
>
> The ones who don't have anything and don't get the chance to make it now. They're the ones who need the help. Not these young ones; they got education and the business world. Farming is gone, but they got other chances. The old folks don't have a chance.[26]

I noticed that all the newspaper and TV coverage of Marks before and during the Poor People's March contained interviews with SCLC national leaders and some with local Black people whom they met by chance or perhaps were recommended by local whites. But there were no interviews with the local Black activists who had worked hard to keep the civil rights movement alive in Marks for years, people like Reverend Malone, Reverend Allen, the Franklins, and the Collinses.

Not surprisingly, the whites of Marks offered reporters classic southern responses. Jack Harrison, a furniture store owner, said he was "a little confused about why... SCLC chose this place. We've had good relations between Negroes and whites. At least I thought so. Seems to me like it would have been closer for them to go to Washington from Memphis instead of coming all the way down here."[27]

Former sheriff T. M. Stanford, owner of a grocery store in the Black section, agreed. "We've got a good bunch of Negroes here, but they aren't that poor. The ones that are poor—well, I'll just tell you why. A colored man and his wife came in Saturday night. They bought $2.50 worth of groceries for them and their six kids and $3 worth of beer. That's why."[28]

That evening, May 2, about one thousand SCLC and Marks protesters marched around the county courthouse singing Freedom Songs, as a public act of self-assertion.[29] It was at this point, I believe, that local whites had to finally give up kidding themselves that "their colored folks" were satisfied. They saw Reverend Ingram, a Black minister never known before to support civil rights, leading a boycott. The teachers, one of the most conservative groups in the Black community, had walked out and closed the schools. Now this demonstration. Some demonstrators were from Memphis, but possibly half the Black adults in Marks were there too, people the whites knew. The whole Uncle Tom pretense was gone.

With all these new civil rights people in town and all this activity, there was increasing fear of retaliatory white violence. Mayor Langford came to talk to local Black leaders about it. He often came to the Black part of town to discuss the Bible with Reverend Ward and was one of the few popular white officials there. When civil rights workers first came to Marks in 1964, Mayor Langford had warned them that he could guarantee the safety of only two civil rights workers at any one time.[30] His statement might sound extreme in other places, but it was not in Marks, Mississippi, in August 1964. That month a white man in Marks had threatened to do the same thing that happened in Philadelphia, Mississippi, where three civil rights workers had been murdered. Their bodies had been found less than a month before that threat was made. Compared to that, Mayor Langford was benevolent.

In 1968, during the crisis after Willie Bolden's arrest, Mayor Langford spent three days with Rev. James Bevel of SCLC trying to prevent violence. The mayor was in his sixties and had heart trouble. "I haven't seen my wife in three nights," Mayor Langford said.[31] His doctor finally ordered him to bed.

"The mayor had no antagonism toward us," Reverend Bevel told the newspaper. "He was just concerned about the possibility of violence here. He said he felt we were honest people and that he thought we were doing right." Reverend Bevel said Mayor Langford's actions were "absolutely commendable."[32] On the night of May 3, the mayor installed toilet facilities, lights, and water in the field where two hundred out-of-town marchers were camped.

The mayor announced that local businesses had raised $14,000 to establish a training center for unemployed people. "We hope to train 100 people for jobs in industry at a time," he said. "Most of these will be Negroes. It's a small thing now but it will get bigger." (Actually, Mayor Langford had first discussed the idea for the training center in 1966, sign of a genuine interest in helping Black people rare among Quitman County officials.) After talking with SCLC people, Mayor Langford said,

"They don't want any violence and I can agree with anybody that's trying to do something right. I think the town will be a lot less tense when I get a chance to explain to people."[33] That helped end the boycott of the white stores.

At the same time, SCLC leaders worked hard to keep things respectable. "I'm going to show you how a lion lives in the jungle," Bevel told the out-of-town marchers. "Tomorrow morning you are each going to knock on a door and tell the people there, 'I'm part of the poor people's campaign. Can I use the tub?' Then when you get back here, you're going to wash out your socks and underthings. . . . We're going to stay clean."[34]

For the next week there was continuous heavy rain, but on May 13, 1968, 115 of the marchers set off for Washington, D.C., in a mule-drawn caravan they called the Mule Train.

CHAPTER 8

"We Was All So Determined"

1968–1972

Resurrection City

The first marchers left in a caravan of fourteen to twenty wagons pulled by fifty-five mules. Among the riders were twenty young children, the youngest only eight months old. The oldest person on the Mule Train was over seventy, but most were young adults between seventeen and thirty. At least forty were women. Two cars and two trucks traveled with the Mule Train. One truck carried feed for the mules and portable toilets. The second carried the travelers' belongings and food. The other twelve hundred marchers left Marks for Washington, D.C., in buses.[1]

Two of the Franklin brothers helped with the mules. Jack Franklin told me about it. "I had to go to Chicago to get bridles and breast chains for them mules and rubber shoes 'stead of iron shoes for the highway. I didn't get no money to help out. I just drove them mules to Washington and didn't have nothing to eat on the way. I just asked people to fix me some cornbread, and they did."

"On that mule train to Washington, some of these young folks couldn't even put a collar on the mule," chuckled his brother Jessie. "They tried to put it on upside down. They never would have got it on if it hadn't been for some of us old heads.

"They scared of mules. When the mule would stop and wouldn't do nothing, they say, 'Beat him up! Hit him upside the head!' Mule tired. He just like you and me. He got to rest. You treat him right, put the gear on him right, you'll work him a long time. My little boy, two years old, he ain't never seen no mule. It would scare him if he saw one. So they still needs some of us older heads to show them things."

Another mule driver was Gable Common, who sang bass in Reverend Malone's church choir. "I worked on the Mississippi River with mules on the levee in the 1920s. The white people said, 'Kill a mule, buy another one. Kill a n—, hire another one.'" But I always did good. I fared pretty good in all the jobs I had. When we went to Washington, I drove the third wagon. We lost two mules in Grenada. One of them didn't want to be shoen. We didn't have no more trouble till we got to Georgia. They thought the deal [police] was gonna whup us when we drive through there. But the Lord wouldn't let them do it.

"They didn't want us to go on Highway 20. They wanted us to go where we would have to climb some mountains on 25. The mules couldn't climb it. They had a group trying to march us where the billy clubs was. I stuck with my wagon after we had done got turned around. I was the last one left when they carried the others away. But somebody told them to let us go on through on 20 anyway."

In a month the Mule Train traveled five hundred miles from Marks to Washington, D.C.

There, close to the Lincoln Memorial in West Potomac Park, SCLC built a community of tents it called Resurrection City.[2] Beatrice Humphreys described it to me: "I loved Washington. SCLC had me a good place. They was tents. Resurrection City looked as big across as from here to Clarksdale. All our tents was built in a row, big tents. They had electric light. I was lucky enough to get the first tent from Marks, Number 200. Beatrice Humphreys was the first tent.

"We stayed at a white folks' place before they got the tents built. The white folks was nice to us—I ain't gonna tell no story. I spoke at Washington during the movement. A man had me speak at the federal court about how I liked them tents and I didn't mind that we didn't have no running water. The man give me fifty dollars for making such a good talk."

"You had a good time in Washington then?" I asked her.

"What you talking about! I had all the time I ever hope to have in my life! We had Indian people, Puerto Ricans there, every kind of denomination of people, some I ain't never heard of.

"But they sent vegetable seeds and clothing to Marks for people that took part in the civil rights movement. And I was marching myself to death, and I didn't get nothing. People got it that never done nothing. And here I slept in mud up to my neck in Washington when it rained so hard. And I got bit by mosquitoes and had to eat that cold food. We got oranges and raisins and peanut butter, good enough food, but all cold.

"We're the cause that this place looks better now. People say we ain't, but we was. I ain't afraid to say this; I'll say it in front of white folks! They some getting stuff and didn't do nothing for this movement!"

She paused and called out to a woman walking down the street, laughing, "I'm the cause of y'all being free—me and the other freedoms!" She turned back to me. "I saw plenty up there in Washington folks don't know about here. And I ain't gonna tell all I know because I'm down here.

"We had a bunch of us from Marks singing. You know they carried us to New York free, to most of the churches. They aks me to sing and lead the peoples in song, and I sung:

> Lord I stretch my hands to Thee
> No other help I know.
> If Thou withdraw Thy hands from me
> Wherever can I go?

and you could just see them peoples falling. I stayed in New York two years. I worked in the Watts Hotel. I would have stayed in New York if my sister hadn't died and I had to come back home."

Lula Belle Weathersby was also changed by her experience. "Resurrection City stomped a picture in my heart that never can be erased," she told me. "As shabby as it was, we was happy as can be. Up at Resurrection City I felt so happy and easy in my mind. I didn't have to sit up at night wondering where my child's next meal was coming from. We was all so determined. Hundreds of us demonstrated in the heavy rain. The rain wasn't nothing to me if I could just get at what we need.

"You know, on that trip to Washington we had the world's attention. That's the first time in my life I was proud I was poor. I know it may sound stupid, but they treated us so nice. It was the first time in my life I ever felt like I was a human being. All your life, if you poor, you got that other society hacking at you, but finally we felt somebody really cared." She began to weep. "You know, we knew that couldn't last, but it holp us feel things could get better." Then she began to laugh. "People from around the world come to talk to me in my shack at Resurrection City, and I know they talked to the other folks there. For one time poor people had the world's attention not doing no violence. You know, killing don't do no good. But we was trying to do good, trying to help ourselves. Martin Luther King, what I like is he wasn't working just for the Black man, he was working for poor people in general. If you was in poverty, he was trying to pull you out.

"When we went to Washington, we had specific demands. One of these was the housing project. If we hadn't gone, we wouldn't have had it. That trip to Washington made the food stamp program better. 'Course, if we stop pushing, things would slip back to where they was. Welfare got better when we come back. We had new jobs come in. All that we had before was the cottonseed oil mill and the compress—that was seasonal work. But then, four new factories open: two in Marks, one in Lambert, and another one, a clothing factory, just up the road. They opened up a little, then they closed it down.

"A lot of the women from Marks wanted to join the National Welfare Rights Organization. You pay a dollar to their national organization and you get a button and some papers about welfare. They told us the money goes for lawyers to help us at the welfare office. Paying that dollar was mighty hard, but I agreed to it, and the people made me and Tommy Young heads of it in this county."

Protesters did worry about violence. James Figgs observed, "You couldn't help think about the Memphis situation with Dr. King and . . . those who were planted in the sanitation workers' march to disrupt that march. And you couldn't help think about where are they. You knew they were somewhere. . . . But after a couple of days . . . you got the feeling that you had a job to do there and whatever you was asked to do, you would do it."[3]

Most whites saw a different threat, with the march coming so soon after the riots following King's death. All around Washington there were troops on alert. J. D. Powells told me, "When we were at Resurrection City, a whole lot of Black soldiers came to talk to us in civilian clothes because their officers didn't want them with us. They said, 'Do what you think is right. You all are our own people. A lot of us have brothers and sisters on the Poor People's March. If the officers think we are going to fire on y'all, they're crazy.'"

But the longer the marchers stayed in Washington, the more harassment they received. Lee Dora Collins described what happened. "I left Marks and went to Atlanta, Georgia, and Washington on the Mule

Train with four of my children. I have fifteen children—sixteen with the girl I raised. I was at Resurrection City. I got hit in the side by a policeman when we was marching around the Building of Agriculture. They knowed the purpose why we was there. We was marching for more jobs and a better deal in the food stamp program and to have our rights, and they didn't like it."[4]

One of the oldest men at Resurrection City was George Nickerson of Marks, whom everyone knew as "Cap." Mr. Nickerson was the most regular person I knew in Marks about attending civil rights meetings. He would come even when it was raining so hard we considered calling off the meeting. He registered to vote as soon as it was possible for illiterate people to do so and voted regularly. But the undocumented world he grew up in gave Social Security bureaucrats an excuse to refuse him help. "I'm used to farming, but I ain't farmed in a long time. I have chopped cotton for fifty cents a day. Wasn't no Social Security exemption for that then. I worked seven years at the Greenwood Compress till I cut my hand. I worked at the Greyhound Bus Station in Indianapolis, Indiana. They paid me dearly, but they don't give me no Social Security. We went to East Texas doing farm work when I was past sixty, picking cotton."

He started trying to get help when he was in Washington, D.C., and he was still working on the problem in 1975 when he talked to me: "I've talked to lawyers about my Social Security. They say they charge me fifty dollars in hand, but they want it before they start. I figure that was just a ploy to get my money. It's been right around six or seven months since I been to Social Security the last time. They told me I could just get $40 a month if I dropped my welfare. I was getting $125 a month welfare. I had to hold myself to keep from cussing.

"So I just give it up. I started asking them for the Social Security money eleven years ago, 1965. They had a heap of excuses. They had so much excuse I can't count it. Vietnam, that's where the biggest of the money went, that and going to the moon. At the march I was supposed to go to the Social Security Administration, but we left Washington before I had time to go.

"I imagine we would still be at Resurrection City now if them old jitterbugs hadn't started chunking rocks at the polices. But when they started doing that, the polices used the tear gas. Them polices wasn't doing us no harm at all, 'cause we was on our side and they was on their side."

Actually, the police had begun evicting Resurrection City residents as soon as SCLC's six-week permit expired. By then many had already left. A few young people tossed rocks and vandalized buildings along Fourteenth Street, and police used tear gas to disperse them. The National Park Service then bulldozed the tents.

Despite the failure to achieve the longer-term goals, Mr. Nickerson felt positive about the experience. "I enjoyed it there. We had lots of good food, all we wanted. We had a plank walk over the mud when it rained hard. It was a nice place when it didn't rain. This Mississippi is a good country, but it's just the people in it. They grouchy. Place of trying to help people, they try to keep them down."

James Metcalf of Marks organized a young people's choir at Resurrection City that continued to perform afterward. They became famous for their cheer, "I may be poor BUT I AM SOMEBODY." Robert Holland sang with them. "I went with the Mule Train in '68," Robert told me. "I was eleven. Resurrection City was all right. I met a whole lot of people—Black, white, Indian. All the people on the Poor People's Campaign was really pulling for us, trying to make some changes here.

"I got tear-gassed when they first bust up and sont all the people out of Resurrection City. When we got tear-gassed, some of the Blackstone Rangers [a Black Chicago gang that became active in civil rights] picked me and another dude about the same age up. . . . [They] took us to the medical tent and put ice on our face to stop that tear gas burning."

Two Steps Forward, One Step Back

The year or two following the Poor People's March brought some improvements to Marks—not as many as we had hoped for—and some setbacks. At the end of May 1968, Mr. Franklin's oldest son Presley was the first Black student to graduate from the formerly all-white high school. He had higher grades than any other student, Black or white, in the county. When he went through the line to receive his diploma, the school superintendent refused to shake his hand. Two white Quaker women who had come to Marks to see what conditions were like after the Poor People's March arranged for Presley to be admitted to Amherst College and get a tuition loan. They helped Presley's younger brother Melvin get admitted to Princeton University. They arranged for him to stay with a white family in New Jersey to finish high school because they believed Melvin could get better college preparation there than from his Mississippi high school. That same month, Mae Ella graduated from the all-Black high school that had once harassed and expelled her. Her father and the civil rights lawyers had gotten a federal court to make the school take her back.

That summer, the MFDP joined with the National Democratic Party of Mississippi, an organization of white liberals who finally felt safe to come out in the open. The 1968 Democratic Convention in Chicago accepted a delegation from this new combination. Fannie Lou Hamer, the heroic Black leader from Ruleville, Mississippi, was accepted as a delegate by the same party that had rejected her and the MFDP in 1964.

Some Black activists from Quitman County were at the 1968 Democratic Convention. Tommy Young from Lambert drove a mule wagon from the Poor People's Campaign to help the SCLC lobby for a strong antipoverty plank. Mr. Young was almost caught in the clash between the Chicago police and the antiwar demonstrators in Grant Park and had to drive his wagon at full speed to escape.

Unfortunately, the main result of the MFDP joining with Mississippi white liberals was the loss of local control and participation by poor Black people. In Marks those still interested in civil rights joined the local NAACP, which replaced the MFDP as the main organization for that purpose.

Meanwhile, the Vietnam War's expenses caused poverty program funding to be cut severely. When Head Start was first funded, there were 400 Marks area children in it, maybe more. By 1969, the funds had been cut so deeply that it could support only 160. And food stamps lived up to people's worst fears. That February I learned that only 36 percent of poor people in Quitman County were able to get on the food stamp program.

I talked with Mrs. Weathersby when I visited there in April 1969. She had moved from Lambert to Marks. She said, "I want it nonviolent, but most of the other people are ready for anything. After all, you can only see your children go hungry for so long. Then some of these people might just go into stores and take what they want. We want to know what can we do to make them give us justice? What do we get at?"

A February 19, 1969, letter from Sylvia Haygood, a Black woman in Marks, to Reuben Anderson, a Black lawyer in Jackson, shows the challenges pressing in from all sides.

My son been drop out of school because his principal requested me to pay $8 and some cent for his book he left in his locker at school which I was not able to pay.

So now I not able to keep him in school. The Well Fair plans to cut the little check he was getting which was what we had to relie on. Because I be out of a job all most 2 years. Everywhere I sign up for a job I never get on. I am a widow and it really hard to me and my son to survive. The check was $25 a month, was raise in Jan. 1969 to $30. Now they plan to cut the check in March.

Stamps was $6 for $28 worth of food. So you can see just what I am handling thru this life. Widow woman catches hell. You know we took sides with silver right [civil rights] all the way. We march. My son even went to Washington with Willie Bolden and everything. He only got $10 from that. That why he got shoved out of school and they laid it on books. He could not even get in school after all of that and no one tried to help me get him in there, the [SCLC] workers nor the welfair peoples. After all they made him stay in the 8th grade 3 years, so you can see why I am so up set.

Signed yours truly
Mrs. Sylvia Haygood

Also our Negro principal at our colored school is still throwing children out of school. We really don't need [the principal] nor [the Black grade school principal] either one, because they is all for the white side, not their colerd people.[5]

Although the attitudes of many white people were changing, especially younger people, the small group of whites that controlled Quitman County was still trying to keep control through the new federal programs. When Peter Joseph asked Ruth Figgs whether the poverty programs had helped her, she responded emphatically, "It have not. The power structure is still fighting it. . . . We're talking about the rich whites. . . . They want it where they can hound us and the poor will still be submissive to them."

"We're used to it, but we ain't happy with it," she concluded. "We don't feel good. You can look at the condition of our living here. . . . They've always had their ways of keeping some of us Negroes down, and they still work it on the same old things."[6]

In 1969 the Quitman County Associated Community Corporation (CC) searched for a program to bring in jobs and income.[7] In neighboring Panola County, movement activists had started an okra-selling co-op for Black farmers, who shared the profits. Mary Jones and Mr. and Mrs. Wilson visited to see how it worked. Mr. Barber of the Panola co-op described his plans, which Mrs. Jones documented in a report:

> I and Mr. Wilson and Mrs. Wilson went up to Mr. Barber to see where he was goin to plant the okra. . . . We stade their until he come and when he got thir he took us all over the place and he talk to us about the okra, how much it wood brang. He talk about houses and training school and shopping center and he talk about hospital, super market, fish lake and factory, cow and hogs.
>
> He said when we got this on feet, he was goin to brang his pastor in. He said that he was a one hundred per cent with us and his son was with us and was goin to help us too. And he said that one acre's supposed to brang you 12 ton at 6½ dollars. At that one hundred acres will brang us 7200 dollars.[8]

Unfortunately, the Panola County co-op only lasted a few years. When Quitman's CC tried to set up a similar co-operative in 1969, insects ruined the crop. Amzie Moore, the civil rights leader from Bolivar County, helped the CC contact Rev. Jacob Oglesby, head of an agricultural community development project in Panola, asking for financial help.

> Dear Sir
>
> We are involved in a vegetable farm trying to find ways and means of buying land to provide jobs for low income families and rehabilitation.
>
> This year we have 80 acres of okra. We were very successful in working and chopping out the okra. We employed at the rate of 100 people a day but for harvest we had bad luck due to unfavorable weather. It rained at least two weeks straight. Then the okra went bad with the boll worms before we could get back to harvest.
>
> We could have employed at least 300 people if the weather had been favorable.
>
> But it was the will of God and you know about what shape it left us in.
>
> We are asking your aid to help us overcome this situation and we will continue to help ourselves with the help of God and man.[9]

But no financial aid came, and, although the CC continued, its okra co-op never got going again.

One program that did help was a federally funded literacy class conducted in several Black churches. The students, paid ten dollars a week for attending, put out a newsletter called *Soul of the Centers*. Willie Thomas's wife Izella learned how to read and write there. One of the first things she ever wrote was a letter to President Nixon asking to be paid more for the classes. That money was the only income for her, her husband, and her six children besides help from relatives.

Mrs. Henrietta Franklin went to the classes as well. She had been to school for only three years as a child. She had been trying to teach herself to read better since she became involved in the civil rights movement. At first she tried using her children's primers, but she felt awkward. She got some books of gospel songs and sang the words to herself at a slow pace without feeling uncomfortable.

The literacy classes were very popular. When I visited Marks in 1969, there was a meeting at one of the larger Black churches about expanding the classes. So many people came that the church was full and there were crowds outside listening at the windows.

Mrs. Franklin was also always searching for jobs. Sometimes she went up to Michigan to pick fruit. Once she tried asking welfare to help her. "I went to the welfare lady and asked her could she find me a job. She said, 'Go back and ask them civil rights people. You with them, so they should find you a job.' She said it was a shame, the colored and white trying to mix together."

Her husband William finally got the family on welfare with the help of a civil rights lawyer. "Welfare tried to refuse to take me and my brother Jessie on. Then we got a woman lawyer and got on them. She made them give me an application. They claimed Jessie's application didn't come in right. We went in with our lawyer and scared them to death. They even called the sheriff in there and had him standing around. Our lawyer was putting it on them so bad, they thought we was trying to fight them. She told them it was some things they could ask us and some things they couldn't. She'd make them shut up. She'd tell them about some things, 'That's not legal.'

"The head welfare lady moved away. One old man in the office went home and had a heart attack. The second time we went there, one of the old ladies in the office had a heart attack, and she died. We went through six departments. Each one was checking on what the other was doing. Finally the last one, he said me and Jessie had heart trouble.

"It's been a whole lot easier for other people to get on welfare since we went. When you pops up there with a lawyer, they gets on their P's and Q's."

Finally the schools integrated. On April 6, 1969, U.S. District Judge William Keady made the following finding of fact on the suit that Black parents brought against the "freedom of choice" plan: "After three years of this school district's having operated under the freedom of choice plan, about 99% of the Negro children continue to attend wholly 'Negro' schools. The faculty, staff and extra-curricular activities of the schools are almost entirely segregated. School transportation, subject to minor exceptions, is controlled by racial considerations."

The earlier court order to put eight white teachers in the Black school and eight Black teachers in the white school had not been carried out. Three Black teachers had been placed in the white school, but no whites were teaching in the "Negro" school. Out of eighty-one county school buses, seventy-eight carried only Black or only white children.

Judge Keady concluded:

> Since freedom of choice in this district has failed to end segregation, it can no longer be used, but other means must be employed by the school district.
>
> The affirmative duty resting on the Quitman County School District at this time is to formulate a new plan and . . . fashion steps which promise realistically to convert promptly to a system without a "white" school and a "Negro" school but just schools.

On June 22, 1969, Judge Keady issued specific guidelines.

> For the school year 1969–1970 only 20% of the enrollment of each of the formerly all-white schools of Crowder, Lambert, Marks and Sledge shall be Negro students assigned by the defendant [the school board] on the basis of proximity of residence, freedom of choice or other method as it may select.
>
> For the school year 1970–71 and thereafter . . . grades 10, 11 and 12 shall be assigned to Quitman County High School Attendance Center [the "Negro" school] at Marks.[10]

Out of 5,075 schoolchildren in Quitman County at the time of Judge Keady's order, 3,397 were Black, over two-thirds of the school-age population. Many whites were alarmed. Rev. Charles Ellis, a white Baptist minister in Marks, testified in federal court just before the two student bodies were to be merged, "We accepted integration right soon after I came to Quitman County without any problem. . . . My older son graduated from Marks High School, integrated school, but this school that our children are zoned to—it's just completely out of proportion. I don't think my children could learn anything in a situation like that."[11]

About half the white parents, mostly those better-off financially, set up a private school called Delta Academy. According to Mr. Franklin, "The old man who used to own the farm where we used to stay asked all the plantation owners to help him start Delta Academy, and seven or eight of the biggest planters went in on it with him. They started out at fifty dollars a child and raised it up from that and the poor white folks couldn't go along with it. I had several of the white children at public school tell, 'Man, we started out at the Delta Academy, but we couldn't stay there.'"

Dr. Phelps, head of the public school board, told the federal court on October 14, 1970, that plans to build a new school building with $500,000 from a 1967 bond issue had "fallen through." Mel Leventhal of the LDF, together with school board attorney Larry Lamb, requested that the court reallocate the $500,000 for urgently needed repairs on the buildings. "I'm glad to be working with you instead of against you," Mr. Lamb told Mel.

Nixon

This was the last major victory Mr. Franklin won in the federal courts. While this suit was going on, Mr. Franklin went to Washington, D.C., with his fifteen-year-old son Hull to complain about the way the white school administration was treating Black pupils. They found the new Nixon administration indifferent, even hostile, to school integration. "It was 1969," Hull explained. "Winifred Green was a lawyer. She was very upset about the way Black kids were treated in school. I think that lady was using us as an example of how the states were not carrying out the federal programs. The State of Mississippi could have applied for free hot [school] lunches as early as 1965, and they wouldn't do it. The money was out there. They just didn't want to take it because they were afraid it would give the federal government the right to run their schools."

"You remember them little pot-gutted children," William Franklin added. "It meant they had some kind of disease from not getting enough to eat. We found seven of them pot-gutted children around Sledge in Quitman County. I wanted to tell the government the children couldn't study unless they got something to eat."

At the white school, Hull told me, "I was the only Black student in that particular grade level that year who had passed. The white kids wanted to tease you, and I didn't like it at that time. Now that I have studied educational administration, I realize things like that time the kids stuck me with pencils means the school administration is incompetent. Dad and myself went with Winifred Green to Washington, D.C. Attorney General [John] Mitchell heard what we had to say, then he aksed us to leave. We had a sit-in with fifteen or sixteen people. The Justice Department office was pretty crowded."

Mr. Franklin continued. "Mitchell wanted to know where we come from. He said, 'You all hungry? We'll feed you.' I told Mitchell about those hungry kids down here. They couldn't learn nothing. Mitchell asked me how did I know that. I said, 'I know it by myself because I know I can't go and do work and be hungry.' Mitchell said that was the awfullest thing he ever heard. I said, 'That's what the matter is with this country. That's why they can't learn at school.'"

Hull chimed in at that. "Those people up there have been taught that people like that are lazy and shiftless and never will amount to something, that it's their own fault. They don't know what it's like."

"I said Mississippi been hungry ever since I been in the world," continued his father. "Mitchell said, 'We'll go to Mississippi'—him and the secretary of agriculture. He said, 'We'll give you some food there. We didn't know all this was going on.'

"I said, 'I know what's going on. I born and raised in the stuff, working for six bits a day and all that.'

"He stood up there and swore he didn't know about all this going on. Mitchell was talking all this old off-the-wall stuff. He said we was doing all this on account of Martin Luther King. He said, 'What you got to offer them folks, Franklin?'

"I said, 'I'm just here to get what you got. I think Black and white looks good together. I want to get every one of these schools integrated. I want them to learn to love one another.'

"He said, 'Oh, you got an education. I know you is.' He was depending that somebody got to have a college education to know what they knowed. And Martin Luther King was telling them folks all the time that the foolish gonna betray the wise. I told Mitchell, 'You just like this attorney Ben Caldwell we got back home.'"

In March 1970, Nixon called for an "open" society "[that did] not have to be homogenous or even fully integrated."[12] Nixon and his closest advisers were convinced that most whites did not want any expansion of school integration. Nixon's administration dramatically decreased the number of school systems it investigated as part of its "southern strategy" of catering to white racism. Nixon ordered the Department of Health, Education, and Welfare (HEW) to stop threatening to cut off federal funds to districts that were not desegregating. The Johnson administration had used that threat often, and Nixon wanted to ease the pressure.[13]

Enforcement of school desegregation was transferred from HEW to the Justice Department under Attorney General Mitchell. Mitchell's Justice Department then argued in the Supreme Court for *less* desegregation. As Mitchell boasted to a reporter, "This country is going so far to the right you won't recognize it."[14]

Agents of the Civil Rights Division of the Justice Department no longer came to investigate local situations and offer help. President Nixon had withdrawn them. In 1971, Mr. Franklin lost his last major federal court case, to bring the Cotton Street neighborhood into the city limits of Marks. That would have increased Black political power and gotten paved streets and sewers.

"They running around here with their little old NAACP making the people pay four dollars, and they ain't doing nothing," Mr. Franklin complained to me. "After we commenced to beating so many cases, every case they got out on us, Nixon said, "No, buddy. You ain't gonna do that." These cats, I tell you they gonna keep the world the way they want it. Nixon banned the civil rights lawyers. That cut us off from the lawyer situation. We can't afford to pay them others. Therefore we don't get no lawing. We got that little piece of justice, and they jerked it back so quick you can't even tell we had it. We all ought to work together to build a better world. 'Ought to' and ain't doing it ain't gonna help none."

Lula Belle Weathersby was a little more upbeat. "At the convention where Nixon was nominated in 1972, a bunch of us was there. I was representing the Welfare Rights Organization. All we did was protest, protest, protest, trying to keep Nixon from being nominated. Don't you reckon a lot of those people wish they had listened to us and not voted for him?

"You know, Joe, all that protesting and going on, I really believe it helped. At least it got people's attention, and you have to get people's attention to tell them what you want them to know. We kept hollering for so long, we annoyed them, and they stuck this little piece of bread in our mouth so us couldn't holler so loud. Nixon tried to push us back some. Under Nixon, we didn't gain nothing. We just had to hold on to what we got and wait for another president."

William Franklin frowned. "Them folks that got the books written up, they say Martin Luther King or some big folks did such and such. A boy was trying to sell me a book like that. I said, 'Look, fellow, them people didn't do nothing. It was poor people like me in every place done it. Where you got their names?' He dropped his face, and I didn't buy the book."

PART III

TEN YEARS LATER

CHAPTER 9

"Things Is Better in One Way and Worser in Another"

In May 1975, I came back to Marks. I could only afford to take the bus as far as Tunica, Mississippi, well into the Delta. I started hitching and the first person to pick me up was a middle-aged Black woman. I asked her, "Is it safe to hitch around here?"

She smiled and said, "You must be thinking of how things *used* to be."

"Now It's No More Fear"

In 1964, James Silver published *Mississippi: The Closed Society*.[1] He argued that state leaders had whipped the white population into such a frenzy to preserve white supremacy that freedom of speech and press were destroyed for everyone, Black and white. Dr. Silver was forced to resign his faculty position at the University of Mississippi and received so many threats to his life he had to leave the state. When I first arrived in Mississippi in 1964 the atmosphere of hostility and suspicion was like a physical weight.

By 1975, the closed society was gone—even in rural areas like Quitman County. Despite the continuing poverty there was a new feeling of openness and freedom. One of the indications of this new atmosphere was that I was free to use the names of almost all the Black people I interviewed. In fact, several of them were eager to have their names included. In the past that would have been much too dangerous. "Now it's no more fear," Reverend Malone told me. He still led the Quitman County Voters' League.

Andrew Kopkind described the change in Lowndes County, Alabama, in the April 1975 issue of *Ramparts*. His words could apply just as well to Quitman: "Its population of Black farmers . . . is still economically subservient to the small white minority," he observed, and the "whites who still control the board of education and the county commissioners give Blacks few benefits . . . , and that grudgingly." But in more profound ways, even in these rural communities the atmosphere was "profoundly new," Kopkind asserted. "The great fear is gone." Kopkind acknowledged that "the use of atmospherics as a measure of progress may seem naive or cynical. We projected 'power' in more tangible terms in those days. But . . . a sense of freedom from fear is the base that supports both blacks and whites as they enter a long transition from the unreconstructed old order to a social design that at best is still sketchy."[2]

As the Black people of Marks talked with me, I was impressed by how open and direct the expression on their faces had become, especially among younger people. Even Black people I had never met before spoke frankly but with a genuine friendliness instead of the Uncle Tomming that was once frequent. I watched them deal with the local whites in the same direct way they talked to me.

Most people in Marks I spoke to in 1975 felt their lives had improved. Certainly, they had many more modern conveniences than they did when I lived there. Many more houses had indoor toilets and telephones. Even the Franklins had an indoor toilet by 1975, although their Cotton Street neighborhood still had no sewer line.[3]

Lula Belle Weathersby credited the movement for much of the improvement. "I know peoples that when this movement started, they was sleeping on the floor, and they didn't have no food unless somebody was to bring it over. Now they got beds and gas stoves and food to cook on them and freezers. You see, when people see someone come to help them, it makes them want to help themselves."

Mrs. Evans agreed. "The white people are better, schools are better, parks are better. Back then we couldn't use them. Motels are better—you get a room in any motel. Cafes, public facilities are better. Jobs is not better."

Reverend Allen nodded. "Things are much better. They recognize you better. They pays a man about what he's worth, and he's not pushed around. And they don't give a cussing to the colored women who work in their houses. They just work them for eight hours instead of from sunup to sundown."

"Even with the recession we're doing better than we was doing back when we was slaving and didn't have enough to eat," Mrs. Weathersby emphasized, "and we worked hard. 'Course I don't have everything I would love to have. And it was a heap better before the recession. But still it's better than back in the thirties and the forties. Better than all of my life." But, as she quickly clarified, "That don't mean I don't have problems."

When I first got to Marks in 1964, the city had only one policeman. Most law enforcement was done by the county sheriff's deputies. A decade later Marks had a regular police force. From 1968 into the 1990s, the police chief was L. C. Pride, the first Black officer ever appointed. Four of the eight members of the force were also Black. By the mid-'80s, one was a Black woman. In 1986, Richard Arvedon, one of my coworkers, went back to Marks to visit the Franklins. He wondered if he would have to worry about hostile whites when he drove into town. When he saw the Black policewoman directing traffic, he said, "All right—it's changed here."

Through the 1970s, Chief Pride remained unpopular in the Black community because of his actions during the demonstrations in the spring of 1968. But when I visited Marks in 1981, long-time community leader James Wilson Sr. told me, "L. C. have come over to the side of his people a hundred percent."

In fact, Mrs. Weathersby told me, speaking of the Black people of Marks, "I can't think of a single person now who's not with this movement." From an underground group in the 1950s, civil rights had become the Black community consensus.

Nevertheless, well into the 1970s some people who had been active in civil rights work still expected harassment. Ruth Figgs told me about her son's and her own experiences. Especially after a 1975 racial killing in Byhalia, Mississippi, she worried. "I works with the exchange program that learns children how to understand and dwell with one another. I gives out clothes to families that has an emergency. And I'm in the National Council of Negro Women. They work on such as garden co-ops and political powers also. I served on a campaign committee for a Black candidate for school superintendent. I've had a lot of discrimination against me, such as I was fired off local jobs. I didn't have any favorable kind of chance on paying my bills. All my bills had to be paid on time to keep them from cutting off water and lights and gas ever since I started working in the movement.

"My son was a social service director for Legal Aid. He offered all the informations on the free lunch program at the school and reported about the low-paid labor in the public school system. Also he was breaking down the balance in the welfare and the food stamps. So they just didn't want him in. They didn't report no special reasons for arresting him. They stopped him and one of his brothers in a car with him for arrest, you know, and they beat him up. When court come they didn't bring up no special thing. We taken it to federal court. He went to a compromise. His Black witnesses from town didn't turn out at all. He didn't have nothing but two young childrens for witnesses, and he was afraid that wasn't enough. The police had been down to arrest some of the childrens on the lower end of town for a fight. That was in December 8, 1970. They still got that same kind of gang around here that they used to, but what they'll do is put the Black police up to it. Like that Black boy mobbed and killed in a white cafe in Byhalia. Some of these peckerwoods here is laying around ready to do the same thing. You can see it in their expression."

One thing I noticed in what Mrs. Figgs said: the civic activity she said she was harassed for sounded normal enough, but for a poor Black woman in rural Mississippi it was almost impossible to have been able to do those things until the changes of the 1960s. When I visited Marks in 1998, her son James had become school superintendent. Mrs. Figgs had passed away by that time. On her tombstone was inscribed:

SHE LOVED HER GOD
SHE LOVED HER FAMILY
SHE LOVED HER COMMUNITY

Now that Black people could register, the voting struggle had shifted to the ballot box. Mr. Franklin ran for justice of the peace in 1971, and his brother Mr. Jessie ran for county supervisor. They both lost. In 1975, several Black candidates ran. Lula Belle Weathersby remained deeply involved. "We have a Black boy running for superintendent of education this year. He sure is a good guy. He have a good chance to win 'cause a lot of the white say they going to vote for him. He been working on that Title I over among the white folks, and a lot of them know him and like him. Title I help less fortunate children in school that need dental treatment or eye treatment. Now if all the Blacks just vote—'course everybody had to re-register, and a lot of the Blacks ain't register yet.

"You know, that's one thing that made it better for us in Mississippi was when we got that voting power. That made it automatically better. When they in office, they do better 'cause they want your vote. You know something? Color don't mean nothing to me. I votes for the man. It may seem crazy to you, but most of us like the sheriff we got now. We got a Black man running, but we figure if we vote for him the whites will put in one of their mean folks, so we all voting for the sheriff we got now."

I talked with Samuel Lipsey, on Marks's NAACP steering committee. "The things that need to be done? We need a lot more Black people in office here. We got a lot of Blacks registered to vote, but there are still Black people that haven't registered. We've got a white sheriff candidate that was swinging a bat at the people marching here in '68."

Only one Black candidate won in the 1975 elections, a constable. Still, this was the first Black elected official in the history of the county. This put the county far behind many places in Mississippi. In nearby Clarksdale, the city council was over half Black by 1975.

By then it was common to see white candidates driving around Black neighborhoods looking for votes. Reverend Allen told me, "All the candidates for sheriff come to the NAACP meeting. They want our vote. I know some whites, they's voting for Negroes for public jobs. And that hain't never been before."

Joe Collins was less impressed. "White folks, they come around and shake your hand at election time, but they don't never do nothing. Whoever this here that running for supervisor now, he claim he going to put in a sewer and blacktop the streets. If there was any white, it woulda done been did by now."

Mr. Collins lived outside the city limits. Inside Marks, the open sewer that once ran through the Black part of town had been put underground by 1975. That terrible stench and health hazard was now gone. Even the Cotton Street neighborhood was paved and no longer flooded with raw sewage in every heavy downpour, even though it was still badly drained, and every rain left pools of stagnant water.

In 1975, Cliff Finch was elected governor of Mississippi largely with Black votes, though he was also popular with working-class whites. He had started out as a segregationist but later did legal work for the NAACP in nearby Batesville. During his campaign, one day each week he would work at some job like driving a bulldozer or bagging groceries. Ernestine Evans approved of these changes. "The white folks, they just want to forget the civil rights trouble and go on ahead. They treat us all right. We all got together, Black and white, to elect Governor Finch. He's a hard-working man. He drove a bulldozer. Peoples like that. White people voted for him as well as Black, because Finch says he'll bring jobs and they out of a job too."

By 1975 even the least educated could see themselves as part of what was happening around the country, which greatly increased their feeling of political self-confidence. In 1976, Jimmy Carter won the presidency based on the southern Black vote. In Mississippi most of this came from the largely Black counties of the Delta. This is still not forgotten by the Black people there. "I been praying so long that Carter would win, but I didn't think he would," Reverend Allen told me later. "Then we had a sunny day and got a lot of peoples to the polls. I stayed up all that night at the TV, then at the very last minute they said they needed Mississippi to win, and when Mississippi come through, I couldn't hold back. I shouted so loud my wife got out of bed to see what was the matter, and we both started shouting."

In 1980 I saw Jesse Jackson and Senator George McGovern in Marks mobilizing people to vote. They spoke to a crowd in the park that Black people would not even enter in the 1960s.

Yet no elected official could come up with any solution to the huge problems facing Marks. Some of those who worked hardest to get the right to vote came to realize that voting was at best only a beginning and at worst a racket. Jessie Franklin took the latter view. "Voting ain't no good. All that politician stuff ought to die. The politician pushing dirt on you when you ought to see daylight. These people get your name, and then they get in there and get some old high-paying job, they forget about you. Folks could do something about it, but our folks don't stand together. If we could get 75 percent of our people to support a supposal to the government, we could stand up to the sheriff, but they ain't together."

"That Far Apart"

"If people was to get together and say 'This is what I want' and stand up—[but] they ain't gonna stand up! They that far apart." Mr. Jessie spread his fingers wide. "You can't compare the state you born in with

Heaven. Up there it's glory and fire; down here it's kicking and beating. Up there it's rest and down here trouble. The white man ain't gonna come by your house and give you good advices. If he done that, the Black folks wouldn't be doing all that crime. Instead he send the polices after you.

"The politician hand you his card, and you gets two dollars and some whiskey to vote for him. My brother was running for justice of the peace, and someone give a old Black man five dollars to vote for the other man. I seen it. Our own folks ain't got no more sense than that.

"Something's gonna happen. It's gonna bust loose some day. I hope I live to see it. It's gonna be a time when all this gonna be showed down. They coming to be a calm between Black and white, but they never will get along because they have done so bad. But if they get right with this next generation and show them the way and teach them, then they will come to love one another."

His brother William was also exasperated. He was still the person Black residents came to with their problems. After getting one such phone call he told me, "This is the dirtiest town I ever lived at in my life—Negroes and whites. That's the reason I ain't fooling with them no more. They say one thing and do another." I asked him why people still called him if he felt this way. "I don't know," he replied. "They ain't gonna do what I aks them to do. And when I get finished doing for them, they don't speak to me. They'll say, 'Oh, Mr. Franklin done some wonderful work for me,' and next day they won't even heist they head to me. Then when they in trouble, they'll be coming to me for help again." About two hours after saying this, he was advising a man about cuts to his Social Security. One night in 1981 when I was visiting, some people came all the way from Clarksdale to ask Mr. Franklin for legal advice.

Many looked to organizing to fill the gap between electoral politics and community need. But, like the Franklins, they worried about the lack of cohesion in the Black community. Particularly with the decline in farm work, some thought there had been a decline in the neighborliness that was still crucial to the survival of rural Black people. One man lamented, "Years ago when we used to plow with mules, we had friends. If I had to pick up a bale of cotton, my friend come by and help me. Now I ain't a friend to him, and he ain't a friend to me." Some people talked fatalistically: "Things is better in one way and worser in another."

People like J. D. Powells, who acquired skills and education in the civil rights movement, hoped to build new community institutions to amplify neighborly behavior. But in the 1970s most were still waiting for a chance to do something. "I dropped out of the tenth grade," J. D. told me, "but I took a GED test. Then I started to Coahoma Junior College when I was twenty-six. I went there a year and a half and then went to community organizers' school at Howard University.

"I want to learn how to do something to be of some use. I want to come back to Marks, and I want to create something that ain't nobody ever did before, something between journalism and organizing. The main problem around here is people just aren't organizing. That's the whole thing, right in a bag. You don't run into the barriers you used to run. But there's a lack of industry. With anything to do, things would be mellower.

"Here in Mississippi, you don't never see a Black man starve because if you run out of groceries, somebody gonna give it to you. You see people send groceries from one house to another. That's the only thing that's helped a lot of people to survive. That's the only kind of organization there is around here." But J. D. was unable to achieve his dream. He worked in his brother's cafe in Marks, still waiting until his death.

His mother, Mrs. Ernestine Evans, was also interested in community organizing. She wanted to use the applications for home nursing training that she distributed to neighbors as an organizing tool, but she doubted it would be effective. She told me, "God don't need nary minute of your help. Here's how you help him down here: help each other. Now I'm studying the state's nursing lessons. People here needs some kind of medical school. They need to be taught how to eat. They need some kind of lesson on how to live to a longer age. We need to teach them how to read, how to amuse themselves—not just drinking and gambling, but how to have church meetings, meetings where they talk over things, women's meetings, getting together with their family to learn how to love one another.

"I got some cards here for women to fill out. There's no education required, just a willing mind. We need three or four women to set up a clinic. They got it over in Tupelo, women doctors—colored—saving lives. Giving shots, delivering babies, all that. Some women here would just throw these cards in the garbage can."

Jobs and Welfare

Economically, frustratingly little had changed since the 1960s. Ora Bea Phipps, the widow of Armistead Phipps who died on the March Against Fear, talked to me as she hoed her garden about the heavy unemployment, how it affected her and the large number of unemployed young Black people in Marks. J. D. Powells joined our conversation. "They think we lazy, but that's wrong," Ora said. "We about the smartest people in the world. That's all we ever knowed, hard work. I went to the welfare and asked them to find me a job. You know I'd rather have that than a handout. But welfare don't help you get a job. I know plenty here would take a job if welfare would give them one. And I drove around to all these factories, down to Lambert and Batesville. But they say I done got too old. And you know that car don't run on air. So I takes $157 from welfare for my four children, and I chops in this little garden and raises me three hogs. Idle brains is the devil's workshop. Now us old soap-sticks out of work wouldn't do nothing, but these young people, they better find something to occupy their time. They want beer, they want cold drinks, and they going to take it if they can't get a job to take it."

J. D. chimed in. "These kids, they got something we didn't have when we was their age, and that's automatic weapons. They just stay over there in the park drinking beer and smoking dope, waiting for the cops to come. They just waiting to start trouble. That little white cop don't dare come around there. He got to go get a Black cop to break them up."

Few traditional jobs were available. The limited number of farm jobs could not support the number of young people who needed them. "I'd say the main problem in Marks is you can't find jobs," Samuel Lipsey told me. "The only thing the NAACP can do is try to get a government program. Industries here, like the cottonseed oil mill, are going out of business." According to the 1970 census, Black unemployment in Quitman was 13.5 percent, the third highest in Mississippi. A decade later, that number was even higher—18 percent—compared to less than 5 percent for whites.[4]

Changing attitudes had also led to the disappearance of some traditional jobs, such as midwifery, or being a "doctor lady," as Black people in Marks used to say. Mrs. Sarah Ann Brown, who worked in the volunteer Head Start in 1966, was a midwife. She had delivered Mrs. Franklin's youngest son Jimmie Lee in 1960. In 1969 she moved north, but she often came back to help administer the property and financial affairs for her extended family. She finally moved back to Marks, where she died. On one visit to Marks in 1975, she told me about midwifery. "Being a midwife is easy work. Of course, sometimes the mother take her time, and then you got to talk to her and help her along, but most times you just got to wait. I remember when a baby wouldn't come out, I taken the mother over to the hospital in Clarksdale. The doctor let me into the room with the mother. He straightened the baby in the womb just right, and the woman had a big old boy baby. We call that doctor Dr. Jesus. But at Marks the doctor wouldn't let the midwife or the woman's mother come in like he supposed to.

"There was four or five midwives working in this county when I left here in 1969. Used to be twenty-five or thirty midwives around here. I don't know how many I delivered. It was in the thousand." Now, however, "most women like to go to the hospital. They want to go to the doctor and get them a shot. They think they more safe at the hospital."

Even businesses developed by Black people had a difficult time competing with whites who had the money to set up bigger operations. Gilbert Hamer explained, "I haul pulpwood. I own this truck. It was Black folks started hauling pulpwood and hauling old junk cars to Greenville with their old beat-up trucks. Then the whites come with their new trucks and started crowding them out."

The prefabricated housing plant in Marks closed down in the early 1970s. The Johnson administration had helped small industrial enterprises in poverty areas with a government loan. The Nixon administration cut the loans off, and the plant in Marks folded. Other small industries that had recently started shut down in the 1975 recession. The textile factory in Lambert closed soon after. It could not compete with cheap textiles coming from other countries under the new global trade agreements.

Mrs. Weathersby and Mr. Young, county leaders of the National Welfare Rights Organization, described the shutdowns and unemployment and the resulting turn to welfare. Mrs. Weathersby began. "We was doing good in Marks for a while. Things was really blooming here for the first time in history. What really started things in Quitman County up was that housing plant where they cut out parts for housing and put them up. But they had a government loan, and when that was cut, ooh, that hurt!"

"The National Welfare Rights Organization never did no good here,"

Mr. Young added. "You see, the people looked mostly for the organization to help them. They didn't see that the organization is for them to help themselves."

Mrs. Weathersby nodded. "That's the main problem. Most people look to an organization for what it can do for them, not for what they can do for the organization. Brother Young, I really think that the Welfare Rights Organization did some good. 'Cause I had people come to me to get them on welfare, and the welfare lady would put them on when she seen me. She knowed I was with the Welfare Rights Organization. I didn't try to hide it from her. I wore my buttons every time I was there. Now the Welfare Rights Organization ain't much here. The old folks is getting supplement from Social Security instead of welfare. The children is still on ADC [Aid to Dependent Children] from welfare.

"They talk about peoples on welfare. They burlesque them. They always talk about them, they get on television and talks about welfare, and it just makes me sick. They was the one put you there. They'll put you on the welfare roll and they won't put you on the payroll. I know two-thirds of the peoples on welfare would rather have a job. That's why I couldn't get nowhere with this Welfare Rights Organization. Peoples would tell me, 'I don't want no welfare! I wants a job!'

"Joe, you know, when I was on welfare, at first I cried so hard. I wanted a job even though I got high blood [pressure] and a heart condition. It took me a year to settle down to be on welfare. My husband worked plumb till he got so sick that he couldn't. Welfare is just a way of keeping us down. Don't you know these peoples in Washington could do something to provide jobs so people could provide for themselves? But all they want to do is give you welfare. Peoples wants to work! It's just like slave. They can tell you what you can buy and what you can't buy. A lot of people aren't contented with welfare. You don't believe that, just let a big job open up here, and you see he have his hands between now and night. I know I'm sick, but when they was hiring, I tried to get a job. You know, the Black man don't know nothing but work. It seem a shame I was working all these years for nothing, and then, when I got a chance to get paid for my work, I can't."

Mr. Franklin agreed that welfare and food stamps were just forms of control, even though in the 1970s they were easier to get than they had been.[5] "Welfare ain't nothing but a big cheat," he told me, "a white folks' racket. They don't break fair with you on that stuff, and somebody else furnishing it. My youngest boy gets thirty dollars a month. The government's tried to get them to point you out a job and get you off welfare, but they don't do it. They say, 'Y'all is supposed to go look for them jobs and come tell us about them, and we'll take you off welfare.' I told them, 'If you over forty, they don't hardly hire you. You all supposed to have a committee appointed to help find jobs, and y'all ain't got no committee yet.'

"That stamp thing is just a controlling thing they got on you. Ary bit of money you get from up north, you got to report it. When they furnished you on a plantation, they didn't give you that much trouble. I got to tell if I get anybody staying with me. If Jimmie Lee, my youngest boy, get a job cutting grass, I lose my food stamps. If my daughter and her husband come, they gonna threaten me, 'Look we are not furnishing food stamps for anybody to eat up. If they furnishing they own self, that's OK.' And before you know it, some of the welfare people be in my house to see is they eating the food I got with my stamps."

His wife jumped in. "Welfare got a mockingbird around here—a poll parrot. Your own color go against you, tell them everything you do."

Mr. Franklin nodded. "They done put people in jail here when they caught them doing that if they don't have no money to pay it back. Everybody wants a job. They don't want to be worried about that old welfare."

"We used to be on food stamps," Harry Hentz chimed in. "We got off in '72, we got so much harassment. Once one of us got big enough to go up north and work, they come to us and harassed us. Like my sister went up the road to work to make money for college, and we had to pay $256 back to the food stamp office."

Some people told me food stamps had prevented starvation but had a lot of faults. "Babies born now, Joe, all of them's fat and fine," Dorothy Stanford told me. "Used to be some of them skinny, tight-skinned babies 'cause they mamas couldn't get enough to eat. They eat them water beans 'cause they couldn't get nothing else to grease their belly. I stand in the store and look. They got them stamps now and load up. Some of them don't know how to use them. They can't budget them off. It just crazy, man. They spend all $200 worth. I think that's the reason the price of meat gone up. My daughter say, 'They think everybody with a food stamp is a fool.'"

Jessie Franklin agreed with both the good and bad aspects of the food stamp program: "People used to suffer so much from pellagra here because they just ate cornbread all the time, but this food stamp thing has kind of brought people out. They gets better food, and their health is a little bit better. Eating better makes their mind better too. Because the food stamp program come in, the people can eat well three weeks and the fourth week they can die like hell. And all the time the property tax got to be paid, whether you like it or not. You got two things you don't want to do: lose your home or starve."

One day in 1975 as I was walking around Marks, Isabelle Johnson invited me up on her porch. She told me she had some things to tell me. She emphasized that even though most people didn't want welfare, with the bad economy and low wages they didn't have much choice. But the welfare system seemed totally stacked against them too. "You ought to write a book on them food stamps," she told me. "They said I was making too much money because my husband hauling junk. There's ten of us. The last time I went over and talked to the welfare lady, she told me the food stamps would cost me $136, and, as high as groceries is, I don't need no food stamps if the food stamps cost that much. I'd say my husband would average about $180 a week hauling old cars. And his expenses got to come out of that for gasoline and tires and to pay the boy that help him. But he don't make a load every week. It's two men haul cars here in Marks, and I don't know how many from Clarksdale. They come over here looking for cars and lots of times they beat my husband to them. In the wintertime, when them dirt roads and the fields muddy, my husband can't get at them cars or he get stuck up. So he go a whole month without hauling cars in winter."

There were few alternative ways to earn money either. "They ain't too many people be hiring you to chop cotton. Last year I sent my children to the field to chop cotton, but this year we ain't found a place to hire them. They say they just going to hire the people stay out there on their plantation to chop cotton."

Her daughter-in-law, who had stopped in, agreed. "The food stamp office, they gypping and jiving, that's what. My grandparents on a fixed income, and they got to pay $60 for $80 worth of stamps."

Mrs. Johnson nodded. "Children be going to school on a empty stomach," she said. "I ain't even got nothing to fix for them sometime. They sitting there in class on a empty stomach. How can you think on a empty stomach?

"After school, look to me like they ought to have some jobs so children can buy clothes and shoes. The white childrens gets part-time jobs, but they ain't done nothing for the Black kids till last year they worked out a program. They big enough to work, they needs a job. You give them something to work at, they keeps out of trouble.

"I ain't never been no one for a handout. I was brought up to work. I likes to work. But if they ain't no work, what can I do? You has to take welfare 'cause you can't do no better. If you go in the white folks' house to cook and clean out, they ain't gonna pay you no more than two dollars a hour. That factory down in Lambert, if you ain't got a good education, you can't go there and work. It's plenty people here in Marks can't read neither write. They know enough to do the work, but they can't fill out the application.

"I passed up to the third grade in school. When I was a kid out in the country on the white folks' farm, they didn't want us going to school. They raise so much sand with your parents, they afraid if they send you to school they can't get no food if they go to the white man. So, I was out there in them old boots in the winter in the field picking cotton instead of going to school. They the causing of the Black not having the education.

"Then too again that Head Start program is something else. You take me; I got the children. They got women working there ain't got no children. How come they won't give me no job? I'm the one got to feed these children. Them women with the job ain't got nary one to feed. President Ford ain't doing nothing for the Blacks without food nor the poor class of white. I tell you it's some white around here as bad off as the Black. But them big sophisticated white, they don't care. They sent money to help Nixon. These here big folks that got plenty land, looks like they could give a Black person some land to raise a truck patch. Maybe the government could buy it for us.

"You go down to the food stamp office, they keep you waiting all day. They act nasty, I tell you. They ask you a whole lot of old stupid questions they shouldn't ask. If they could put some factories in here where people could earn they own money, they wouldn't need the food stamps. You take a girl finish school here, she can't get no job here. She got to go up the road north to get a job. They don't want to go. They rather stay here. My daughter was in Rust College. She come home because she ain't got no nice clothes and she shamed to go there. And she is so smart in her books it's a crying shame."

In 1981, I interviewed a younger Black woman. She asked me not to use her name. She had many of the same problems as Mrs. Johnson, even though her income was above average for Black families in Marks.

"I stopped school in the seventh grade," she told me. "I pay $150 and get $250 worth of food stamps. My husband work at Vintage Homes where they make trailer houses at near Clarksdale. But it's not a good steady job because he was laid off two months. He makes $2.95 a hour. He wouldn't be making that much if he wasn't some sort of group leader. I get welfare for two children I had before I was married. That don't provide for them two children. What is $48? Their father's dead, but he didn't leave no Social Security. I have three more children by my husband and expecting another. I've applied everywhere for jobs. At the factory they tell me to fill out applications and come back. I've filled out so many applications I'm tired of it. I worked at the white dairy bar for a while. They didn't pay but $1 a hour for short-order cooking. The majority of the people who work around here don't have unions. My husband say they was trying to organize a union where he work. They had a meeting, but they ain't got it yet. At least he don't pay no union dues.

"The majority of the white peoples here don't want to help the poor people. When you go to the state, they think you lying. If you wasn't in need, how would you go there when you have to tell them all your personal business? I know I wouldn't.

"See?" she laughed. "I'm helping you write your book, and you could make millions off of it, and I may get nothing."

Despite the lack of jobs, less than a quarter of Black poor families in Quitman County received welfare, most of whom were female household heads with children.[6] Even disability and other benefits that in theory were guaranteed were very difficult to qualify for. Mrs. Ella Mae Haynes told me her story: "I wish you'd a been here when I tried to get on disability. They said I could live on my husband's check. I said, 'Lord, if I'd a knowed that, I would a never paid nothing on Social Security when I was cooking at the hotel all these twenty-some years.' I had to quit cooking in '75. I had sugar [diabetes], and the doctor told me I couldn't keep walking on concrete. My feets was all swole up.

"That lady at the office told me I don't need money when she found out my husband had a pension from the railroad. She just about give me a heart attack. And here these white folks been taking Social Security out of my paycheck every Sunday since it started."

"She would go out chopping cotton if I didn't stop her," her husband Will chided gently. "I don't want her falling out. She have high blood."

She nodded. "I cooked many a meal for twenty dollars a week. I worked every day, Sunday and all, Christmas Day. I never got to go to church. Leave here walking in the rain and all. Worked so hard. Right now I can't hardly work around my house. When I try to make my bed, I have to sit down. When that lady told me I didn't need the money, I didn't say nothing. She was white, and I was colored. I told her the truth. If I'd a told her a lie, I might a got the money, but I believe in telling the truth."

In those years, not just welfare but all the government programs that were supposed to relieve the distress of poor people were extremely limited, thanks to federal spending for the Vietnam War. Head Start funding in the 1970s fell far below the amount that Alex Shimkin and I sought, for example. Still, the program did some real good. Mrs. Lee Dora Collins continued to do volunteer work as a Head Start community auxiliary in the 1970s, even though, like most poor women, she couldn't get one of the paid jobs. She also did a lot of civic and church work after a lifetime of heavy labor on the plantation. "I've just worked," she told me, "worked so hard till I ain't no account. I have broken veins in my leg and something wrong with my nerves. I can't do like I used to. I can't go out to chop cotton. I done picked so much cotton till I don't never want to see nobody else's cotton field again. I'm glad I have a part-time job in the high school cafeteria. If I could get welfare I would."

She also served as the volunteer secretary for the parents' committee for Head Start. I asked her if she thought the program had made a difference. "Yes," she replied, "Head Start have really improved the life of the children. The children gets their meal twice a day. They gets the juice, the milk, the vegetables. Right now in the PTA we in the process of getting free school lunch for the grade school. We ain't never had it before." Free school lunches did not come to the Black children of Marks until 1975.

A government housing program also helped some poor people in Marks and partly changed the appearance of the Black part of town. It built a neighborhood of frame houses painted in cheerful colors to the west of the tarpaper-covered shacks that housed most of the Black community. Mrs. Weathersby and her family got a house under this program. "When we got ready to build this house, we didn't have nothing but ten dollars. I just shed a tear, Joe. But I looked up and here come a truck full of lumber to get us out of the heat and the cold and the mosquitoes. I just looked at it and felt so proud. And I felt the same thing when I looked at the truck taking the lumber to other people's houses.

"All we had to pay was $25 a month. The government was paying $32 a month on each house. But the government loan run out, and the housing project for low-income peoples done slowed down. But now I'm pretty sure it will start up again, for Congress appropriated another loan. You can just move in without any down payment whatsoever—just start your monthly payment. And all my life I been hearing, 'You too poor,' when I wanted a house that would keep us out of the weather."[7]

However, some of the houses were constructed from cheap, green lumber. The walls of those houses were bulging and sagging in places and had to be propped up with boards. James Herron, a Black plumber, described the defects of the housing, both how the workers were treated and how the houses were built. "I did some work on the low-income housing project. They wasn't paying me nothing. They want me to furnish the material, and they give me about $500. I didn't do but two or three. I couldn't make no money like that. I be losing. Some of them houses, you go in them now, the tile is coming up, the paint is peeling off the wall, the paneling is coming loose. They insulated all them houses good, but you can't build a house out of two-by-fours, and they built all them houses out of two-by-fours." Once again, lack of funds limited the good such programs could do.

Longing for Home

Many young people who grew up in and around Marks wanted to stay. But the decline of jobs in agriculture and the inadequacy of federal programs to create new jobs left their economic prospects bleak. Clara Rucker told me she went to a conference in 1976 on how teachers could help Black youth prepare for a life in Mississippi rather than move north. Many white stores had failed, and those still in business understood the need of having Black youth stay. Mrs. Rucker and the other teachers had some effect with their message. When I visited Marks in 1981, twelve-year-old Loretta Phipps told me emphatically, "We can have just as good a life in Mississippi as any place else." She said she had learned this from her teacher. But Loretta was not able to find a job in Mississippi when she grew up. She moved to Virginia to study to be a medical lab technician.

As a result, through the 1970s the numbers of young Black people (and low-income whites) leaving for northern cities grew. The county population, which had been declining since the 1960s, shrank to 12,636 in 1980, less than half that of 1950.[8] William and Henrietta Franklin's daughter, Mrs. Lenora Wells, explained why she moved to Gary, Indiana. "Money, that's the thing. There's money up there. Here there's not much of nothing. Up there they have opportunities for jobs."

"And amusement?" I asked.

"Right! Up there, there's lots of places to go. Here there ain't nowhere to go, ain't nothing to do."

I asked her if she saw any disadvantages to leaving. "I would say so," she answered. But when I asked her what they might be, she hesitated. "I don't know. I would just rather be in the city, period. I got some postcards to send home to Gary, and I found one that said, 'MARKS—POVERTY CAPITAL OF THE COUNTRY.' I didn't buy them. I don't want my friends to see nothing like that. With the cottonseed oil mill laying off, if something don't change soon, this town is going to die."

But many of those who left for the North later returned. Some, like Mrs. Brown, were older and found they could not find jobs. More often, what brought Black people back to Marks and other southern towns was the combination of a longing for the comforts of a small town and the impact of the economic recessions. Mr. Jessie's sons, Man and Jessie Jr., talked with me in 1975 about both the draws and the challenges of the North. Man was planning to go up there soon, and Jessie Jr. had recently returned to Marks. Man told me, "Five or six years ago this place was full of young people, but now Marks ain't even got a factory. Just a place that make T-shirts, Pacific Building make these new houses, and the oil mill is the only things really going in this town, and you see how the oil mill run down.

"I like a little small town. I don't like no big place like Chicago or New York. I like a little town where I can find my way around. [But] I'm going to Chicago soon. Ain't nothing around here, Joe. I'm a welder. I make from $95 to $104 a week. Up there I could make $8 or $9 a hour. If I don't find a job, I can always come back home. I'll try to find work in Chicago where my brother-in-law working. If I can't work there, I'll go to Wisconsin and try to get a job where my brother Sonny Boy is."

But Jessie had come back. "That steel mill in Chicago closed down. I seen old Cass's brother here in town. He say they laid him and the others all off."

One day Charles Jamison invited me over to his family's house. His whole family had been very active in the movement. It was the weekend of his aunt's funeral. Many relatives had come in from Memphis and Chicago. Charlie pointed out among a group of children one who was his uncle, another who was his youngest brother, and several nephews and nieces. "I was passed to the eighth grade," Charlie told me. I asked him why he quit. "I don't know. I got grown, I reckon."

"His family didn't have no money," his sister explained.

"I started to work," Charlie continued, "at the Federal Compress making bales of cotton. That the first job I ever had. I was fourteen years old. I worked as a head-runner. After they press cotton and it come out, I have to pick it up with a header—that's a hook on a cable—and put it on a trailer. It was first hard. After I got to be a man, it wasn't so bad. When I first started they paid me $1.60 a hour. Then I went up to $2.15.

"I got married and divorced. I got a seven-year-old boy over at Clarksdale. I supposed to support the child, but I ain't gonna tell no lie, no, I don't. When I get myself together, I'm gonna get my little boy in there with me. Your own home feel better than anyplace else. You can do what you want to in your own house. I don't want to be staying at my mother's all the time.

"I went up to Chicago less than a year ago. I worked at a steel mill for $4.56 an hour. I liked it, but I couldn't handle it. It was too much heat in there for me. I didn't like Chicago. As many people as I saw get killed, I didn't like it. Over in the juke house I saw three or four get shot down. Yeah, I likes it here. Where I raised and born, I got to like it. I'm working on the railroad at Coldwater now, 45 miles from here, laying new track."

"Is it hard to find jobs now?" I asked.

"Yeah, sure is. Nine times out of ten, people drawing unemployment. I think things tougher than they used to be. Used to be peoples asking if you want to work. Now they ain't got nothing to do. My eyes is getting bad." He gestured toward his bloodshot eyes and swollen lids. "The creosote on the crossties, that stuff burn my eyes. I got to stand up ten or fifteen minutes and quit working cause my eyes hurts me. I'm gonna try and get on disability."

James Herron was a younger man deeply committed to life in Marks. He knew everyone from the wealthy white Self family to the very poorest Black families. He was full of hope for Marks's future yet frank about its disadvantages. "I don't believe Marks has improved that much," he told me. "I put it this-a-way. It different from up north. The sheriff here say he going to close all these places at nine o'clock. If these cafes close, those youngsters won't have no place to go, and they'll be out doing a whole lot badder things."

Harry Hentz, a young farmer, made a similar point. "It's a lot of things could liven Marks up. A lot of the older people, Black and white, dig boxing. So we could put up a boxing ring and bring peoples together."

He too had hopes of staying in Marks and making a difference. "I was in the marines. I'm going to use my veteran's benefits money for college. My brother is twenty. He don't want no more school, so he'll stay at home and farm full-time and I'll come home and farm part-time. I want to study social work. This place need some, and maybe I can start some involvement.

"Or maybe I can get into law enforcement. In this place, the law enforcement is still too biased to one race. Marks is like this: a rich man can run that red light, and won't nobody do nothing to him, just wave at it and keep going. If a poor man run it, they stop him and he get a fine. I want to be a police not just for a rich man but for a poor man. A poor man ain't even able to pay a ticket, and he get one. He ain't hardly even able to get bread."

Mr. Herron emphasized, "Some things is better. White folks here, they speak to you now. I say yes and no to them, and they say yes and no to me. I treat everybody the same. I don't bite my tongue. We all just the same. The kids are much healthier-looking now. I like my work as a plumber. I love it here. I wouldn't go anywhere else. Because I believe it isn't going to go anywhere else but better. I have home buddies that moved up to Chicago coming back home. I have ate at the Self family's table, and they treated me just like anybody else. If you stand up for yourself, they don't bother you.

"The Black people here just don't get together. If they would have a big meeting like a family reunion, they could demand that the city do something for them, 'cause they pay taxes too. They should get just as much as the other man. I love my people, and that's the reason I'm not leaving here. I dream like you do of seeing a better world. I really don't think the white folks are going to try anything. A lot of white folks is really scared of Black folks."

Land

Broader land ownership could have solved at least some of the community's problems. Despite employment shifts away from farming, both land ownership and the independence it brought remained crucial to the stability of the local Black community. The Delta country is some of the richest soil in America. But it still belonged to a few big owners like the Selfs. In the best areas, Blacks were long ago swindled and bullied out of land. One of Mr. Franklin's most vivid childhood memories was seeing a Black man lynched because he refused to sell his land to whites. In Quitman County, only 83 of 586 farms were Black-owned in 1969, and that number dropped to 55 only five years later.[9]

Harry Hentz described how hard it had been to get land. "Me and my father own a small farm, 40 acres," Harry explained. "We raise ten acres of cotton. We get about thirteen bales on the average each year. We hand-pick it and hand-chop it. We can't never get no cotton-picking machine. Most every year we make a good crop. We've had our own farm for sixteen years. We sharecropped all our lives until '61. Then we started paying for the farm. It was hard scuffling to pay for it. We finished paying in the year of '66. I never will forget that year.

"We raise corn, peas, watermelons, potatoes, tomatoes, okra. I enjoy it now. At times I wondered. But now my father retired, and me and my brother work. Most all my sisters and brothers done got up big and left home. They come by on vacation and give a helping hand.

"When we first got our farm it was nothing but wood. We cleared about eight acres with a crosscut saw and ax, and then we got a chain saw and done the rest. We moved off a big plantation near Lambert. Three of my brothers was big enough to work along with my father and four of my sisters. The boys cut wood, and my sisters piled the brush and burned it, and we took two mules and snaked them logs out and cut them up in stovewood blocks and sold to peoples to burn in wood heaters, and we burned some of it ourselves.

"For the first seven years, we plowed with mules. Many days we went without food. We had a big note we had to pay on each year. To pay that note we had to do without many things. Many times I went to school with wire tying the toes of my shoes up and cardboard in the soles to cover up the holes. We lived a mile out in the fields, so we had to leave our truck parked in the gravel a mile away when it rained. I think it was worth it."

Junior Mayes told me he needed a second job to supplement the income from his farm. "I stayed in St. Louis for six month, but that place too rough for me. But then, I don't like the city no ways. Farming is all right. It's just knowing the right thing to plant. Any way you look at it, it's a gamble. Like this year, dry weather burnt up half our cotton. We just try to keep the other man's hand out of our pocket—stay out of debt. That's how they want you. I have one brother and one sister there with me and my mother. I have one child with me and my mother and the other one with her mother up in Chicago. I don't enjoy farming. It's just the only thing I can do. But then, I likes it. My father done it before me. But then, you have to put up with it whether you likes it or don't.

"I worked at the oil mill, but I been laid off ever since the first of the year. When I was laid off, twenty-nine other mens was laid off with me. They lay off thirty or forty every time they lay off. They moved the cottonseed oil mill to Arkansas, but the soybean oil is still here. I was up in Memphis, and a cop stopped me and said, 'Boy, where you from?'

"I said, 'Marks, Mississippi.'

"He said, 'Boy, ain't that where Mr. Self from?'

"I said, 'He is.'

"He said, 'Don't he own about everything around there?'

"I said, 'He don't own me.'

"And he said, 'Boy, how come he don't own you?'

"I say, 'I own my own self.' I always wonder why the white people hate Black people. The way I feel about it, one color ain't no more than the other. The younger white people, half of them don't care about color, though enough of them do."

Owning rather than tenanting land could have provided greater independence and self-sufficiency for many Marks families. But agricultural policies kept too many in debt. The fact that a few wealthy families owned most of the land meant those policies had been set for them, not for Harry Hentz and Junior Mayes and certainly not for the Black farm workers who still were the largest group of employees in the county.

Owning land is also about power. In the Delta, land has always been the source of social and political power. In Washington, the Delta was represented from the 1940s to the 1970s by Jamie Whitten, who owned Rabbit Ridge Plantation in Tallahatchie County, next door to Quitman. While he was in office, planters mechanized under policies he helped set. That pushed Blacks and poor whites off the land and into northern cities. For those left behind there has been a long, weary waiting for a job or the chance to use their talents, a wild scrambling for the benefits of inadequate government programs.

There had once been an alternative land policy tried in Holmes County, Mississippi. During the Great Depression, the government bought several bankrupt Holmes plantations and sold them to the sharecroppers on easy terms. This project was not tried elsewhere.[10] By contrast, in Quitman County the Selfs bought the bankrupted plantations.

Land ownership made the difference in what Black people gained from the civil rights movement. In Holmes, the many Black farm owners couldn't be intimidated by the threat of being kicked off the plantation. If anyone was arrested, there was land to put up for bonds. Black farmers donated land and money for a handsome community center. So, after the Voting Rights Act of 1965, people there rapidly registered to vote and built strong local organizations. In 1967, Holmes elected Robert G. Clark, the first Black member of the state legislature since the 1890s. By 1975, a number of local officials there were Black. In Quitman, where so few Black people owned land, the movement had a difficult time. Until 1975, there were no Black officials, and that year only one was elected.

Gilbert Hamer talked with me in 1975 about the importance of land reform. "You won't see a white man driving a tractor. The whites won't work for so little, fifteen dollars for a fourteen-hour day. Talk about the Black man lazy, that the only one working. It's a whole lot better than it used to be, 100 percent better. But it's still hard yet. You go out on them plantations, ask people how they living, and they can tell you a lot, if they ain't scared somebody will tell the Man. It's still a lot of people not getting enough food. That what make so much sickness. If the government would divide this land up, I know plenty of people getting welfare who would move out there and work the land. I tell you what keeps it hard; it's the older-type white people. The younger white people growed up with colored, they ain't like that. The younger people don't want it the old way, white neither colored."

Mr. and Mrs. Dean agreed. "All the peoples in New York and Chicago out of a job and prices so high," said Elnora. "For my part, I bets on this ground. That's what I raised all my children with. We never got rich, but we could make a living. I raised all my children in the field."[11]

"You know what they could do, Joe," Alec suggested, "Put all the land back in circulation and let the peoples go back to work farming. I'd go back to work if I could, raise corn, chicken, hog, everything else. Let the peoples raise they own food and get off welfare."

"You know the government could do it if they wanted to," Elnora put in. "You let the peoples work the land like they used to, they won't need welfare."

Alec nodded. "I think the world is looking for something to do. They looking for it to change one way or another, white and colored."

CHAPTER 10

"The Home House"

When I was a civil rights worker, sometimes on my down days I would wonder what good the whole thing was, since most likely all the young people would move away. But I saw when I visited Marks in the 1970s and 1980s that these small communities were surviving and continuing to play an important role in Black life. Such places remained focal points for Black extended families throughout the North.

Family and Community

Large families like the Franklins continued to work as a unit even when they were widely scattered. Mr. Franklin's sister in Cleveland, Ohio, and his uncles on farms in Mississippi's hill country took in some of his children and helped them find work. In turn Mr. Franklin took in one of his in-laws' nieces when the family was in financial trouble. This remains common even today, far more than among white middle-class people. For most of the people in this book, like Mr. Franklin, Mr. Dean, Mrs. Evans, and Mrs. Collins, their families must be understood as several households pulling together.

When I was in Marks in 1983, a young man pointed out his house to me, but he said that his grandmother's house was his "*home* house"—that is, the headquarters of his extended family. This pattern is very old, as Mr. Franklin's son Hull says. "Black people—they say they didn't bring nothing over from Africa because they didn't have it written down on tablets, but they had it in their mind. Like that family thing. Let's say we're brothers. Well, if I die, I know you'll raise my kids. All African people are like that. Like my uncles and my father and all of our family, we stick together."

Although both Black and white poor families were often large, many Black families consisted not just of mother, father and children. Grandparents, aunts, uncles, and cousins were helping each other out or raising each other's children. In this sense, almost all of the Black community of Marks belonged to a few large extended families.

In and around Marks are pieces of land these families own, the graves of ancestors, and churches where family weddings and funerals take place. Some people working in the North bought land in Marks, which relatives then tended. Those who stayed behind were often the strong individuals who kept the extended family together. They took the phone calls from relatives in the North who fell on difficult times or were simply lonely or disliked city life. There was always space for them if they returned to the old family center, like during the 1970s recession when many children were sent south to stay with grandparents, aunts, and uncles. One sixteen-year-old girl living with her parents up north gave her baby to her older sister to raise. Children were sometimes adopted from needy friends who were not related.

Partly this was because of the difficulty of finding employment or apartment space in the North, but partly it was because the parents wanted to get the children away from urban violence. I was told about this in 1975 by thirteen-year-old Sonny and his younger brother Charles, who were playing hopscotch with other Black children on a bumpy side street in Marks. Unlike in big cities, people in the Black part of Marks had little worry about getting run over except on the four-lane road that leads to Lambert. They often walked or played in the middle of the street. Sonny explained, "My daddy had a job up in Chicago, but he got sugar [diabetes]. He don't work up there now. He on unemployment. I like Chicago, but too many people get killed up there. We be around the corner when they get killed." He pointed to his younger brother Charles. "He say when he was in Chicago somebody sot a bomb behind the house." I asked if the bomb had killed anyone. "No," Charles replied. "No. It like to. My nephew got killed in Chicago."

I saw many different forms of informal adoption, from occasional support to living as a member of the family. In nearby Clarksdale, a widow's son had grown up and moved out. Left with extra food, she said she "hated to see anyone hungry." So a family that lived nearby sent their little boy to spend the day with her, and she fed him. In turn he fed the woman's chickens and ducks, solemnly and with an air of intense fascination.

Sometimes young Black people from Marks found city life untenable, and they too returned. Ruby Lee explained, "I found the world wasn't like what I thought it was. I come back from Detroit because I didn't like it there. Too much killing and robbing up there. When I first got there I couldn't get a job. It was a year and two months before I could get a job. I locked up in my room and I stayed locked up except when I was at work. I wouldn't even be looking out the window. I be too scared somebody be shooting up at me or knock my head off with a rock. I didn't know nobody's name on the street where I stayed. I seen my relatives, but I lived a long way from them.

"I be afraid these people gonna rob me 'cause, see, these old dope addicts stay in the place I lived, and they see when my check come, and they know that's when they gonna rob me. I be scared to watch the news. I turned it off and listened to the music. I felt like I was in a prison. I feel much safer down here."

In all these families, every member pitched in. It was not unusual to see a five-year-old girl staggering along with a baby over her shoulder. Until advanced old age, any Black inhabitant of Marks was likely to be called on to take care of children of the extended family.

The extended family also continued to provide a place where the elderly and those with disabilities or mental illness could live in a safe environment and enjoy friendship and encouragement. In the 1960s, I saw children intellectually compromised because of lack of adequate food. These children were young adults by the 1970s when I returned. In Marks they could be supervised, attain self-respect, and enjoy friendly relationships. Mentally ill people led happier lives than they could in institutions and were safer than on city streets. I knew of only two elderly Black people in Marks who were in nursing homes in 1976. One was in a nursing home where his daughter worked. The other had refused to let friends and neighbors take care of her after she became feeble.

Mrs. Annie Belle Stuart described the way most people in Marks took care of older people. About a third of the Black elderly received public aid (although more than 90 percent lived in poverty). Those that received welfare used it to pay to remain in their homes; the rest relied on community generosity. "I could get $110 from the government for taking care of my cousin that stay here with me," Mrs. Stuart said. "They paid me for taking care of my uncle. And that old lady that stay across the street—have to go over and take care of every move she make, and I don't get nothing for that." Relatives and neighbors were always sending food or hauling firewood for these people. Young people would pay them a few dollars a month to rent a room and then take care of them if they were sick or had an accident.

Many elderly people stayed active working and in community affairs longer than those in white communities. Alec Dean argued that older people could actually make their way easier than younger people. "The older man know what he doing more than the young man, even if the young man go to school for it. I don't catch no steady work now, just piecework. I make twenty-five bucks a day if I can get in about ten hours. I'm digging holes to put in light posts at the hospital at Senatobia and concreting around. I worked for the tree nursery man, and when I worked for him I had a good influence to him. And when he see an opening for a job, he point it out to me. But it ain't no jobs here.

"You know, a older man can get a job here quicker than a young man. 'Course, I was raised up for working from a kid. I don't never go to the doctor. I just get my teeths pulled. I ain't got but three teeths left, and I'm getting them pulled next week. I'm picking up weight. I'm thirty-four around the waist.

"I had a hard way to pay for this house, and a easy one. Easy because I could pay for it in whatever way I wanted to. I didn't have no worry about it. Now I got the house paid for, I'm happy as a lark, and I'm *living*."

In 1977 a Black promoter opened an old folks' home. A similar home had opened in neighboring Tallahatchie County, but apparently only a few older Black men and women moved in. Many in Marks were skeptical. The year before, ninety-one-year-old Jack Brown had explained to me, "We had several people from here go in them old folks' places up north, but they died—soon died." J. D. Powells expressed the general attitude at that time. "It's just the white folks mostly that send their old folks to the old folks' home. With us it's a tradition that when people get old, they move in with their relatives. I know of Black folks from here that moved into the old folks' home up north, and didn't none of them last but two months. They don't last long in them places.

"The first time I ever seed a old folks' home was up in Chicago, and it really upsetted me because I wasn't used to that kind of thing. Peoples told me, 'I'm going to see my uncle or my aunt,' and I asked where, and they said, 'The old folks' home.' And I aksed how could they let a member of their family go in a place like that. I'd take them in no matter how little space I had left.

"You remember Mrs. Red, the old lady that lived with us. We took her in even though she had other kinfolks in this town. It's a lot of old folks here staying with people that ain't no kin to them. They just took them in. It's a Black guy that's organizing the old folks' home. I think he just did it as a loophole to get federal funds. I don't see a need for it."

People in Marks were strongly committed to maintaining their extended family structures. In one case an older couple died. Their last three children living in the area moved north. Another of their sons moved back to manage the small pieces of family land and see that the parents' graves were cared for.

Many families continued their tradition of family reunions. Memorial Day was a major time for members of the extended family to come back and visit the old gravesites. One problem came up in this respect. When the Civil Rights Act was passed in 1964, Black people could be buried in previously all-white cemeteries. Before that, many had been buried in plots provided by planters. After 1964, some planters told Black families to rebury their dead in the formerly all-white cemeteries, which some of them couldn't afford. In those cases, planters simply removed the headstones, plowed the gravesites and planted crops. Tractors rolled over the grave of Mr. Franklin's mother. Some local Black ministers protested, but, as was so often the case, it was no use. The Black cemetery on the plantation had been simply a gift from the landowner. It had never been formalized as a transfer of land, so the family who owned the plantation could just take back the land when they wanted to. This has been going on since slavery times. I knew a Black minister in Holly Springs, Mississippi, who looked around and found a number of old Black cemeteries and cleaned them off and left flowers there.

The Fourth of July was another time for reunions of extended families to gather. That is when the Franklins have their family reunion. That weekend in 1975 I was at Alec Dean's family reunion. His children showed up from their homes in Mississippi, Indiana, Arkansas, Iowa, Michigan, and Tennessee. Mr. Dean's three-month-old grandson, who had been kept for a month by an aunt in Michigan, was returned to his mother who had come down from Iowa.

At this reunion, Mr. Dean told me about the Delta Burial Association he and many others in Marks belonged to. It worked like an insurance company; members paid a small amount per person on a regular basis, and the association provided the money needed for a funeral and burial. It was a communal and social institution as well, ensuring that members and their families would be taken care of regardless of their circumstances. "I works at the Burial Association sometimes," Mr. Dean said. "We used to keep some whiskey there, and when we finished embalming and washing a body, we'd lock the door and drink it, but we don't do it no more. The boss of the Burial Association, he a Black man. He got him a plantation. He give me a whole house from his plantation. I hauled it here into town and fixed my house with it.

"I pays $5 to the Burial Association for my children and the grandchildren you see here and $3.35 for myself and $6.10 for some of the granddaughters. I ain't got all fifty grandchildren down on that policy. Them that's got daddies supporting them got they own policies. I got nine of my children living and eleven dead. My youngest about twenty-seven years old. I been married fifty-five year."

Most Black extended families want to give the largest and best funerals for their members. Even the poorest Black people in Marks, if they were well-known and liked, had large crowds at their funerals. This is one reason the owner of a funeral home or head of a Burial Association was such a powerful man in the Black community. James Wilson Sr., who did so much work with community development organizations in Marks, gained much of his influence because for a while he was the head of the Burial Association. I was barely aware of him while I worked in Marks, yet he made our work possible from his important but quiet and unassuming position. I did know his son, James Wilson Jr., whose half-brother J. D. Powells had introduced me to people around Marks. But I now realize that it was James Wilson Sr. and some others who kept us able to use the Masonic Hall despite the fact that the conservative Black leader Percy Nelson was a prominent Mason. It was probably his influence and that of a few others that kept us from getting in much more severe trouble than we did when Reverend Carter was going to the law about his broken toilet. And it was also James Wilson Sr. who both organized the Quitman County Head Start program and later managed Reverend McCloud's removal from the program when he failed to train and hire poor mothers to teach there.

Modernization

In 1977, construction began on a hospital in the Black section of Marks, which brought about much of what Ernestine Evans had hoped for. Previously, there had been one very inadequate clinic where most poor Black people went. Mrs. Evans had described the conditions there: "It's a sin the way babies are delivered here. The government is paying the doctor, and he don't take no trouble. I nearly lost my daughter there when she had her baby. There were six women there, and they never give them no kind of nothing to help them no way. I had to help bring the baby to the world. I didn't see no doctor around, just this colored woman I guess they have for a nurse, asleep. The doctor be's at home. He don't care about colored people. Government doctor, if he at home, he still get his pay. Then on top of that he still charges you. So I brought my daughter home. We don't have doctors at night, period, and don't have enough in the daytime." But, as Mrs. Brown had already told me, there were fewer midwives around to help women deliver at home. The new hospital, which provided inexpensive medical care to people in poverty, was a necessity.

When the hospital opened in 1977, Black people praised the efficiency and devoted care of its nurses, both Black and white, although it was small and lacked the equipment or services of big city hospitals. People had to go to Memphis for that. To help with the new hospital, a Black doctor moved to Marks, the first Black doctor in the history of Quitman County. The Mes Zenith Club, an organization of Marks's more well-to-do and better-educated Black women, let the doctor use their clubhouse for an office.

Despite the new hospital, health remained a major problem for many Marks residents. Most Black people there still relied on pork and cornbread and beans cooked in pork fat. This is a cheap, high-energy diet for people doing heavy labor in the fields. Because fewer people were now doing such work, the rate of high blood pressure in the Black community was twice that of whites. And instead of urging a better diet, TV commercials pushed children to eat sugary junk foods. As one person told me, "The average children now don't like this old-time cornbread. They rather have cookies and Cheetos."

Modernization had other negative effects, including a decline in rural folk culture. When I visited Mrs. Evans in 1975, two of her daughters were discussing astrology they had read about in magazines. They were curious to know what my sign was, but they said they had no idea about the kind of astrology well known among the farm people of the South—an astrology that Mr. Jessie was practicing only a few blocks away. He was giving a neighbor advice on when to castrate a hog. "The almanac, it tell you about such as birthdays," he explained. "Peoples can understand it a lot better than they can the calendar. I know I can use it a lot better. I still can read the signs: Bull Sign, Fish Sign, Twin Boy Sign, Balance Sign, Ram Sign, and all. It tell you what day to do work on. You cut a hog when the sign in the feet. Today the sign in the knee. Then tomorrow the sign in the feet. Then it's in the head all over again." Now such folk astrology for planting and tending animals is declining, partly because so many people have had to move off the land.

Mr. Jessie had been overseeing the butchering of a hog, and this provided some opportunities to pass on rural practices to a new generation. They hung the hog up by the legs, and the children brought boiling water to soften the hog's hair so it could be scraped off. One of the adults joked, "The one that eat the morest meat eat the morest hair—and God bless them!" The older people were glad to have the children there helping. This was one thing the adults could pass on that they could never get from school or TV.

Around the end of the butchering, a woman stretched open one end of the hog's chitlins—the large intestines—and started pouring boiling water in to wash the dung out. A boy told her he couldn't eat those chitlins because the whole thing looked so dirty. He said he would rather have chitlins from a store because he thought they would be cleaner. The woman answered, "Chitlins in a store got stuff left in them. With these, I know they clean because I cleaned them myself."

The use of herbs for medicine had also declined, Mrs. Elnora Dean told me. Her mother-in-law was an herbal healer. "Ain't no people round here that use herbs like the old people use to. Them old people all dead, and this younger race don't believe them herbs any good. This medicine you get on Medicare ain't no good. You follow the direction on the bottle, and it make you crazy. I stopped taking mine. I know several others say the same thing, Four of us give our medicine back to the doctor."

One change in the older ways I was glad to see was the decline of hair straightening. I remember in the 1960s when small children would reach up and touch my hair and say sadly, "You got that good hair, and I got this bad old nappy hair." I saw women getting their daughters ready for school heating the iron straightening comb on the stove. Then they would comb Dixie Peach pomade, a kind of perfumed Vaseline, through their daughters' hair. Once I told a minister I didn't like the idea of hair straightening. He said, "The Bible say that a woman's hair is her glory. Ain't we got a right to as good hair as the white folks?"

By the 1970s, most Black youth of Marks were wearing their hair natural. Many, both men and women, tied it in long braids all over their scalp as at one time only pre-school girls did. When I first went to Marks, most Black women wore bandanas around their heads like a turban. In 1975, I saw this style only among older women. Although bandana wearing is probably of African origin, to young people it was apparently a reminder of slavery.

Some cultural and community practices remained. The Black community of Marks still had very little crime because it would be difficult to burglarize a house without being spotted. Once I saw two Black men start a drunken brawl in the middle of the street. Immediately neighbors stepped off their front porches to separate the two men rather than call the police. Teenage Black girls walked around alone on errands for their parents at midnight, something that would have been much too dangerous for them in many northern urban neighborhoods.

One tradition that surely dates back to Africa and survived strongly (and I suspect still does today) was that children were taught to dance before they could walk. It was very common to see a young woman with her baby brother or sister or her own child in her arms and the radio turned up, dancing around holding the baby's hand like a dance partner. When the baby could barely stand up, the young mother or older sister helped the child stay afoot on the floor, and they danced through the long afternoon to the radio music. Preschool children gathered in circles and chanted verses as each child took a turn in the center of the circle doing the fanciest dance steps he or she could.

If I can see any common theme in Black culture, it is the loose-jointed but highly coordinated movement the child learns in the center of the ring play. It can be felt in Black music and Black community life from the way the scattered households of the extended family work together to the preacher with his circuit of independent congregations. White people have eagerly adopted the rhythms of Black music. They should learn even more the combination of flexibility and close coordination of independent democratic centers that runs along with the music through so much of Black life.

Change Agents and the Church

Besides the extended family, the other major force in the lives of the Black people of Marks has long been the church. But I wondered about its future. Most Black ministers in Quitman County were older. Many religious people stayed at home on Sunday and listened to preachers on the radio. In 1975, one devout young man told me, "These churches here in Marks getting too dim. The people won't hardly come. These kids go around the streets drinking liquor; it ain't no good. They should be in church. It learn the young kids to be nice to the older people, not get around their mama and daddy and cuss them out like some of these young mens does."

Many people "professed religion"—that is, they had had a conversion experience—but they usually didn't go to church. That was true of the Franklin brothers and Mrs. Henrietta Franklin. Ministers who didn't take part in the civil rights struggle were discredited among many people. Jessie Franklin explained, "Back in the civil rights movement, wouldn't but a few stand up. These old preachers wouldn't go up to Washington. The white man ask him why he ain't back preaching. He just want to tell all them chickens in the church house what God say and take up money. The preacher got chicken to eat, and the sisters rides him up and down the road, but he ain't doing no good. He done fool the people, and the white man done fool him."

Yet the church is where large numbers of Black people learned the basics of democracy and leadership. For a long time it was the only place where African Americans could participate in anything like civic affairs. In *Freedom Summer*, white SNCC volunteer Sally Belfrage noted her surprise that Black activists knew about parliamentary procedure at the MFDP convention of 1964, even though they had not been allowed to vote. She would not have been so surprised if she had seen the workings of the church.[1]

A Black church in rural Mississippi takes a great deal of members' time in meetings of all kinds. As poor as the people are, they put a lot of their money into the church and closely monitor how it is spent. In 1964 I saw a congregation of twenty-nine of the most ragged poor Black people I had ever seen in Panola County, Mississippi, raise eighty-seven dollars for a special offering, which would be hundreds of dollars today. The church was often one of three or four the minister visited, and some Sundays he might not be there at all, so leadership fell very heavily on lay people, including women and young people. At one time some congregations had a female leader, called a mother, who was often the head of the largest extended family in the area.

The church has also been important because it has given rise to many other community-minded organizations. For example, most churches have ushers, usually women, who make sure people overcome with emotion don't hurt themselves. These ushers are organized. Annie Belle Stuart described it to me in 1975. "The Swan Lake Usher Union is the association of the ushers in a lot of the area. I just got the Valley Queen and New Paradise churches in this town. I'm the director. We use the $1,000 to give scholarships to childrens every year. The association give scholarships to from thirty to forty children around here a year. The scholarship is for one to two years. You know, two years is a heap when you ain't got no money to go to college in no way. And, you know, none of them childrens is grateful enough to send back $10 to help the next child with his scholarship. And some won't go to school far enough to go to college—jump out of the seventh and eighth grade. I had three adopted children never made it to the ninth grade.

"The Swan Lake Association been giving the scholarships since 1948 when I become the chairman.[2] We going to have [Alabama] Governor [George] Wallace speak to the association. He's all right down my alley. I don't know if I would vote for him for president. I don't like none of them candidates too much." Several neighbor women were standing around as Mrs. Stuart said she approved of Governor Wallace. They told Mrs. Stuart they strongly disagreed with her.

In the early 1970s, a Marks woman persuaded a Nation of Islam minister to hold services in her house. She was hoping the Nation would set up a co-operative farm or business in Quitman County as they had elsewhere. But the minister told her that the Nation of Islam didn't have enough money to do that. Several local Black men offered to buy a lot with a building on it for the Nation to use. They explained they would keep control and responsibility for the property, as was the democratic pattern of their own churches. The minister insisted any property bought for his use would have to be turned over to the Nation of Islam. The local men refused, and the minister left Marks.

Instead, in 1977, Mrs. Clara Rucker, William Redd, and Rev. Ezra Towner, who had been leader of the local NAACP, set up the Quitman County Development Organization (QCDO). "We saw ourselves as a change agent after the civil rights movement took place," Robert Jackson told Richard Arvedon, "and we were in place to make sure some of the changes became part of the permanent fabric of this community."[3]

The community-based QCDO would have been impossible without the sacrifices so many Black people had made for the civil rights movement. When Black citizens didn't have the vote and the white leadership had absolute power over them, a schoolteacher like Mrs. Rucker would never have dared to launch such an ambitious project in the Black community. Her teaching job would have been too vulnerable.

Rev. Carl Brown, pastor of Valley Queen Church, one of the largest Black churches in Marks, became head of the QCDO. Reverend Brown was born in Marks, moved to Los Angeles in the 1950s, and later returned. He became universally popular. "If you talk to him, you'll be meeting a good man," Mrs. Sarah Ward told me. She and her husband, the late Rev. G. W. Ward, had taken me into their home when I first came to Marks.

The QCDO was set up after years of frustration in getting government benefits like affordable housing, jobs, day care, and help with education. It offered a variety of social services and youth programs, helped develop new housing, and offered microfinancing for new businesses. It had been set up thanks to the skills of those church people. I worried that those skills could be lost if church membership continued to decline.

Integrating Schools—and People

Before I knew of the QCDO, my main hopes for the Black community of Marks were based on the changes that integrated schools had made. Older people like Beatrice Humphreys could already see some of it in 1975. "When they integrated the school, the Black kids and the white kids was chunking at one another, but I just said it was natural for kids to fight. After two years, they stopped fighting. My grandchildren go to school with the white kids now, and they get along just fine with them."

Mrs. Weathersby agreed. "It's a beautiful sight to go across town and see the Black childrens and the white childrens walking the streets playing with each other, just having a ball. The old folks kind of stare at them, but the kids enjoy each other. If we let these childrens alone, they going to make it. When they first integrate the school, you go by the schoolyard, and you see the Black kids over in a corner all by themselves, but now you see them all mixed up, running and playing together. When school was going on, my boy had a white friend. Some days at school they didn't like what was for lunch, and they'd come over to my house and eat."

As in much of the South, most white students from better-off homes attended the private all-white Delta Academy. But at the public school, Black and white students studied under teachers of both races. Their high school literature textbook had selections from Black writers like Martin Luther King, Frederick Douglass, Lorraine Hansberry, Ralph Ellison, and Langston Hughes.

Jimmie Lee Franklin described the integrated public school from a student perspective. "You don't find too much football talent going to the private school," he explained. "They ain't got much to choose from. They got too few kids coming there. Public school, they got some troops, about eight hundred. It's really up there. Maybe a fourth is white. All the kids at school, whites and Blacks, they get along pretty good.

"In the public school, you got thousands of attitudes. You got people coming from all different points of view. On a team of forty people, you got forty different attitudes. At the private school, they all supposed to believe the same thing, that hating people. But at the public school, you got all kinds, kids from poor families, some kids from better-off families. If we have a white boy on our team, it don't matter if he good. If he go over to Delta Academy, the private school, he be the star of the whole school. They get at the white boy behind our back. They make him offers. They give him a scholarship or something if he go over there.

"We got about five white football players that been on our team for about three years. All of them good. All we like brothers together. We ain't got nothing against each other. The white players wouldn't leave our school for nothing. They hate the private school like a dog. We got one we lost to the private school, but he come back 'cause he didn't like the school. We got more white going to our school now than we did. We had a case of a white boy that played basketball in junior high. Then he went to the private school. He was a star over there, and he come back to public school, and he couldn't even make second string in basketball. That show how much more competition they got in public school."

The vast majority of those students, both white and Black, were graduating, a dramatic change from pre-movement days. In fact, as Hull Franklin pointed out to me, "All of us that went to Marks High School for more than two years went on to college or graduate school." Considering the low level of education of most Black Marks residents just a decade before, this was an incredible triumph.

It didn't happen immediately. Of the sixteen Black students who entered the previously all-white school in 1966, all but Presley and Melvin Franklin either returned to the Black school or failed out. Willie Thompson told me most of the twenty-five or thirty Black children in his grade that entered the white school together faced a great deal of harassment as well. That had changed by 1972 when Hull and his class graduated. Among that group at least one became a PhD, one a lawyer, and one an assistant school superintendent. One became a state legislator and another a Mississippi Supreme Court justice. I told Hull recently that Robert Maniece growing up on Cotton Street and becoming a PhD was as remarkable to me as the United States having a Black president.

Integration not only improved the lives of Black young people in Marks, it also changed Marks. Several young people talked to me about it. Hull went to St. Olaf College in Minnesota on a scholarship. When he came home on a visit in 1976, he reflected on the changes he saw in Marks. "The white kids seventeen and younger, they don't know about race prejudice like it was. I can attribute that to three reasons. First, Daddy took us and put us in school over there on the white side, and they saw that all Black people wasn't like they thought, a big threat, you know—that we're human too.

"Then the new sheriff in here has done something about it. Black people are getting more involved in voting questions, so white people have to get involved with the Black man if they want that office. With the school integrated, more poor whites are having to intermix with Black kids. But none of the rich whites are sending their kids to public schools. The most highly radical people who opposed the Black man's involvement in politics were the poor whites in this county. The most highly radical for segregation in this county were the Black so-called teacher men. Because I had one myself tell us in the sixth grade that he didn't want us going to school over there with the whites. The big thing that helped Black people out all over the United States was Africa. The government had to do better for Black people if they wanted to get that oil from Africa."

Not all the change he saw was good. "I've only been back in the South for two months, so I haven't gotten the hang of things yet. I don't see so much change. People are still as illiterate as they ever were. Of all the Blacks I have seen graduate from Quitman County High School, I have never seen one that would come back here and organize something for their people. They just hang around here, or they go to Chicago, always thinking there's a better place somewhere else. They could make a good place here, but it would take time and work. I've seen lots of Black people in college who had all kind of knowledge about math and chemistry and stuff, but they didn't know about people.

"I get sick when I see so many Black people leave this area and never come back. Most of the smart ones have left. The young people graduating from high school don't know about the civil rights era. The civil rights era got rid of a lot of old, slavery-time ideas about Black people, that's what it did. I'd say there is less racist ideas in the South than in the North. Blacks and whites down here, we have to know each other. We're involved in each other's lives. I'll say one thing, as much trouble as I had from a few kids when I was in the white high school here, I never heard sick jokes like at college up North, like, 'Have you used too much suntan oil?' I majored in social studies teaching. Anthropology and sociology—I wasn't interested in that in college. I know if I was to take courses in sociology, I could tell them things they didn't know. The students used to come around and ask me things like is this or that so. They have this old stereotype of the South like every white person has a whip and every Black person is begging, 'Don't whip me no more!' And I have to tell them it's not that way. Like the South is not the best place in the world and all, but . . . I want to take a cotton stalk to college to remind me when I don't want to pick up a book. I had a cotton sack on my back. I could pick 200 pounds of cotton in a day, and 200 pounds of cotton ain't easily got. I'd pick in November when it be cold."

Harry Hentz had similar thoughts about changes in the South. "My father wouldn't let me come in contact with civil rights. I wanted to, but I was sort of young. My older brother went to Washington, D.C., and got put in jail when they refused to leave Resurrection City." His first exposure to another way of thinking was the armed forces. "I was green when I went to San Diego in the marines. I felt free. I didn't have to say 'yes, sir' and 'no, sir' when I went to buy gasoline, just 'yeah' and 'no.' I got away from being so brainwashed. It was like paradise.

"Once you get away and learn—Marks, Mississippi, it's all right. I met brothers in the service, and I learned how to face the problem, and I can do all right here. I can handle it. I don't never have to say, "Yes, sir, Mr. Jimmy." Young people these days, they opened up, the majority of these young whites. All this old slavery-time stuff, they ain't for it. I got some of the coolest white friends you could ever meet, right here in Marks.

"About two weeks ago, we was out in the park—four of us Black brothers with six white dudes, and we talked about getting together a soul group and a hard rock group to play on Saturday evenings and everybody kick back in the park. So Marks is getting better and better every day. The older generation is dying off, and the younger generation is overtaking the older one."

There were still dangerous flash points. The breakdown in racial barriers caused an increase in interracial boy-girl contacts, although this remained rare. These incidents might be harmless from the viewpoint of young people of both races, but they still outraged many older whites, and the police occasionally got called in.

"What it is now, white folks seem to be going to school with Blacks," Reverend Allen told me in 1975. "I don't know what they think, but when a white gal have anything to do with a Negro, they want to blame him. It's always on the Negro every time. And the thing that's so hurty is you can see more white babies than a little in Negroes' rooms and nothing said about it. If it is, it's kind of quiet. But it better not be the other way around. And all that make Jack a dull boy. That's the main reason they don't like the Negroes going to their school is on account of that white gal. That's one of the main things."

In one such incident Reverend Malone described to me, a Black high school boy called a white girl to ask about their schoolwork. He supposedly asked about a date, and her father overheard on the extension and called the police and had him arrested, probably on a charge of using insulting language on the telephone, which is a crime in Mississippi. When the youth was in jail, the girl's father somehow got into his cell and beat him up.

Reverend Malone and other NAACP leaders told the boy's father they would investigate whether the jailer deliberately let the girl's father into the cell. If this was so, they said, the boy's father could sue the sheriff's department. Reverend Malone found out the jailer had been in another part of the jail and left the cell open since the boy couldn't run away because an armed deputy was downstairs. The jailer had returned to find the girl's father there and chased him away. Reverend Malone was satisfied. Until a few years before, such an incident might have caused a lynching, and few Blacks would have been willing or able to investigate.

Black and White Together?

This relatively smooth process of social integration could only have happened because the white young people of Quitman had gone through changes of their own. In 1969, one of the staff of *Kudzu*, an underground paper in Jackson, Mississippi, was a young white man from Marks. He wrote me, "Young Marksists are taking part in a nation-wide youth culture. . . . Power to joy!"

One day in 1975, I was sitting with a Black woman in Marks on her porch. Two white youths came by, hitching to Lambert. They didn't have any luck, so they asked to sit on the porch out of the sun for a while. They told me about low-income white life in Quitman, which had many similarities to Black life. I was struck by how much the civil rights agenda spoke to poor whites' concerns and hoped a broader movement of Black and white poor people could tackle these social and economic problems together, just as Martin Luther King had called for with the Poor People's Campaign.

Danny Robinson, who did most of the talking, went to an integrated night class to get his GED. Compulsory schooling had been abolished in Mississippi in 1955 to avoid school integration. There was seldom pressure to keep poor children in school. Many of them, both Black and white, dropped out and remained illiterate or nearly so. Only after Governor Cliff Finch was elected in 1975, thanks to Black votes and some poor whites like Danny's mother, did compulsory schooling laws return.

"I got to the sixth grade and quit," Danny told me. "Me and the principal didn't get along. I didn't really care about school. I could figure out anything really important. Like if someone was to cheat me out of money, I know how much money I'm supposed to get out of it. I'm a traveling man. In Lambert everybody knows everybody, and it's a busybody town. That's what I don't like about it.

"I ran away to Tuscaloosa, Alabama, just getting away from home. Me and this boy got stopped in Tuscaloosa and put in jail, and my brother come after me. He was raising all kinds of sand. The next day the principal come in and said, 'I'm gonna suspend you for four days.' So I just said, 'I ain't gonna go.' I got to the sixth grade.

"My brother knows this guy, and he's helping me pass the twelfth-grade test and get in the army. You get shipped to different places in the army. You never know where you're gonna be from one day to the next. I want to go in the army 'cause there's gonna be a war soon. People says there ain't, but the world's gotta end sometime. If you read the Bible, the Bible don't tell you no lie. I was brought up on it, so I know the world's coming to a end."

"I'm thinking of going back to school," sixteen-year-old Terry volunteered. "I quit the sixth grade. I don't like it. I don't like the principal the way he does. He gets on the kids too much for nothing." I asked him if there were many young people his age in sixth grade.

Danny jumped in. "Man, there's some twenty years old!"

"I want to be in the army," Danny continued, "especially so I might get to go to Mexico and learn Spanish, learn to speak them pretty words.

"The biggest part of the fields I've worked in is stomping trailers. You know, when a cotton picker is filled up and unloads in a truck, I stomp down the cotton, pack it down so they can put a little more cotton in. It ain't hard work. They pay $1.60 an hour.

"Mama used to get food stamps till I started to work. Then they come up with this junk, 'If he don't stop working, we're gonna cut you off.' She said, 'I ain't gonna stop him.' So they cut us off. I'm the onliest one left. I had nine brothers and four sisters, but they're all grown up and married."

Terry joined in again. "School was pretty easy, but I didn't like it. Daddy found a pretty good job up in Chicago. We lived up there for nine months, but people too mean up there. That's why we left. Whatever I know, I learned myself. I can't read that good. I don't know enough, that's why I'm going back."

"I went to school more than he did," Danny observed, nodding toward Terry. "When I moved down there to Lambert, he wasn't really going that much, and I talked him into going. We'd sit there and copy off each other.

"My brother has been to Vietnam. He was shot in the leg, and his buddy right close to him was shot right between the eyes. After my brother got out of the hospital they put him right back on the line. He won't even watch a war movie on TV. I can see why. All them people got shot. I can't see the use. If there was a war, though, I wouldn't be scared to fight. The sergeant, he's supposed to be your guardian, and when he says fight you got to, or they can shoot you.

"I went to night school in Marks about a month. That's where I got what reading I got. They paid good money, two dollars a night. I'd read more than I'd do anything else. When you had your head in a book, they wouldn't say nothing to you. I liked night school better than regular school. They wouldn't tell you to do nothing. They'd ask you. They don't put such authority to you.

"My father's dead. One thing different about my mama, me and her talks things over with each other. Like if we need money, my mother talks to me. Here's why I'm going in the army. On December 30, they're cutting us off everything, welfare and Daddy's Social Security. There's a new law, see, I'd be eighteen then. So I got to do something. I'm just the kind of person that talks to people. I don't care what color they are or nothing.

"I really like Governor Finch. Mama even voted for him. She liked the way he was talking. He was more serious than any of the others. We need to clean all the things out and start again. They bring up this old stuff about Watergate. They should just drop it. That president's already out. I think Ford had something to do with it. A lot of people here in Mississippi don't like Ford. They'll vote for whoever runs against him. All these presidents do is just sitting on their do-nothings."

The following year, Mississippi supported Jimmy Carter for president. Most of that vote was Black, but many were whites like Danny Robinson. I hoped that poor white young people like Danny could get together with Black young people, now that the walls of segregation were gone, not just for socializing but to create a new society in Quitman County.

EPILOGUE

"We Ain't Never Going Back to What We Was"

Even now I see hope.

Marks is still one of the poorest towns in the nation, within one of the poorest states in the nation. Unemployment remains too high, life expectancy too low. America's crumbling infrastructure is more visible here than in many other places. But Marks remains rich too—in its soil, in its people, in its possibilities. There are individuals and organizations still fighting to improve conditions there, although many more resources are needed. And race relations are vastly improved. When I spoke with her in 2015, Mrs. Phipps told me, "The white folks used to be nice at Christmas. Every day is Christmas here now. The white people is really nice." We spoke just after my coworker Richard Arvedon visited Marks. He found the same thing. "When I approached folks who had no clue about me, they looked me in the eye and spoke to me as if I were a person, not a white person, as they would have in the old days." Hull Franklin agreed. "No hate, no prejudice going on. People are one-on-one toward each other instead of a social thing." The movement brought Marks a long way. We need a new sort of movement to bring it to where it should be.

Economic Instability

In 1998, Hull Franklin, who had become assistant superintendent of schools in West Tallahatchie County, drove me to Sumner, the county seat. It is only about thirty miles from Marks. There was an eerie feeling—all the stores in Sumner were shuttered because their white owners had moved out. We drove back into Quitman County and went to Lambert. It was the same there—all the stores on the main street were closed. Almost all the white people in Lambert had moved away.

In Marks, about half the stores on Main Street had closed. The middle levels of white society who had owned the stores were gone. What were left were mostly chain stores. The rich whites were still in Marks; the Selfs had their mansion where they sometimes received U.S. Senator Trent Lott.[1] And some poor whites were still there. Further drops in both the Black and white population have continued. In 2021 Marks's population is 1,299, and, because so many whites left, the proportion who are Black has increased dramatically to just over three-quarters. County population trends are virtually identical.[2] The public schools had gone from about 75 percent Black in 1977 (by Jimmie Lee Franklin's estimate) to 95 percent in Hull's 1998 estimate. Today, in Quitman's single unified school district, 98 percent of the students are Black.[3]

Still, when Richard visited Marks in 2015, the economic scene was not as grim as during my visit seventeen years earlier. "Driving into Marks from Tunica on Highway 3," he told me, "you first drive through the town of Crenshaw. Crenshaw struck me as a rural version of the South Bronx in the 1970s. Decay and desolation. I feared that Marks would be the same. But once you follow the highway south to Sledge the houses and churches all begin to appear to be in good shape. Sledge to Lambert looks like a viable, if shabby, commercial district."

Robert Jackson, who grew up in Marks and is now a state senator, put it less kindly. The "downtown is dismal," he insisted, with a local bank owned by the Selfs since about 1910, a CPA firm, a casket shop, pizzeria, and senior citizens center—"that's basically it."

Despite its size, Marks is considered "urban"; only 4 percent of those employed work in agriculture. Farming is only slightly more important in the county as a whole. In 1990, farm workers were the largest category of county employees. Today agriculture and fishing account for 5 percent of county occupations.[4] Of those who do farm, the cost of crop production, on average, exceeded the value of those crops, and many still do not own the land they work on.[5]

During the agricultural crisis of the 1980s, several plantations in Quitman County went bankrupt. The Franklins were able to buy fifteen acres of the plantation where they had once been sharecroppers, paid for by their oldest son. But most of the land was snapped up by the bigger plantations. And for the Franklins and other small owners, given high oil prices and too few outside jobs to help make ends meet, the challenge of maintaining the family farm is now even greater than it was.

The civil rights movement had certainly opened new nonfarm opportunities for African Americans that would have been inconceivable in the early 1960s, including jobs in public service and law enforcement. There are even a few Black lawyers and doctors. But there are hardly any good employment options, particularly for those with limited education. This is one legacy of segregation: although education levels have improved dramatically since the 1960s, in Marks almost a quarter of all African American adults never completed high school. Only 9 percent have graduated from college. The cottonseed oil mill has been torn down, and there is very little manufacturing. The largest single employer is the school system.[6]

There have been two relatively new sources of jobs: gambling casinos and the nearby prisons, but they have proven unstable. In the 1980s, when the Reagan administration slashed federal funding for many programs, some states, including Mississippi, legalized gambling to help replace lost revenues. Black people in Marks found work at the casino in Tunica, about fifty miles away. Others worked at Lady Luck, near Clarksdale (now closed). Today perhaps eight casinos within long range of Marks provide employment for local people, although few of them are well paying.

There is also the prison farm near Lambert, a "step-down" facility for Parchman Penitentiary prisoners about to be released. It was relatively small and didn't hire Black people until after the movement. Then, in the 1980s, its mostly Black population exploded with the escalation of the War on Drugs, which became especially a war on crack cocaine and the African Americans who smoked it. Just over a half-hour drive from Marks, Parchman itself, notorious for its horrific treatment of prisoners, has also expanded.

At first these new opportunities meant good news for employment. In 1990, the Quitman County unemployment rate was about 6 percent. The poverty rate fell from earlier decades, and the Black county population halted its dramatic decline and stabilized at around six thousand people.[7] But economic downturns hurt the job market, and declines in state and local tax revenues meant the prisons also cut back on hiring. Casino jobs are particularly fragile, vulnerable to both competition and recessions. When nearby states legalized gambling, Mississippi's revenues fell. Because of this variability, unemployment rates in Marks (and Quitman County) rose and fell dramatically year by year. In 2019, Marks's unemployment rate approached 10 percent, and it was almost twice as high for African Americans.[8] Marks's Black poverty rate of 31 percent (11 percent for non-Hispanic whites) is substantially lower than what it was in the movement days.[9] But that is still a very high rate. Almost half of all children in Marks live in poverty, as do more than half of families headed by a single parent.[10] It just demonstrates how badly off Black people were before. "The community is fine," Hull insisted. "I don't see any major thing wrong with it except jobs." Robert Jackson agreed. "There are no jobs here in this county, that's for sure," he told Richard.

Because it is mostly the richest and the poorest whites who stayed in Quitman, poor whites are struggling with the same local economy. As Richard concluded, "So now it really isn't civil rights, it's human rights—jobs, economic opportunity." Hull nodded. "You said the heart of it. You give a man a job, and then we bring in more and help more and give back to the community." Now the struggle is about both racial and economic justice, and the civil rights strategies we used could provide the basis for new organizing efforts.

Housing and Health

When I visited Marks in 1998, I was struck by the great improvement in the appearance of the Black part of town since the 1970s. Following a flood in the early 1990s, the first Bush administration created (and the Clinton administration expanded) a program that trained local people to rebuild low-income housing. Most of the shacks and the poorly built houses from the 1960s programs had been fixed up by young people getting employment and learning carpentry at the same time. Others now live in trailers and mobile homes, but they are still better than those shacks.

As a result of the decline in the white population, many better-off Black families had moved into formerly all-white neighborhoods, and those from the poorest areas like the Cotton Street neighborhood moved into houses they left behind. After the death of William Franklin, his widow Henrietta moved with her son Hull and his wife Annette all the way from Cotton Street into a large two-story house that had belonged to Sheriff Harrison. For the first time, Mrs. Franklin had white neighbors.

Their Cotton Street house is empty, but the Franklins can't decide what to do with it. The house holds great emotional significance for them because it was built by Hull's grandfather, Elijah. And behind that house, in the former Freedom House and community center William Franklin built from boards salvaged from the countryside, lives the youngest of the Franklin children, Jimmie Lee.

By the 1990s, there was also a new area of well-built brick houses largely for senior citizens. This was the achievement of Mrs. Clara Rucker, who had by then retired from teaching. The old folks named the street Clara Rucker Circle. For those who can no longer live in their own homes, there is now a nursing home. Families still care for their elders but have accepted the benefits a nursing home can offer. Thanks to these changes I believe more of the elderly are better served than before. Today, Richard told me, there are no segregated neighborhoods in Marks.

The neighborhoods may be in better condition, but it is not clear that the residents in them are. Only a third of all Quitman County residents have private health insurance, and about 17 percent have no coverage at all.[11] In 2010, First Lady Michelle Obama addressed a statewide meeting in Jackson about the problem of food deserts in Delta areas like Quitman, with nourishing food difficult to obtain and junk food easy to find.[12] Much of the land still belongs to planters who raise staples like cotton and soybeans to be shipped out of state. Fresh fruits and vegetables often have to be trucked in from outside, which makes them expensive.

This began to shift in 2015, when the Delta Regional Mule Train Market and Museum opened. Senator Robert Jackson helped establish this regional market so local farmers who had been growing those goods for export could instead "grow produce that we can sell so people would have food in this food desert." This has been a great boon to the community. As Helen Godfrey-Smith, president of Shreveport Federal Credit Union said, "The people of Marks, Mississippi, . . . have hope, they've got faith, they've got trust—they can see whatever it is they have in their hands, and they can use what they have to make a great and mighty future for them and for their children and for their community."[13]

Nevertheless, nutritious food remains harder to get, and more expensive, than other alternatives. There are thirteen convenience stores or dollar stores in Quitman County that offer prepackaged or prepared food, as do a few gas stations, but only three grocery stores (one is in Marks). In nearby Lambert all the food stores have closed. There is also a McDonald's in Marks. The nationwide movement for a better diet led McDonald's to add salads to its menu, but when PBS reporters checked in 2010, the Marks McDonald's did not actually have them to serve.[14]

Because junk food is so cheap and there is still so much poverty in the area, African Americans in the Delta face some severe health hazards. For one, they have one of the highest rates of obesity in the United States. A 2013 University of Washington study ranked Quitman as one of the nation's worst counties in this regard: 42 percent of men and 58 percent of women there are obese.[15] And local health care is abysmal. The tiny hospital—the only one in the county—closed in 2016. Even when it was open, it did not adequately serve the population. "If anybody sick here, except if it's a small thing, the hospital is like a holding cell," Mrs. Phipps told me. "They bring a helicopter when there's something serious."

Still, some younger people have been trying to be healthier, and the Reclaimed Project sponsors summer sports camps and recreation projects for children. Groups often gather on athletic courts near Valley Queen Church to play volleyball and tennis. When I visited in 1998, I found twenty-five-year-old Pete Phipps there, whom I had known since he was two. He got his mother to start going on walks for her health when she was past seventy. She is now in her nineties and still active. Today her vegetable garden covers her entire yard, front and back. Still, the 2013 study reported that in terms of "sufficient physical activity," Quitman women ranked third to last of any U.S. county and its men thirty-first from the bottom.[16]

Health problems related to poverty continue to plague Marks residents. Almost three-quarters of Quitman adults suffer from hypertension, resulting in dismayingly low life expectancy rates of 75 years for women and 68 for men.[17] That is far below the national average, putting both in the bottom 1 percent of all U.S. counties. For women, life expectancy rates have actually declined since 1985, while men's rates have risen only very slightly.[18] Even in comparison to the rest of Mississippi, Quitman's residents have poor health outcomes. In 2020, the country ranked 78th out of the state's 82 counties for "health outcomes" and 80th for "health factors."[19]

Community and Opportunity

By the 1990s, more African Americans were returning south than moving north. Part of it was the lure of prison and casino jobs in an otherwise bad economy. Hull told me others had come back because so many northern factories laid off their workers. I know still more who returned to help their families or to "be of service to my community," as Robert Jackson and Reverend Brown did. Jackson planned to commit ten years to Marks. Almost forty years later, he is still there.

Hull's own family showed both the pull and the challenges of the South. The older Franklin children were as eager as other Black youth of their time to move north, but the three youngest wanted to stay. Jimmie Lee played football at Southwestern Oklahoma State University but dropped out and returned to Marks. He got a job driving a tractor on the Self plantations. Later he became a security guard at the Tunica casino.

His older sister Ruby got a college degree and began medical school. She realized her poor educational background had put her at such a disadvantage that she left and became an algebra teacher in a small community near Marks. The other teachers there were having problems with their principal. They asked Ruby, "Are you from that family that always stands up for themselves?" She tried to help them, but they lost, and Ruby moved to Chicago. She moved back to Lambert in 2007 and has a master's degree in education.

After graduating from St. Olaf, Hull taught in Iowa. He returned in 1988 because his father was sick, and he looked for a teaching job. The following year, just before his father died on April 3, Hull's older brother Azki (formerly Presley) also returned. He had been a minister in the Nation of Islam. After he quit being a minister he went to law school. When Azki came back to Marks, he became the school board's attorney.

One of the first things Azki did was launch a suit against County Attorney Ben Caldwell, a white man who had been one of the most intense opponents of the civil rights movement, for some dubious land deals. After removing Mr. Caldwell from his job, Azki took up the case of Black residents who could not get school jobs because they had been given to the friends and relatives of a popular Black preacher. He won their case but antagonized some Black families. This meant his brother Hull could not get a teaching job in Quitman. Instead, Hull became a grade school principal in Tallahatchie County.

Today, Jimmie Lee still works nights as a security guard, and Azki continues to practice law. Hull and Ruby are officially retired. Ruby now manages a thrift store and U-Haul store with her brothers' help. "The Franklin family always seems able to visualize what could be," Richard observed. "The stores were created from the vacant hulk of a corrugated shed." Although Hull complained that townspeople are "greedy," Richard told me the Franklins return 10 percent of all store profits to the community. "Just from the few hours I spent in the stores it seemed clear that the venture provides a service to the community. People can buy quality secondhand goods and then rent the truck they need to haul the furniture home."

Both the infrastructure and the culture of these small southern towns are struggling. Widespread poverty and unemployment have led to demoralization. Some have turned to alcohol or drugs, most recently to opioid abuse. Most seriously, we have seen the rural white vote of desperation for Donald Trump. Part of what he represents is the negative energy released by decades of destructive policies toward rural America.

Few young people join gangs, but there is some crime and drug-related violence, and many express a scornful attitude toward school. Some coming from the North pick fights with the southern Black kids and make fun of them because they are religious. One of Hull's nephews considered becoming a preacher to keep up his spiritual strength in the face of the taunts of the kids from the North.

Marks has fared a bit better, although the schools struggle to meet the many needs of their students. All the 266 students in M. S. Palmer High School (now serving the entire county) qualify for free or reduced-price lunch programs, and 87 percent make it to graduation. Twelve percent test as proficient in math, and 17 percent are proficient in reading. Not all the teachers are certified. The building is old, and there are few extracurricular options.[20] This is not surprising, since the school system, like most of those in Mississippi, is seriously underfunded.

Ironically, more Black students are also attending private school. In its quest for federal funds, the previously all-white Delta Academy has been reaching out to Black children. Still, between white flight and the use of private schools, the public schools are almost as segregated as they were during the Jim Crow days, even though there is now only a single public high school.[21]

But there are committed and energetic teachers at Palmer who genuinely care for the children. There are support programs for those who want to take the ACT. Many do, and approximately 30 percent go on to local community colleges or, if they have high enough scores, the University of Mississippi or historically Black colleges like Jackson State. Almost no one leaves the state to attend college, and none go to nationally high-ranked schools. About the same number attend trade schools.[22]

Many who leave don't come back because there are no jobs. Too many others can't afford to go on for more education or choose not to because they see so little hope. Most of those end up unemployed or only marginally employed. There are still substantial institutional problems holding Black people and poor people back that haven't been adequately addressed, from inadequate funding for schools and infrastructure to punitive welfare policies, policing methods, and similar practices that perpetuate discrimination and poverty. The movement still has a role it can play.

Still, Marks retains its sense of community. Unlike nearby Clarksdale, which struggles with gang and drug violence, or even Batesville or Lambert, which have high crime rates, Marks "is more laid back," Hull explained, with few problems beyond shoplifting. Why the difference? "Community," he answered, even though he believes it has weakened. "You have to be careful who you put your faith in because you might end up being disappointed. People are not respectful to each other. Little children now are not as respectful to older people as they used to be." But families and neighbors still watch out for each other, and children still play outside under watchful adult eyes.

Most of the people from Marks who stayed up north also maintain strong connections. When Richard visited Hull and Annette in 2015, he told me that the house was "full of children playing. Annette's family was visiting from Georgia. That weekend Hull and Annette were hosting a barbeque for 150 relatives and friends." Hull explained that their extended family's "home house" was now divided between his house in Marks and Ruby's in Lambert. "Any of them wanna stay, they got a place to stay," Hull said. The "home house" remains a reality and lifeline for extended families based in Marks.

These northern transplants also keep ties with other people from Marks who have moved north. In 2010, when Alice Maniece, a well-known Black woman in Marks, died, her funeral was held in Milwaukee, where most of her family lived. People who had been away from Marks for at least thirty years traveled to Milwaukee, like William Franklin's sister-in-law Margaret and his son Melvin. Armstead Phipps Jr., whose father died on the Meredith March, came from Chicago. "Marks remains isolated and poor," Richard told me, "but it is a place where I could understand people wanting to live."

Political Action

What hope there is for progress, I still believe, lies in political action, on both the grassroots and electoral levels. I think about the churches, which provided young people with leadership expertise during the movement. Today there are eighteen churches in Marks and sixty-seven in the county. "But they're not doing anything," Hull lamented to Richard in 2015.

In fact, Hull said, there's "not a whole lot" of organizing going on right now. "Everybody's too much on their own. It's not like what was there years ago." Hull believed the issue was generational. "Young kids, they don't care," he told Richard. "They don't realize how the struggle was to get here." The challenge is to galvanize young people with the sort of energy he and others had during the movement.

Several important projects are still active, including the Quitman County Development Organization. Now operating in four counties, the QCDO has financed dozens of duplex homes and repaired hundreds of existing homes. It also owns and manages single-family homes for low-income renters. The QCDO established a credit union in 1981 in the midst of a severe recession and has helped many families get through difficult financial times without depending on loan-sharking finance companies. By 2009 it had made more than $47 million in loans, largely for first-time home buyers. It then merged with the Shreveport Federal Credit Union, and it continues to operate its Marks branch.[23]

The QCDO also supports students with programs like its Save the Children tutoring and reading programs, Mississippi Delta Foster

Grandparent Program, and Children's Village after-school program. Focused on improving educational skills and opportunities, these projects are necessarily comprehensive. Other organizing projects have been underwritten by national and international organizations, from the Children's Defense Fund based in Washington, D.C., to ChildFund International, which focuses on the needs of poor children around the globe.[24] For example, in 1992, Youth Opportunities Unlimited (YOU), a national group serving underprivileged youth, came to Mississippi. It established a multipurpose center in Marks offering tutoring, sports, and dropout prevention programs, GED preparation and other services for at-risk young people and their families, and a day care center. A ChildFund International grant supported mentoring and tutoring programs at the North Delta Youth Development Center (YDC) in Lambert, directed by Robert Jamison from Marks, one of the first Black children to integrate the white school.

Reclaimed has bought a building in town to provide rent-free housing for seven teachers and volunteers and offers tutoring, summer programs, and community events. It sends young teachers from around the South to work at Palmer and other Quitman County schools.[25] Funding is always a problem for these organizations, and most rely heavily on volunteers. Not surprisingly, then, the YDC, YOU, and a youth-run sweet shop have closed, although the QCDO absorbed some of YOU's programs into its Carl Brown Educational Center. "For thirty-eight years we've been scrambling [for money]," QCDO director (and current state senator) Robert Jackson acknowledged.

But even with better funding these programs cannot solve the structural problems that keep so many families trapped in poverty. One of the goals of the movement was to help the people marshal the necessary resources to resolve these issues through electoral politics. There the record has been mixed.[26]

In some ways, the political scene has changed radically. The most significant change has been the huge leap in the proportion of Black adults registered to vote in Mississippi, skyrocketing from less than 7 percent in 1965 to 83 percent in 2020, four points higher than for whites.[27] The state has more Black elected officials than any other, and in several recent elections, Black voting rates exceeded white.

Locally, this made a huge difference in the power structure. In 1997, thanks to the sharp decline in the white population, Marks elected its first Black mayor. Today every alderman there is a Democrat; one is

James Figgs, son of activist Ruth Figgs. Marks's mayor, Joe Shegog Jr., its chief of police, and Quitman County's sheriff are Black. Elections feature multiple Black candidates.

In the new atmosphere of freedom, another descendant of slave owners besides me came to Quitman, where he helped elect the nation's first Black president. While I was in Marks I came to know Rev. Albion Crudup, a Black minister active in civil rights and community development. He was a sharecropper on a farm owned by one of the county's few Black landowners, Dudley Shegog (related to the current mayor). I met Mr. Shegog and saw him at civil rights meetings.

In early 1966, when I returned to Oklahoma to see a dentist, I met a white man named David Shegog. I learned one of his ancestors had opposed the Confederacy and refused to go into the Confederate Army. When Confederate troops came for him, his family hid him under a heap of wheat.

I did not see David Shegog again until the spring of 2008. He told me then that one of his slave-owning ancestors had had children by an enslaved woman. David worked for the Obama campaign in the 2008 Democratic primaries. He decided to find descendants of his ancestor by this slave woman and get them to mobilize their families and friends to vote for Obama. So David Shegog came to Quitman and met with the children and grandchildren of the Black man Dudley Shegog whom I had known. These people were David's distant cousins, and he mobilized them to work for Obama.

There have been important political victories. Since 1993, the Delta has been represented in Congress by Bennie Thompson, a Black man from Hinds County. Since 2004, QCDO director Robert Jackson of Marks has served in the Mississippi Senate representing parts of Coahoma, Quitman, Tate, and Tunica Counties. Jackson, son of sharecroppers and a former a movement participant, struggles against the same old foe: the Delta Council, which is the old white Citizens' Council now in an integrated disguise. The council is "tantamount to the Mafia, basically," Jackson explained. "While they don't go out and shoot people, they set policies in place to keep folks powerless and dependent, and it's been tough fighting that kind of situation." The big landowners and their front men still control Quitman's economy. The result, Jackson claims, is fear. QCDO no longer holds mass meetings because "people are so afraid now," he says. "We've slipped back into the fifties or sixties. . . . It's like the days of the West—anything can happen."

"The Delta is the way it is because that's the way the leaders want it," Jackson told Richard Arvedon. And having Black officials does not necessarily change that. Three of the five members of the Quitman County Board of Supervisors are Black, but "all the decisions basically they made, they all pretty much vote 5–0, and most of those decisions are against the people I serve, African Americans. The system is very shrewd. People are not very strong willed; they don't know what's going on. When they get elected the system sort of takes a man and turns him around, and they become part of the system and the problem as opposed to being a part of solving the equation.

"There are a lot of good people here who would like to see changes, but at the same time we are dealing with a force that's almost invisible. People don't know the grasp that organizations like the Delta Council have on the local community." He shrugged. "Just have to meet it head on. There's just no other way." Fortunately, Jackson and other current Black leaders have gained experience and a certain amount of freedom of action because of the civil rights movement.

Black voting participation and other electoral engagement have transformed local and even state and national politics in many ways, but it is still true that the power structure remains largely white, from the governor to the state's two senators to the county courthouses. Despite the steadily rising proportion of Black voters supporting Democratic presidential candidates, the state has voted Republican in every presidential election since the early 1960s (except 1976 when Mississippi supported southerner Jimmy Carter).

This white control is not only about the power of groups like the Delta Council. It is also in large measure thanks to various methods the Republican Party has used to disenfranchise African American and rural voters. For example, voting precincts are carefully designed to protect (white) incumbents, and voter identification laws often hurt poor rural people who lack appropriate documents. And especially after the Supreme Court struck down voter protections at the heart of the Voting Rights Act, various laws to make voting more difficult have proliferated in Mississippi and elsewhere in the South (and parts of the North as well.) Robert Jackson and his wife, who ran for tax assessor, have also faced harassment and false accusations.[28] The county now sharply limits its absentee voting, although more than a third of Quitman residents voted absentee in previous elections. Registered Black voters don't appear on the lists, and absentee ballots disappear. "It's all by design," Jackson insists. And those efforts have only intensified since 2020.

As Bob Moses, SNCC leader and architect of Freedom Summer, put it at a 2014 conference at Tougaloo, "The problem in the country—and it's not just a Southern problem—is that what we need now is an affirmative right to vote. What we have right now is a negative right to vote. That is, if somebody interferes with your right you can bring it into court but it doesn't say that the government protects your right to vote. We need to raise this to the level of the Constitution—the idea that the right to vote is fundamental and it needs to be affirmed. . . . Instead, we're using all of our energy on the legal front putting out brush fires."[29]

It is also true that younger Black eligible voters are not going to the polls in large numbers. "It's getting worse with these younger people, trying to get them to participate," Jackson observed. Why they were apathetic was "a question my generation has been pondering. Hopefully when they see situations like Ferguson happen, they'll be motivated to be part of the answer. I'd like to put a challenge to the young people to find themselves in the struggle and find ways to become a part of it and to bring about the change that we need so that everybody living in the community can not only survive but thrive. And I think as humans, we should do that. And especially if you see your race being victimized like we are in so many ways not only here but throughout the country, you would find some way to assist."

One illustration of the potential power—and limitations—of the Black vote was the victory of Republican incumbent Thad Cochran against a Tea Party challenger in the 2014 congressional primary. By all accounts, Black support pushed Cochran over the top. Black Mississippi Delta voters remain deeply Democratic, but they recognized that Cochran was far preferable to his challenger, Chris McDaniel, who opposed virtually every antipoverty and antidiscrimination program. They hoped their support would put pressure on Senator Cochran to vote more sympathetically on those issues.[30] And there has been some payoff from political action. After negotiations with state officials, Amtrak reopened rail service to the Delta in 2018, with a station in Marks. There is hope that this will spur economic development, although the COVID pandemic has limited its impact so far.

As Senator Jackson observed about the circuit courts, the local political structures are broken when it comes to African Americans. "But that's the only thing we have. So we have to go through the process." Yet, even locally, I fear little will change so long as basic power remains in the hands of the planters. They still own the land.

Back to the Land

The more I think of Marks and of such people as the Franklins, the more I think of how they functioned as part of a community. Yet the aim of most people in high places since World War II has been to do away with the rural community as something obsolete. Once it was decided in the years just after the Civil War not to give land to the former slaves, that basic element of a rural community was not there. If Martin Luther King had proposed land reform in the Deep South, he would have been seen as not only as a communist but also as insane.

Once the decision was made to mechanize the cotton plantations, the destruction of such rural communities as Marks was taken as a foregone conclusion. The hope of liberals was to do away with discrimination and give rural Blacks access to education so they could go somewhere else. Their very existence in the places where they lived was seen as a social problem. This is true not only among conservatives but also among liberals. And it was not only African Americans in the South. Everywhere in the United States, social forces backed by government policies have been destroying rural communities. No one saw the farming skills of a man like Mr. Franklin as a valuable resource that should be preserved.

There have been some efforts to rectify the situation. In 1975, the Emergency Land Fund (ELF) was established to help Black southerners with land problems. It was coordinated by former civil rights workers like Jesse Morris. The ELF did not ask for land reform but tried to help Black small farmers keep the land they had and encouraged farming cooperatives. The fund's pamphlets explained basic information about property taxes, wills, land policies, and other questions affecting small farmers, just as the civil rights movement put out leaflets for new Black voters explaining how county, state, and federal governments worked. The ELF still exists, now called the Federation of Southern Cooperatives/Land Assistance Fund.[31]

Another hopeful sign is the success of a class action lawsuit by Black farmers that the Department of Agriculture systematically discriminated against them in providing loans and crop subsidies. The consent decree in *Pigford v. Glickman* was the largest civil rights settlement in history, and claims are still being filed.[32]

A meaningful movement for land reform would have to be nationwide, on the scale of the civil rights movement. Such a movement would have to unite Blacks, whites, Hispanics, and Native Americans and bring together farmers and organizations working on environmental issues, including water rights and opposition to strip mining and fracking. All these problems are rooted in control of land by too few people.

It would certainly be difficult. Those government policies that favored wealthy landowners and threw Black people off the land were both economically and culturally destructive. Young Black people from Marks seem to have no wish for agricultural life. I was sad to discover that one of the scornful names among young Black men is "farmer." When you think of the tremendous knowledge of the soil someone like Mr. Franklin had, you realize how much has been lost by African Americans and everyone who still works the land.

I don't think it's impossible to turn things around, though. Although for a while most residents were "industrial-minded," Hull explained, more are now coming back to the idea of the land. He and Jimmie Lee have been discussing farming land near their Uncle Jessie's. "It's on our mind," he said.

The growing threat of climate change makes the need for land reform more pressing, and it might also make organizing that sort of movement easier. We must find ways to develop more local food sources. Even in Detroit, city planners are trying to reimagine a city where "everyone who wants one has a quarter-acre garden, and every kid lives within bike distance of a farm."[33] Malik Yakini, a Detroit school principal who runs a two-acre farm, explained to reporter Mark Bittman that his goal "is to help Black people stand up, to demonstrate that creating reality is not the exclusive domain of white people." That is very much like what we believed in the movement. Maybe we can fight for a rational redistribution of the land based on Mr. Bittman's assertion-that "food is central. Justice, security, a sense of community, and more intelligent land use have become integral to the food system."

Land reform is not the only answer. Nonfarming jobs are now the norm, but they remain too hard to come by. Areas like Quitman County need more job training and other social services. I hope the new Amtrak service will help. But so long as political power lies in the land, and so long as places like Marks continue to serve as anchors for extended families, getting and keeping land in the hands of the Black community—and the working-class white community—is crucial.

During my 1998 visit, the Franklins drove with me to a small Black cemetery just south of Marks, across the road from one of the Self family cotton fields. In the field had been two ancient Indian burial mounds. I was told one had been flattened by tractors, but the other still faced the Black graves across the road.[34] I recognized some of the names on the headstones. Ruth Figgs, community activist. True and Emma Ware, who had been active in the movement. Hobie Haines, the son of Ernestine Evans. And there was the grave of William Franklin, one of the major influences in my life.

When Mr. Franklin died, so many civil rights activists from around Mississippi went to the funeral that it had to be held in Silent Grove Church, one of the largest Black churches in Marks. At the gravesite, each of the Franklin children took turns shoveling earth into their father's grave. Hull looked around the cemetery. "There's a lot of history here," he said.

But in the words of William Franklin, "One thing for sure, we ain't never going back to what we was." Black citizens of Quitman County have gained leadership and experience from the civil rights movement. But the movement has won only the first step for Black people and working-class white people in Mississippi: freedom from fear so that now they can get together to try for more.

Despite its challenges, I believe Marks will survive and continue to have something important to give, not just to Black America but to all America. The choir of Clarksdale's Silent Grove Baptist Church once recorded a song for the Archive of American Folk Culture that sums up the spirit of the Black people of Marks, their patience and courage and their will to keep on keeping on:

> Ain't no grave can hold my body down
> Ain't no grave can hold my body down
> When the first trumpet sound
> I'll be getting up walking round
> Ain't no grave can hold my body down.

NOTES

Prologue

1. Hubert Humphrey, address to the Democratic National Convention, Philadelphia, Pa., July 14, 1948, https://www.youtube.com/watch?v=8nwIdIUVFm4.

Chapter 1. "God Promised You a Living and a Killing"

1. See the "Interviewees and Families" section for a list of names with years of birth and interview. Their words are reproduced here verbatim, although when several are quoted on the same topic, they were not necessarily all present at the same interview.

2. "Leopold Marks, 1852–1910," https://www.findagrave.com/memorial/153250673/marks.

3. No professional historical sites claim this, but numerous others do. See, for example, "Politicians Killed by Poison or Overdose," Political Graveyard, https://politicalgraveyard.com/death/poison.html; "John Anthony Quitman," Aztec Club (Quitman was the first president of the club, founded in 1847 for Mexican War veterans), http://www.aztecclub.com/bios/quitman.htm.

4. Population.us, "Population of Marks, Mississippi," http://population.us/ms/marks/. See also U.S. Bureau of the Census, *Census of Population and Housing*, 1910, 1930, https://www.census.gov/prod/www/decennial.html.

5. National Bureau of Economic Research, U.S. Census, *Decennial County Population Data 1900–1990* (digitally modified from original published in 1995), https://data.nber.org/census/pop/1900-90.txt.

6. U.S. Census, 1930, *Reports for States with Statistics for Counties*, vol. 1, pt. 2, 655; U.S. Census, 1930, *Census of Agriculture*, vol. 2, Mississippi County Ta-

ble 1, 1054; Charles Hall, ed., *The Negro Farmer in the United States* (Washington, D.C., 1933), 39, 69.

7. For more on the dispossession of Black farmers, see Sydney Nathans, *A Mind to Stay: White Plantation, Black Homeland* (Cambridge, Mass., 2017); Kenfra Taira Field, *Growing Up with the Country Family: Race and Nation after the Civil War* (New Haven, 2018); Pete Daniel, *Dispossession: Discrimination against African American Farmers in the Age of Civil Rights* (Chapel Hill, 2015); Vann Newkirk II, "This Land Was Our Land," *Atlantic*, September 2019, 74–85; J. Schor, "Fantasy and Reality: The Black Farmer's Place in American Agriculture," *Agriculture and Human Values* 9 (1992): 72–78. See also James Cobb, "Somebody Done Nailed Us on the Cross: Federal Farm and Welfare Policy and the Civil Rights Movement in the Mississippi Delta," *Journal of American History* 77, no. 3 (December 1990): 912–36.

8. Hall, *Negro Farmer in the United States*, 35. The situation did not improve: in 1960 Alex Shimkin reported 131 nonwhite farm owners, 49 partial owners, and 1,077 farm tenants. "Report, Quitman County," February 11, 1966, 2, in MFDP, "County Reports, Feb. 11, 1966," Mississippi State Sovereignty Commission Records (hereafter SCR) 2-165-6-6-2-1-1. All SCR records are now online at the Mississippi Department of Archives and History website: https://da.mdah.ms.gov/sovcom/scagencycasehistory.php. To find a specific file, go to https://da.mdah.ms.gov/sovcom/; under "search name," enter a person's name or go to the full list of Quitman County records (2-82-0): https://da.mdah.ms.gov/sovcom/imagelisting.php; click on the relevant document number.

9. He may have meant a Foster steam tractor or more likely Ford's Fordson steam tractor. See David Fletcher, "Early Experiments Part I," *Tank 100*, July 17, 2017, https://tank100.com/towards-the-tank/early-experiments-part-I, which calls the Foster tractor both a Forster and a Foster; Roger Tate, "The Early Years of Ford Tractors," *MotorCities*, March 27, 2017, https://www.motorcities.org/story-of-the-week/2017/the-early-years-of-ford-tractors-1907-1961.

10. Pellagra, caused by lack of niacin, results in dermatitis, diarrhea, and other ailments.

11. For more on Randolph and the Brotherhood of Sleeping Car Porters ("and Maids" was added later), see Robert Allen, *Brotherhood of Sleeping Car Porters: C. L. Dellums and the Fight for Fair Treatment and Civil Rights* (New York, 2015); David Welky, *Marching across the Color Line: A. Philip Randolph and Civil Rights in the World War II Era* (New York, 2013); Cornelius Bynum, *A. Philip Randolph and the Struggle for Civil Rights* (Urbana, 2010); Andrew Kersten, *A. Philip Randolph: A Life in the Vanguard* (Lanham, Md., 2007); Eric Arnesen, *Brotherhoods of Color: Black Railroad Workers and the Struggle for Equality* (Cambridge, Mass., 2001); Larry Tye, *Rising from the Rails: Pullman Porters and the Making of the Black Middle Class* (New York, 2005); Beth Tompkins Bates, *Pullman Porters and the Rise of Protest Politics in Black America 1925–1945* (Chapel Hill, 2001); Melinda Chateauvert, *Marching Together: Women of the Brotherhood of Sleeping Car Porters* (Urbana, 1998); Paula Pfeffer, *A. Philip Randolph: Pioneer of the Civil Rights Movement* (Baton Rouge, 1996); and Jack

Santino, *Miles of Smiles, Years of Struggle: Stories of Black Pullman Porters* (Urbana, 1991).

12. U.S. Census, 1930, *Reports for States with Statistics for Counties*, vol. 1, pt. 2, 655; *Agriculture*, 1054; Hall, *Negro Farmer*, 69: U.S. Dept. of Agriculture, *Census of Agriculture, 1940, Mississippi*, vol. 1, pt. 33, 391, https://agcensus.library.cornell.edu/census_parts/1940-mississippi. The dramatic rise in white acreage, with only a slight increase in the number of farm owners, attests to the consolidation of land by families like the Selfs. For more on Mississippi during the Great Depression, see Richelle Putnam, *Mississippi and the Great Depression* (Charleston, S.C., 2017); Alison Collis Greene, *No Depression in Heaven: The Great Depression, the New Deal and the Transformation of Religion in the Delta* (New York, 2016); Lawrence Gordon, "A Brief History of Blacks in the Great Depression, 1929–1934: Eyewitness Accounts," *Journal of Negro History* 64, no. 4 (Autumn 1979): 377–90.

13. Mississippi never passed an anti-lynching law; Mrs. Weathersby was probably referring to prosecutions by the Civil Rights Division of the Justice Department, established by President Roosevelt in 1939. The CRD prosecuted lynchings as violations of civil rights but didn't obtain its first conviction until 1946. The NAACP had been working for anti-lynching legislation since its creation in 1909, but no federal bill was ever passed.

14. For more on the STFU, see Donald Grubbs, *Cry from the Cotton: The Southern Tenant Farmers' Union and the New Deal* (Fayetteville, Ark., 2000); James Ross, *The Rise and Fall of the Southern Tenant Farmers Union in Arkansas* (Knoxville, 2018); Howard Kester, *Revolt among the Sharecroppers* (1936; repr., Knoxville, 1997).

15. U.S. Census, 1960, *Mississippi: General Social and Economic Characteristics*, table 35, 26–110, https://www2.census.gov/library/publications/decennial/1960/population-volume-1/37745223v1p26ch4.pdf; James Marshall, *Student Activism and Civil Rights in Mississippi: Protest Politics and the Struggle for Racial Justice, 1960–1965* (Baton Rouge, 2013), table 2. For 1960 population statistics for Quitman and Marks, see MFDP, "The Mississippi Delta," Report, n.d., 4, 9, in MFDP Lauderdale County Records, 1964–66, Wisconsin Historical Society (hereafter WHS) Freedom Summer Digital Collection (FSDC), micro 55, reel 2, segment 42, https://cdm15932.contentdm.oclc.org/digital/collection/p15932coll2/id/54586/rec/83. To find any document in WHS FSDC, go to the search page: https://content.wisconsinhistory.org/digital/collection/p15932coll2/search; enter the name or place. Identify correct collection and location. That link will list the relevant document. Quitman's population has continued to drop since, down to 10,117 in 2000 and 6,176 in 2020. "Quick Facts: Quitman County, Mississippi," U.S. Census Bureau, https://www.census.gov/quickfacts/fact/table/quitmancountymississippi/PST045221.

16. Population.us, "Population of Marks, Mississippi"; MFDP, "The Mississippi Delta," 4.

17. U.S. Census, 1960, *Mississippi: General Social and Economic Characteristics*, table 35; table 83, 26-178; table 87, 26-206. State median education: 8.9

years; thirty-nine white Quitman residents were then in college; twenty nonwhite Quitman adults had completed college. See also MFDP, "Mississippi Delta," 9.

18. Wilson Minor, "Mississippi: Activist Governor," *New York Times*, November 13, 1983.

19. U.S. Census, 1960, *Mississippi: General Social and Economic Characteristics*, table 36, 26-111; table 88, 26-213. Poverty: households earning less than $3,000. (Statewide the figure was 52 percent.) The average county household earned $1,517. Alex Shimkin reported the same figures: "Report, Quitman County," February 11, 1966, 2, in MFDP, "County Reports, Feb. 11, 1966," SCR 2-165-6-6-2-1-1.

20. U.S. Census, 1960, *Mississippi: General Social and Economic Characteristics*, table 36, table 87. (Two-parent families: 82 percent of all Black families included husband and wife, according to table 87.)

21. Ibid., table 88. See also MFDP, "County Reports, Feb. 11, 1966," SCR 2-165-6-6-2-1-1: 3,131 Black employed workers, 2,238 in agriculture and 414 in personal (household) service (515 in all service work).

22. Sixteen nonwhite Quitman men and twenty-eight nonwhite women worked in "professional technical and kindred" fields. U.S. Census, 1960, *Mississippi: General Social and Economic Characteristics*, table 88.

Chapter 2. "I Got Tired of White Folks on My Back"

1. COFO, "Mississippi Handbook for Political Programs," n.d. [Summer 1964], 25, Wisconsin Historical Society (hereafter WHS) Freedom Summer Digital Collection (FSDC), https://content.wisconsinhistory.org/digital/collection/p15932coll2, Lucile Montgomery papers, micro 44, reel 1, segment 3.

2. I recorded this statement in 1964. We frequently took statements regarding incidents of harassment, violence, discrimination, or intimidation, especially in voting, to show to SNCC staffers or civil rights lawyers. If they decided to pursue a legal case later, these statements would prove we had not made the incidents up. Even before the Voting Rights Act of 1965, the Justice Department was going into counties which had obvious cases of discrimination. I appreciated Mrs. Parker's courage in coming to me on her own initiative to make a statement.

3. Mississippi State Sovereignty Commission records are online: https://da.mdah.ms.gov/sovcom/scagencycasehistory.php.

4. Zack J. Van Landingham to Director, Mississippi Sovereignty Commission (hereafter MSC), Memorandum, March 10, 1959, Mississippi State Sovereignty Commission Records (SCR) 2-82-0-3-1-1-1. Spelling and capitalization are all as they appear in the records.

5. Tom Scarbrough to MSC, Memo, July 14, 1960, 2, SCR 2-82-0-9-2-1-1.

6. Ibid., 1.

7. Ibid., 1.

8. *Alston v. School Board of City of Norfolk*, 112 F.2d 992 (4th Cir. 1940). On June 18, 1940, the 4th Circuit Court of Appeals ruled that paying African American teachers less than white teachers violated due process protections.

9. Every civil rights narrative includes Black churches and the engagement of Black ministers and worshippers. For books that focus on religion and civil rights activism per se (Black or white), see David Chappell, *A Stone of Hope: Prophetic Religion and the Death of Jim Crow* (Chapel Hill, 2004); P. Allen Krause, *To Stand Aside or Stand Alone: Southern Reform Rabbis and the Civil Rights Movement* (Tuscaloosa, 2013); Johnny Williams, *African American Religion and the Civil Rights Movement in Arkansas* (Jackson, Miss., 2003); Charles Marsh, *God's Long Summer: Stories of Faith and Civil Rights* (Princeton, 1997); and James Findlay Jr., *Church People in the Struggle: The National Council of Churches and the Black Freedom Movement 1950–1970* (New York, 1993). See also chap. 10, note 2, in this book.

10. For more on Reverend Howard, see David T. Beito and Linda Royster Beito, *Black Maverick: T. R. M. Howard's Fight for Civil Rights and Economic Power* (Urbana, 2009). Reverend Allen, who had been ordained with Reverend Malone, told me he had joined the NAACP in 1955.

11. Till was accused of flirting with a white woman; much later she admitted in an interview with historian Tim Tyson that she had made it up. Tim Tyson, *The Blood of Emmett Till* (New York, 2017), 7. There are dozens of books on the lynching of Emmett Till and the importance of that event in energizing an entire generation of civil rights workers. In addition to Tyson's book, see Elliott Gorn, *Let the People See: The Story of Emmett Till* (New York, 2018); Devery Anderson, *Emmett Till: The Murder That Shocked the World and Propelled the Civil Rights Movement* (Jackson, Miss., 2015); Darryl Mace, *In Remembrance of Emmett Till: Regional Stories and Media Responses to the Black Freedom Struggle* (Lexington, Ky., 2014); Mamie Till-Mobley and Christopher Benson, *The Death of Innocence: The Story of the Hate Crime That Changed America* (New York, 2003); Christopher Metress, *The Lynching of Emmett Till: A Documentary Narrative* (Charlottesville, Va., 2002); and Stephen Whitfield, *A Death in the Delta: The Story of Emmett Till* (Baltimore, 1991).

12. The trial received press coverage across the United States and internationally, beginning with a photo of Till's battered face in *Jet* magazine. Many civil rights workers credit that photo with inspiring their activism. Black newspapers covered the movement extensively; white papers did so only much later. In both cases, news coverage proved crucial to bringing change. See Clint Wilson II, *Whither the Black Press? Glorious Past, Uncertain Future* (2020), chap. 5; D'Weston Haywood, *Let Us Make Men: The Twentieth-Century Black Press and a Manly Vision for Racial Advancement* (Chapel Hill, 2018); Gene Roberts and Hank Klibanoff, *The Race Beat: The Press, The Civil Rights Struggle, and the Awakening of a Nation* (New York, 2006); and Todd Vogel, ed., *The Black Press: New Literary and Historical Essays* (New Brunswick, N.J., 2001).

13. For more on James Meredith and the integration of the University of Mississippi, see James Meredith with William Doyle, *A Mission from God* (New York, 2012); Henry Gallagher, *James Meredith and the Ole Miss Riot: A Soldier's Story* (Jackson, Miss., 2012); James Charles Eagles, *The Price of Defiance: James Meredith and the Integration of Ole Miss* (Chapel Hill, 2009); William Doyle, *An*

American Insurrection: James Meredith and the Battle of Oxford, Mississippi (New York, 2003); and Frank Lambert, *The Battle of Ole Miss: Civil Rights vs. States' Rights* (New York, 2009).

14. For more on SNCC, see Sharon Monteith, *SNCC Stories: The African American Freedom Movement in the Civil Rights South* (Athens, Ga., 2020); M. J. O'Brien, *We Shall Not Be Moved: The Jackson Woolworth's Sit-in and the Movement It Inspired* (Jackson, Miss., 2013); Iwan Morgan and Philip Davies, eds., *From Sit-Ins to SNCC: The Student Civil Rights Movement in the 1960s* (Gainesville, Fla., 2012); Faith Holsaert et al., eds., *Hands on the Freedom Plow: Personal Accounts by Women in SNCC* (Urbana, 2010); Wesley Hogan, *Many Minds, One Heart: SNCC's Dream for a New America* (Chapel Hill, 2007); David Halberstam, *The Children* (New York, 1998); Cheryl Greenberg, ed., *A Circle of Trust: Remembering SNCC* (New Brunswick, N.J., 1998); Cleveland Sellers, *The River of No Return: The Autobiography of a Black Militant and the Life and Death of SNCC* (Jackson, Miss., 1990); Clayborne Carson, *In Struggle: SNCC and the Black Awakening of the 1960s* (Cambridge, Mass., 1981); Howard Zinn, *SNCC: The New Abolitionists* (Boston, 1964); and Vanessa Murphree, *The Selling of Civil Rights: The Student Nonviolent Coordinating Committee and the Use of Public Relations* (New York, 2006). See also "Further Reading" in this book.

15. Most of the stories told to me are also referenced in archival records. For ease of reference, the documents in which those references appear are cited in the notes, with "cf." For example: for Panola, cf. Council of Federated Organizations Panola County Office—Voter Registration and Harassment, 1964–1965 (includes both COFO Panola County Office records, 1963–1965 and Legal Materials, 1964–1965), Wisconsin Historical Society (hereafter WHS), Main Stacks, Mss 521, esp. boxes 1, 2.

16. Freedom Vote figures from Barbara Ransby, *Ella Baker and the Black Freedom Movement* (Chapel Hill, 2003), 312; Carson, *In Struggle*, 98; Zinn, *SNCC*, 100. For more on mock election, see Committee to Elect Aaron Henry Governor of Mississippi, "Planning Details for Freedom Vote for Governor," October 10, 1963, and "Freedom Ballot for Governor: Platform," n.d. [1963], both WHS, MFDP Records 1962–1971, micro 788, reel 1, segment 2, pt. 1. For more on COFO and Freedom Summer, see Bruce Watson, *Freedom Summer: The Savage Season of 1964 that Made Mississippi Burn and Made America a Democracy* (New York, 2010); John McClymer, *Mississippi Freedom Summer* (Belmont, Calif., 2004); John Dittmer, *Local People: The Struggle for Civil Rights in Mississippi* (Urbana, 1994); Nicolaus Mills, *Like a Holy Crusade: Mississippi 1964—The Turning of the Civil Rights Movement in America* (Chicago, 1992); Sally Belfrage, *Freedom Summer* (1965; repr., Charlottesville, 1990); and Doug McAdam, *Freedom Summer* (New York, 1990). See also chap. 3, note 32, in this book. Document collections include Michael Edmonds, *Risking Everything: Freedom Summer Reader* (Madison, Wis., 2014); John Dittmer, Jeff Kolnick, and Leslie Burl McLemore, eds., *Freedom Summer: A Brief History with Documents* (New York, 2017); Elizabeth Martinez and Julian Bond, eds., *Letters from Mississippi: Reports from Civil Rights Volunteers and Poetry of the 1964 Freedom Summer*, rev. ed. (Brook-

line, Mass., 2014). For a broader overview, see "Further Reading" in this book. Many digital archives of the civil rights movement include COFO papers, files, and other materials. See, for example, WHS Freedom Summer Digital Collection, https://content.wisconsinhistory.org/digital/collection/p15932coll2; SNCC Digital Gateway, https://snccdigital.org/events/mfdp-founded; Civil Rights Movement Archive, https://www.crmvet.org/; University of Southern Mississippi Libraries Digital Collections (hereafter USM), https://usm.primo.exlibrisgroup.com/discovery/search?vid=01USM_INST:DIGI. For all, search for "COFO," "Freedom Summer" or a particular name.

17. For more on the MFDP and Atlantic City, see Lisa Anderson Todd, *For a Voice and the Vote: My Journey with the Mississippi Freedom Democratic Party* (Lexington, Ky., 2014); Fannie Lou Hamer, "To Praise Our Bridges," and Charles Sherrod, "Mississippi at Atlantic City," both in *The Eyes on the Prize Civil Rights Reader: Documents, Speeches, and Firsthand Accounts from the Black Freedom Struggle, 1954–1990*, ed. Clayborne Carson, et al. (New York, 1991), 176–79, 186–89. Digital archives also have materials by and about the MFDP.

18. For more on Fannie Lou Hamer, see Kate Larson, *Walk with Me: A Biography of Fannie Lou Hamer* (New York, 2021); Keisha Blain, *Until I Am Free: Fannie Lou Hamer's Enduring Message to America* (Boston, 2021); Maegan Parker Brooks, *A Voice That Could Stir an Army: Fannie Lou Hamer and the Rhetoric of the Black Freedom Movement* (Jackson, Miss., 2014); and Kay Mills, *This Little Light of Mine: The Life of Fannie Lou Hamer* (Lexington, Ky., 2007). For more on COFO and Marks specifically, see, for example, reports and depositions in Sally Belfrage papers, Microforms, micro 599, reel 1, and "Registered Voters of Quitman County," n.d. [1964], Amzie Moore papers, Mss 551, box 8 (which reported 384 Black voters in Marks in 1964, and 425 in West Marks, substantially higher than 1960), both in WHS FSDC. In USM, see, for example, Marks COFO to Jackson COFO, "Project Report, January 23 to February 3," February 3, 1964, and letters from Marks summer volunteer Matthew Zwerling.

19. Cf. Yvonne Klein, "Minister's Wife Loses Jobs in Marks," August 6, 1964, WHS FSDC, Sally Belfrage papers, 1962–1966, Clarksdale 1964, micro 599, reel 1, segment 13.

20. The lawyer sued Mr. McArthur, who had to sell his house to pay the damages. "Mississippi Summer Project Running Summary of Incidents," August 1964, 24, WHS FSDC, Hank Werner papers, Z: Accessions, M71-358, box 2. Civil rights workers Dave Bradshaw and Richard Moore told me later that they corresponded with Bob McArthur, who had also harassed other civil rights workers. Later, Mr. McArthur became much friendlier toward them. A letter from McArthur to Bradshaw can be found in "Transcript of Bob McArthur," n.d., 2, WHS, Susan Gladstone papers, 1963–1965, Archives Main Stacks SC669.

21. There are hundreds of reports and affidavits concerning violence, arrests, harassment, and intimidation in WHS FSDC files, many under "Incident Reports" or "WATS Line" Reports. See, for example, [COFO], "Intimidation August 1964," 1–3 (includes Mrs. Allen's firing); "Violence and Intimidation," n.d., 1, both in Belfrage papers; Kathryn Quinn, "Project End Nears for Freedom Worker,"

Suburban Times, August 20, 1964, 14, WHS, Elizabeth Sutherland Martinez papers, 1964–66, Martinez-Correspondence, micro 790, reel 1, pt. 4; Doris Newman, "Marks Voter Education Program," n.d., cited in Simon Cuthbert-Kerr, "The Development of Black Political Organization in Quitman County, Mississippi, 1945–1975" (PhD diss., University of Strathclyde, Scotland, 2006), 33.

22. Howell Raines, ed., *My Soul Is Rested* (New York, 1977), 279–81. What she was referring to was not simply white men having sex with Black women but a gendered form of violent racial repression similar to lynching. During slavery, white men raped enslaved Black women. From the Civil War onward, as Danielle McGuire compellingly argues, white men used the harassment and rape of Black women as a means of racial control. Many of the main events of the civil rights movement, including the Montgomery Bus Boycott, were rooted in such experiences and resistance to them. Danielle McGuire, *At the Dark End of the Street: Black Women, Rape and Resistance: A New History of the Civil Rights Movement from Rosa Parks to Black Power* (New York, 2010). For more on gender and civil rights, see also Jeanne Theoharis, *The Rebellious Life of Mrs. Rosa Parks* (Boston, 2013); Bettye Collier-Thomas and V. P. Franklin, eds., *Sisters in the Struggle: African-American Women in the Civil Rights–Black Power Movement* (New York, 2001); Holsaert et al., *Hands on the Freedom Plow*; Peter Ling and Sharon Monteith, *Gender in the Civil Rights Movement* (New Brunswick, N.J., 1994); Belinda Robnett, "African-American Women in the Civil Rights Movement, 1954–1965: Gender, Leadership and Micromobilization," *American Journal of Sociology* 101, no. 6 (May 1996): 1661–93; Jo Ann Gibson Robinson, *The Montgomery Bus Boycott and the Women Who Started It* (Knoxville, 1987); Steve Estes, *I Am a Man! Race, Manhood and the Civil Rights Movement* (Chapel Hill, 2005).

23. Lewis Sitzer, Deposition, August 1964; Yvonne Klein, "Lew Sitzer Arrested in Marks," August 6, 1964, 2; Sitzer, Affidavit, July 3, 1964; Klein, "Hank Kassler Arrested in Marks," August 6, 1964, 1–2; Haskell Kassler, Deposition, August 1964, all in WHS FSDC, Belfrage papers, micro 599, reel 1, segment 13; "City of Marks v. Haskell Kassler," in "Federal Removal and Habeas Corpus Cases," 14, WHS FSDC, Social Action Vertical Files, circa 1930–2002, Mss 577, box 16, folder 3. See also Elizabeth Sutherland Martinez, ed., *Letters from Mississippi* (Brookline, Mass., 2002), 164; and note 20 above.

24. Mr. Aronson came from the NAACP Legal Defense and Educational Fund, Inc. He shared this statement with us when it was taken. Cf. CORE, "Mississippi Docket Sept. 21, 1964," 7, WHS, Congress of Racial Equality, Southern Regional Office records 1954–1966, CORE S. Regional Office MFDP Legal Matters, 1964, Archives Main Stacks, Mss 85, box 8, folder 10.

25. Cf. "State of Mississippi v Rose Kendricks," in "Federal Removal and Habeas Corpus Cases," 13–14.

26. Doris Newman, "Marks Voter Education Program." Police took down license plate numbers virtually any time there were civil rights meetings. Reverend Saddler's secretary's car was identified at the Baha'i meeting this way, for example. See chap. 3, note 8, in this book.

27. The former Klansman was Bob Williams, mentioned in the prologue of this book.

28. For more on this, see notes 17 and 18 in this chapter.

Chapter 3. "If You Want Some Fighting, We're Here to Give It to You"

1. Cf. WATS Report, September 1, 1964, 3, Wisconsin History Society (hereafter WHS) Freedom Summer Digital Collection (FSDC), Freedom Information Service (FIS) WATS Reports, September 1964, micro 780, reel 1, segment 7.

2. Cf. Jackson WATS Report, November 12, 1965, 2, WHS, SNCC Social Action Vertical Files (hereafter SAVF), Mss 577, box 48, folder 13.

3. Cf. WATS Report, November 12, 1965, 3.

4. The damages to the bathroom were important enough to make it into the weekly report on civil rights activities in Marks. See Marie Gertge, "Marks Project Weekly Report," cited in Simon Cuthbert-Kerr, "The Development of Black Political Organization in Quitman County, Mississippi, 1945–1975" (PhD diss., University of Strathclyde, Scotland, 2006), 38.

5. Cf. WATS Report, November 27, 1965, 1, SNCC SAVF, Mss 577, box 48, folder 13.

6. We took many of these statements although we could not get them notarized.

7. My affidavit is in my possession.

8. A. K. Saddler, Application for a Notary Public Commission, May 3, 1961?, Mississippi State Sovereignty Commission Records (hereafter SCR) 2-82-0-18-1-1-1. Car: L. K. Barney, "Bahai Organization Report," January 23, 1961, 1–2, SCR 2-82-0-11-1-1-1. Barney asserted, "[The] Bahai organization . . . has a deadline of 1963 for total integration of the United States." See also Albert Jones, Memorandum, January 25, 1961, SCR 2-82-0-14-1-1-1; Scarbrough, Report, February 6, 1961, 1, 2, SCR 2-82-0-15-1-1-1.

9. Tom Scarbrough, Investigation, February 6, 1961, and May 17, 1962, SCR 2-82-0-41-1-1-1; Ben Caldwell to Albert Jones, May 18, 1961, SCR 2-82-0-25-1-1-1; Jones to Gov. Ross Barnett, June 2, 1961, SCR 2-82-0-27-1-1-1.

10. Caldwell to Jones, May 18, 1961; Jones to Gov. Barnett; Eavenson to Jones, n.d. (reply to May 5, 1961 query), SCR 2-82-0-22-1-1-1.

11. E. C. Black to Heber Ladner, May 29, 1961, SCR 2-82-0-26-1-1-1.

12. Cf. SNCC, "Incident Summary—Mississippi October," November 1, 1964, 1, WHS, SNCC SAVF, Mss 577, box 47, folder 5; WHS, FIS WATS Report, October 2, 1964, 4, micro 780, reel 1, segment 8. The report also described police threats at the meeting. Clondike's story is also related in City of Marks v. Allan Goodner, 1, SCR 2-82-0-55-1-1-1, and SNCC, "Incident Summary, October 1964," 1, WHS, Pamela Allen papers M85-013.

13. Cf. WHS, FIS WATS Report, October 4, 1964, 2.

14. Cf. WHS, FIS WATS Report, October 5, 1964, 2.

15. Cf. City of Marks v. Goodner, 1–3; WHS, FIS WATS Report, October 7, 1964, 1, 2; October, 9, 1964, 4; October 11, 1964, 1; October 13, 1964, 2; SNCC, "Incident Summary, October 1964," 3; State of Mississippi, County of Hinds, Affidavits "Abbott Clondike" [*sic*], SCR 9-31-2-123-1-1-1 (Joe's arrest is also there).

16. City of Marks v. Goodner, 2. See also SNCC, "Incident Report, October," November 1, 1964, 2, WHS FSDC, SNCC SAVF, Mss 577, box 47, folder 5.

17. City of Marks v. Goodner, 3.

18. Aryeh Neier, whom everyone in Marks called "Harry," later became the ACLU's national director. Mr. Neier also represented Chester Green's daughters in their school integration suit. WHS, FIS WATS Report, October 17, 1964, 2, mentions Neier.

19. WHS, FIS WATS Report, October 10, 1964, 1.

20. Cf. WHS, FIS WATS Report, October 15, 1964, 3.

21. Cf. WHS, FIS WATS Report, October 22, 1964 (mislabeled as "Oct 23" in finding aid), 2.

22. WHS, FIS WATS Report, October 13, 1964, 3. "Information Report by Project Area," September 28, 1964, 20, offered a similar assessment but did note that despite these lacks they were conducting voter registration drives, testing public accommodations, conducting community leadership training, building a library, launching a Freedom School, and planning a Community Center. WHS, Mary King papers 1962–1999, Mississippi Summer Project, Misc. Files Z: Accessions M82-445, box 1, folder 21.

23. Cf. CORE, "Running Summary of Incidents during the 'Freedom Vote' Campaign, October 18–November 2, 1964," October 20 [1964], 89, WHS, SAVF-COFO papers, Mss 577, box 16, folder 7.

24. Cf. WHS, FIS WATS Report, October 21, 1964, 1.

25. Cf. "Summary of Incidents," October 21, 1964, 89, CORE MFDP Memoranda and Repts., 1964–66, micro 793, reels 2–3, segment 37; WATS Report October 21, 1964, 1, WHS, FIS; Jerry DeMuth, "Notes from Mississippi," *Independent*, November 1964, 6, WHS, Jerry DeMuth papers 1962–1987, SC3065; "Running Summary . . . Oct. 20," 89; "Notice of Intention to Contest Election of Jamie L. Whitten in the 2nd Congressional District of Mississippi," 9, WHS, MFDP Records, Mss 586, box 1.

26. Cf. SNCC "Incident Summary, October 1964," 2.

27. Richard Kennedy, COFO, "Affidavit: . . . a summary of the record of arrests since October 1, kept in the office of the COFO Legal Counsel," 3. (October 27, 1964), WHS FSDC, Benjamin Smith papers 1955–1967, Mss 513, box 1, folder 14. Apparently I was originally arrested for "contributing to the delinquency of minors." WHS, SNCC SAVF, WATS Report, March 4, 1965, 1, Mss 577, box 48, folder 13. I still have my (undated) sworn affidavit.

28. My "trial" is chronicled in WHS, FIS WATS Reports, March 7, 1965, 2, micro 780, reel 1, segment 11–13.

29. Tom Scarbrough, "Investigative Report," October 30, 1964, 2, SCR 2-82-0-57-2-1-1. He noted that my lawyer was Jewish and reported that it was the

opinion of the sheriff and others that I needed "mental treatment. . . . the boy is nuts."

30. See WHS, FIS WATS Report, November 9, 1964, and following, micro 780, reel 1, segment 9-10.

31. Not without a fight. [Hamer to Whitten], "Notice of Intent to Contest Election," n.d. [1964–65], Michael J. Miller Civil Rights Collection, Digital Collections, University of Southern Mississippi Libraries.

32. Marks's Freedom School: Cf. COFO Staff Report, "Freedom Centers: What's Happening," September 1964, 1, WHS, Samuel Walker papers 1964–1966, Staff Repts., 1964–65, Mss 655, box 1, folder 6. For more on Freedom Schools in general, see William Sturkey and Jon Hale, *To Write in the Light of Freedom: The Newspapers of the 1964 Mississippi Freedom Schools* (Jackson, Miss., 2016); Jon Hale, *The Freedom Schools: Student Activists in the Mississippi Civil Rights Movement* (New York, 2016); and chap. 2, note 16, in this book.

33. Both quotes from John Bettersworth, *Mississippi: A History* (Austin, Tex., 1959), 12, WHS micro P84-1640 N78-133.

34. Cf. Marks COFO to Jackson COFO, Memorandum: "Project Report, Jan. 23–Feb. 3, 1964," Civil Rights Movement Archive, https://www.crmvet.org (hereafter CRMA), re situation in Marks, with its debts, lack of program director and freedom house, and so on.

35. Cf. Friends of the Mississippi Project, "Yellow Springs Ohio Newsletter," January 20, 1965, 2, WHS, Lucile Montgomery papers 1963–1967, micro 44, reel 3, segment 48.

36. Cf. COFO Project Report, February 3, 1964, 1–2, WHS, Alicia Kaplow papers 1964–1968, Mss 507, box 1, folder 4, re setting up the office, introduction of R. T. (Robert) and John, and tentative action plan. Copy in CRMA, "Marks Mississippi Project Report."

37. Cf. WHS, FIS WATS Reports, November 12, 1965, 3.

38. Cf. COFO, "Incident Summary Feb 21–March 11, 1965," 1, Walker papers, Mss 655, box 1, folder 4.

Chapter 4. "We Was Glad That We Had to Stand Up for Ourselves"

1. For more on the Selma march and Jimmie Lee Jackson, see Steve Fiffer and Ardar Cohen, *Jimmie Lee and James: Two Lives, Two Deaths, and the Movement that Changed America* (New York, 2015); Craig Swanson, *The Selma Campaign: Martin Luther King, Jr., Jimmie Lee Jackson, and the Defining Struggle of the Civil Rights Era* (Bloomington, Ind., 2014); Barbara Harris Combs, *From Selma to Montgomery: The Long March to Freedom* (New York, 2014); John Lewis, *Walking with the Wind* (New York, 1998), chaps. 15–16; Bernard LaFayette Jr. and Katherine Lee Johnson, *In Peace and Freedom: My Journey in Selma* (Lexington, Ky., 2013), chap. 6.

2. Cf. Wisconsin History Society (hereafter WHS) Freedom Summer Digital

Collection (FSDC), Freedom Information Service (FIS) WATS Report, March 3, 1965, 1, MFDP Lauderdale County, micro 55, reel 3, segment 66.

3. Jail: Cf. WHS, FIS WATS Reports, March 12–14, 1965, 3, Walker papers. Protest: WHS, FIS WATS Report, March 9, 1965, 1; SNCC "Incident Summary, March, 1965," 3. Both in WHS, SNCC SAVF, Mss 577, box 48, folder 13.

4. All narrated in Frank Garner, "Joe Freed from Mississippi Jail," *Daily Oklahoman*, March 14, 1965, 1–2, *Oklahoman* Digital Archives, https://digital.olivesoftware.com/olive/APA/Oklahoman (search title or date); Garner, "Mississippi Jail Life Described," *Daily Oklahoman*, March 13, 1965, 1–2 (includes Caldwell quote, 2). The *Daily Oklahoman* did three other stories on Joe: Wayne Mackey, "Civil Rights Worker from OU Lands in Mississippi Jail," March 12, 1965, 1, 2; Robert Allen, "$350 Bail Ready, Joe Promises to Leave Mississippi," March 13, 1965, 2; Garner, "Lecture Greets Civil Rights Worker," March 15, 1964, 1–2.

5. Cf. WHS, FIS WATS Report, September 5, 1965, 1, SNCC SAVF, Mss 577, box 48, folder 13; "Mississippi Freedom Labor Union," 1965, Civil Rights Movement Archive, https://www.crmvet.org (hereafter CRMA). The MFLU was founded in January 1965. Ultimately, the "tent city" effort failed for lack of money, as did the MFLU in 1966. WHS, MFDP Quitman County Chapter: Records 1965–66, Mss 539, box 1, segment 7, includes papers of the MFLU. Thrown off the land: many reports show this happening to activists in different places and times. See, for example, MFDP County Reports, November 21–December 4, 2, 1965, WHS CORE–MFDP Memoranda and Reports, micro 793, reels 2–3, segment 37; "County-by-County Reports, December 16, 1965–January 9, 1966," 6, WHS, MFDP General papers, micro 788, reel 2, segment 2, pt. 1.

6. "Mississippi Freedom Labor Union Pledge," n.d. (1965?), CRMA.

7. There are hundreds of documents about the challenge. See especially WHS, MFDP General papers, micro 788, reel 1, segment 2, pts. 1 and 2.

8. For more on the Justice Department Civil Rights Division: Michael Eric Dyson, *What Truth Sounds Like: RFK, James Baldwin, and Our Unfinished Conversation about Race in America* (New York, 2018); Leadership Conference on Civil Rights Education Fund, *Long Road to Justice: The Civil Rights Division at 50* (Scotts Valley, Calif., 2014); Brian Landsberg, *Enforcing Civil Rights: Race Discrimination and the Department of Justice* (Lawrence, Kans., 1997).

9. Mae Ella's retelling of her experiences appeared in the October 1965 issue of now-defunct *Insurgent* magazine.

10. Mrs. Fannie Clay only avoided paying tuition for her adopted child by talking to the LDF lawyers. Presley Franklin, "2 Students Suspended at Marks High School," *Southern Courier* (Montgomery, Ala.), September 30–October 1, 1967, 5. Used with permission from the Southern Courier Association.

11. See, for example, "House Dismisses Challenge of Freedom Democrat Party," September 18, 1965, unidentified Meridian newspaper, WHS, MFDP-Lauderdale County, Congressional Challenge, November 1964–September 1965, micro 55, reel 1, segment 6; and note 7 above.

12. Cf. WATS Report, November 12, 1965, WHS, SNCC SAVF, Mss 577, box 48, folder 13, 3; WATS Report, October 27, 1965, 3, and November 22, 1965, 2, both

WHS, SNCC SAVF, Mss 577, box 48, folder 10; MFDP County Reports, November 21–December 4, 1965, 2; Mississippi State Sovereignty Commission Records (hereafter SCR) 2-165-5-49-2-1-1. See also note 5 above re evictions.

13. WATS Report, October 29–November 1, 1965, 1, SNCC SAVF, Mss 577, box 48, folder 10.

14. Excerpt from letter by Dave Harris, n.d., in unnamed document, SCR 2-82-0-56-1-1-1, 1–2. That Marks family had lost five of their eight children and earned $100 a month chopping and picking cotton.

15. The Delta Ministry in Edwards, Miss., ran the Mount Beulah Center, where they conducted various civil rights programs and workshops. Alex wrote drafts of letters before he mailed them; I copied this (and others) when first putting this manuscript together. Other letter drafts are in the non-digitized portion of the Freedom Summer Collection at WHS, but I was unable to locate this one there. I suspect it is in the Freedom Information Service Library Project archive, in Jackson, Mississippi, since Jan Hillegas, who hosts the Library Project archive, shared several of Alex's letters with me.

Chapter 5. "Trying to Take It from the Power Structure"

1. For more on the War on Poverty in Mississippi, see Annelise Orleck and Lisa Hazirijan, eds., *The War on Poverty: A New Grassroots History, 1964–1980* (Athens, Ga., 2011), part 3; Thomas Ward Jr., *Out in the Rural: A Mississippi Health Center and Its War on Poverty* (New York, 2016); Michael Gillette, *Launching the War on Poverty: An Oral History*, 2nd ed. (New York, 2010). See also James Cobb, "Somebody Done Nailed Us on the Cross: Federal Farm and Welfare Policy and the CRM in the Mississippi Delta, *Journal of American History* 77, no. 3 (December 1990) 912–36.

2. CAP challenges, for example: MFDP, Counties Reports March 22, 1966, 1, 2, Wisconsin Historical Society (hereafter WHS), MFDP General papers, micro 788, reel 2, segment 2, pt. 1 (also in MSC, SCR 2-165-6-28-2-1-1). Other examples: WHS FSDC, WATS Reports, April 13, 1966, 1, and April 19, 1966, 1 (the latter also discussed Cotton Street sewage issues); SNCC Social Action Vertical Files (hereafter SNCC SAVF), Mss 577, box 48, folder 11.

3. For more on CDGM and Head Start, see Crystal Sanders, *A Chance for Change: Head Start and Mississippi's Black Freedom Struggle* (Chapel Hill, 2016); Polly Greenberg, *The Devil Has Slippery Shoes: A Biased Biography of the Child Development Group of Mississippi, a Story of Maximum Feasible Poor Parent Participation* (Washington, D.C., 1990). Freedom Information Service (FIS) also followed many of the efforts related to Head Start, health, education, voting, and so on in its newsletters. See, for example, "Mississippi Newsletter," No. 1, June 22, 1966, at USM, Miller Civil Rights Collection. More Freedom Information Service files are in the WHS FSDC.

4. FDP Counties Report, March 22, 1966, 2; CDGM and Head Start: see note 3 immediately above. One thing I realized only recently was how close together the homes, businesses, and churches of the better-off, more moderate peo-

ple associated with the Voters' League were. Valley Queen was the church of Reverend Hill, who had expressed some hostility toward the civil rights movement. He was a member of the Voters' League. His church was only a couple of blocks from New Paradise Church, where the pastor was Rev. O. W. Ingram, head of the Voters' League. Also within a couple of blocks was the grocery store of prominent Voters' League member Percy Nelson and the store and home of Mrs. Flora Shaw, another prominent Voters' League member.

5. Thanks to Mr. Wilson for allowing me to quote from his personal papers.

6. See, for example, H. Russell Embry, Mid-State Opportunity, Inc., to O. M. Melchor, January 3, 1968, WHS, Amzie Moore papers 1941–70, Correspondence 1968, Mss 551, box 1, folder 8. A number of the letters there discuss the Head Start program, including an anonymous letter to Moore, January 30, 1968, complaining about Mrs. Figgs and Mrs. Brown: "[They] are hell they want to Boss and Run every things and didn't give the clothes . . . and food . . . out Right."

7. Despite the infighting, MFDP noted, "The most important thing is that the people are organizing the people against CAP." WHS FSDC, FDP, "County Reports," March 22, 1966, 1.

8. Shimkin notes for letter to OEO, n.d., WHS, MFDP Quitman County Chapter Records 1965–66, box 1, folder 3, Mss 539.

9. None of these efforts succeeded. See, for example, Ross Coggins of OEO to Reverend Coleman refusing to fund the Quitman County Community Action Board, December 14, 1967, WHS, Moore papers, Correspondence 1967, Mss 551, box 1, folder 7.

10. Shimkin to George Williams, Jackson FDP Office, n.d., WHS, MFDP Quitman, box 1, folder 5.

11. For more on voting and its consequences, see WHS, FDP, "County Reports," MFDP General papers, micro 788, reel 2, segment 2, pt. 1. The December 16, 1965 to January 7, 1966, update for Quitman County, for example (posted from Marks), reported twenty complaints. See also WHS, FDP "County Reports," November 21–December 16, 1965, 2, CORE MFDP Memoranda.

12. Cf. WATS Report, November 11, 1965, 2, WHS, SNCC SAVF, Mss 577, box 48, folder 13, re Brown and general fear around running for office.

13. "Lists of families and income needs," n.d. [1967], 3 (Marks), attests to the deep need. WHS, Amzie Moore papers, Moore Correspondence 1967.

14. Shimkin to William Seabron, Dept. of Agriculture, April 14, 1966, WHS, MFDP Quitman, box 1, folder 3.

15. Cf. WATS Report, May 26, 1966, 1, SNCC SAVF, Mss 577, box 48, folder 11; MFDP "County Reports" Jan. 9–21, 1966, 2, MFDP General papers, micro 788, reel 2, segment 2, pt. 1.

16. This is the second letter from Alex I used when writing this book but cannot find now. Like the letter in chap. 4, note 15, it is uncatalogued, either in the WHS non-digitized collection or the FIS Archives. Note that it came only four months after that upbeat letter he wrote in February.

17. That May, the MFDP had filed a lawsuit to postpone the primary until il-

legal bars to the registration of African American voters were lifted, but the suit failed. "Mississippi Vote Suit to Be Heard," *Memphis Commercial Appeal*, May 16, 1966, 14; FIS, "Mississippi Newsletter," No. 1, June 22, 1966, 3, University of Southern Mississippi Libraries Digital Collections, Miller Civil Rights Collection.

18. "Mississippi Story: The Word Is Fear," *New York Times*, June 12, 1966. For more on James Meredith and the March Against Fear, see Aram Goudsouzian, *Down to the Crossroads: Civil Rights, Black Power and the Meredith March Against Fear* (New York, 2014) and Meredith's autobiography, written with William Doyle, *A Mission from God: A Memoir and Challenge for America* (New York, 2012). See also chap. 2, note 12, in this book.

19. See, for example, Ramon Himel, "Sniper Halts Meredith with Shotgun Blasts: Shelby Countian Held," *Memphis Commercial Appeal*, June 7, 1966, 1.

20. Kenneth Toler, "5 Incumbents Win Primary in Mississippi," *Memphis Commercial Appeal*, June 8, 1966, 1. In this first election since the passage of the Voting Rights Act, the Justice Department sent observers to all twenty-four Mississippi counties under federal scrutiny. Toler, "Mississippi Ballots Today in 'Reconstruction' Fervor," *Memphis Commercial Appeal*, June 7, 1966, 5. For an example of Black voting power, see Hasan Kwame Jeffries, *Bloody Lowndes: Civil Rights and Black Power in Alabama's Black Belt* (New York, 2010).

21. Toler, "5 Incumbents Win Primary in Mississippi."

22. Ramon Himel, "Marchers Cover 15 Miles, Bed Down At Batesville," *Memphis Commercial Appeal*, June 11, 1966, 4.

23. Quoted in Goudsouzian, *Down to the Crossroads*, 53.

24. David Pollard, "King Leads 9-Mile Trek, Leaves to 'Plan March,'" *Memphis Commercial Appeal*, June 10, 1966, 8.

25. Mrs. Phipps, phone conversation, April 14, 2015.

26. Howell Raines, *My Soul Is Rested* (New York, 1977), 422. For more on the Deacons for Defense, see Lance Hill, *The Deacons for Defense: Armed Resistance and the Civil Rights Movement* (Chapel Hill, 2004); Charles Cobb Jr., *This Nonviolent Stuff'll Get You Killed: How Guns Made the Civil Rights Movement Possible* (New York, 2015); Robert Williams, *Negroes with Guns* (New York, 1962).

27. Quoted in Goudsouzian, *Down to the Crossroads*, 86. The audio can be found in the King papers at Stanford: Martin Luther King Jr., "Eulogy for Armistead Phipps," Martin Luther King, Jr. Research and Education Institute, Stanford University, http://okra.stanford.edu/en/permalink/document660612-005.

28. For more on Carmichael, see Stokely Carmichael and Charles Hamilton, *Black Power: The Politics of Liberation in America* (New York, 1967); Stokely Carmichael with Ekwueme Michael Thelwell, *Ready for Revolution: The Life and Struggles of Stokely Carmichael (Kwame Ture)* (New York, 2003). For more on Black Power, see also Peniel Joseph, *Waiting 'til the Midnight Hour: A Narrative History of Black Power in America* (New York, 2006); Peniel Joseph, ed., *The Black Power Movement: Rethinking the Civil Rights-Black Power Era* (New York, 2006); Jeffrey Ogbar, *Black Power: Radical Politics and African American Identity* (Baltimore, 2004); William Van Deburg, *New Day in Babylon: the Black*

Power Movement and American Culture (Chicago, 1992); Julius Lester, *Look Out Whitey! Black Power's Gon' Get Your Mama!* (New York, 1968).

29. Stokely Carmichael at Free Huey rally, Oakland, February 17, 1968, transcript: American Archive of Public Broadcasting, https://americanarchive.org/catalog/cpb-aacip-28-4m91834b8n. Comment comes at 50:40.

30. Stokely spoke at a number of campuses. A transcript of his speech, "From Black Power to Pan-Africanism," given at Whittier College on March 22, 1971, can be found at American RadioWorks, http://americanradioworks.publicradio.org/features/blackspeech/scarmichael-2.html.

31. See, for example, Frank Lynn, "Cops' Tear Gas Routs Negroes," *Newsday*, June 24, 1966, 1; James Cazalas, "Tear Gas Scatters March Crowd Seeking to Defy Canton Tent Ban," *Memphis Commercial Appeal*, June 24, 1966, 1, describing King as "shriek[ing] . . . 'We shall overcome.'"

32. John Dittmer, *The Good Doctors* (New York, 2009), 153–54; Frank Cormier, "LBJ Steers Middle Course as Black Power Cry Rises," *Memphis Commercial Appeal*, June 26, 1966, 1.

33. There had been some improvements; for example, the Justice Department reported that more than four thousand Black voters had registered in Mississippi in the first three weeks since the march began. "Negro Sign-Up Exceeds 4,000," *Memphis Commercial Appeal*, June 27, 1966, 1.

34. For more on Parchman Prison, see David Oshinsky, *"Worse than Slavery": Parchman Farm and the Ordeal of Jim Crow Justice* (New York, 1996); Carol Ruth Silver, *Freedom Rider Diary: Smuggled Notes from Parchman Prison* (Jackson, 2014); William Ferris, *Give My Poor Heart Ease: Voices of the Mississippi Blues* (Chapel Hill, 2009).

Chapter 6. "This Corner of the Great Society"

1. Alex Shimkin, "Report, Quitman County," MFDP County Report, February 11, 1966, 3, Mississippi State Sovereignty Commission Records, 2-165-6-6-3-1-1, reported sixty to seventy "regulars" at meetings.

2. QCFO records are located with Quitman County (QC) MFDP records at the Wisconsin Historical Society (hereafter WHS). QC files are themselves scattered throughout the WHS and FSDC collections: SNCC Social Action Vertical Files, Mss 577; MFDP Records, Mss 586 and micro 788; MFDP Lauderdale County, micro 55; COFO papers, Mss 521; Freedom Information Service, micro 780; Amzie Moore papers, Mss 551; Mississippi Free Press (oversize pamphlet collection micro P70-964); *Student Voice*, micro N71-508 and N82-521; Pamela Allen papers, M86-013.

3. Cf. FDP County Reports, January 9–January 21, 1966, 2, and January 20–February 5, 1966, 1.

4. Mrs. Pryar [?], Lambert, to Joe Bateman, July 8, 1966, WHS, MFDP Quitman Chapter, box 1, folder 3.

5. Cf. Alex Shimkin, "Report, Quitman County," February 11, 1966.

6. Richard Arvedon, handwritten notes, n.d., WHS, MFDP Quitman Chap-

ter, Mss 539, box 1, folder 4. Names left out to protect privacy. These and the below examples are taken from different pages of notes and are clearly from multiple (undated) meetings.

7. Richard Arvedon, handwritten notes, n.d., WHS, MFDP Records, Mss 586, box 1, folder 4. "Bonds" in Mss 539.

8. "Notes," Mss 586. The notes also contained follow-ups to several of these situations but did not describe the outcomes.

9. Clara Collins, handwritten notes, WHS, MFDP Quitman Chapter, Mss 539, box 1, folder 4.

10. Presley Franklin, "School Days in Mississippi," *Southern Courier*, September 9–10, 1967, 4.

11. Bateman, "Report to Jackson FDP," September 1966, in Simon Cuthbert-Kerr, "The Development of Black Political Organization in Quitman County, Mississippi, 1945–1975" (PhD diss., University of Strathclyde, Scotland, 2006), 47 (erroneously dated there as 1964).

12. For more on civil rights, race, and the Vietnam War, see Daniel Lucks, *Selma to Saigon: The Civil Rights Movement and the Vietnam War* (Lexington, Ky., 2014); *"No Vietnamese Ever Called Me 'Nigger,'"* (documentary directed by David Weiss, 1968, restored 2018); Lawrence Eldridge, *Chronicles of a Two-Front War: Civil Rights and Vietnam* (Columbia, Mo., 2011); Jonathan Rosenberg, *How Far the Promised Land? World Affairs and the American Civil Rights Movement from the First World War to Vietnam* (Princeton, 2006); Simon Hall, *Peace and Freedom: The Civil Rights and Antiwar Movements in the 1960s* (Philadelphia, 2005); James Westheider, *Fighting on Two Fronts* (New York, 1997); Wallace Terry, *Bloods: An Oral History of the Vietnam War by Black Veterans* (New York, 1984); Herbert Shapiro, "The Vietnam War and the American Civil Rights Movement," *Journal of Ethnic Studies* 16, no. 4 (Winter 1989): 117–41.

Chapter 7. "Boy, We Got Things Rolling"

1. The Voters' League was the longstanding group of generally moderately well-off African Americans who had managed to register to vote. They were more conservative politically than most of us in the movement but were certainly still seen as a potential threat by white folks. For more, see discussion in chap. 2.

2. The Quitman County Voters' League was more sympathetic to, and active in, movement efforts. See chap 2.

3. Quitman County population in 1960: 21,019; in 1970: 15,888; in 1980, 12,636; in 1990: 10,490. National Bureau of Economic Research, U.S. Census, *Decennial County Population Data 1900–1990* (digitally modified from original published in 1995), https://data.nber.org/census/pop/1900-90.txt

4. In 1964, Quitman County had 435 Black voters, 384 in Marks (and 425 white Marks voters); the county had approximately 600 Black voters a year later. Mississippi races can also be followed in the MFDP papers at WHS, especially micro 788, reel 2.

5. This was the issue Alex Shimkin had written to the Agriculture Department about. See chap. 5.

6. Melvyn Leventhal email to Reuben Anderson, Cheryl Greenberg, Fred Banks, October 20, 2014.

7. Presley Franklin, "Problems in Quitman County," *Southern Courier*, September 9–10, 1967, 4.

8. *Franklin v. Quitman County*, Leventhal to Anderson et al. For decision, see chap. 8.

9. I used these records, now missing, from the Jackson, Mississippi, law firm of Anderson, Banks, Nichols and Stewart. Leventhal and Anderson verified the general facts. Leventhal to Anderson et al.

10. Petition, n.d., copied in 1975. Now unavailable, probably in Freedom Information Service Library Project archive, Jackson, Mississippi.

11. James Wilson Sr. personal papers, used with permission.

12. Ruth Figgs's private papers, used with permission.

13. For more on the Poor People's Campaign, see Gordon Mantler, *Power to the Poor* (Chapel Hill, 2013); Robert Hamilton, *Dr. Martin Luther King Jr. and the Poor People's Campaign of 1968* (Athens, Ga., 2020); Sylvie Laurent, *King and the Other America: The Poor People's Campaign and the Quest for Economic Equality* (Oakland, 2018); Colleen Wessel-McCoy, *Freedom Church of the Poor: Martin Luther King Jr.'s Poor People's Campaign* (Lanham, Md., 2021); Chuck Fager, *Uncertain Resurrection: Dr. King's Poor People's Campaign 1968* (Durham, N.C., 2017); Gerald McKnight, *The Last Crusade: Martin Luther King, Jr., the FBI and the Poor People's Campaign* (Boulder, Colo., 1998); Roland Freeman, *The Mule Train: A Journey of Hope Remembered* (Nashville, 1998), part 2; Michael Honey, *Going Down Jericho Road* (New York, 2007), chap. 8; Michael Honey, *To the Promised Land* (New York, 2019), chap. 4; Drew Dellinger, "The Last March of Martin Luther King, Jr.," *Atlantic*, April 4, 2018, https://www.theatlantic.com/politics/archive/2018/04/mlk-last-march/555953.

14. Martin Luther King Jr., "Remaining Awake through a Great Revolution," Sermon, National Cathedral, Washington D.C., March 31, 1968, reprinted in *Congressional Record*, April 9, 1968, 9396.

15. Ralph Abernathy, *And the Walls Came Tumbling Down* (New York, 1989), 412, 415.

16. James Batten, "Symbolism Is Rich Mixture in 'Poor People's Campaign,'" *Memphis Commercial Appeal*, May 7, 1968, 27.

17. *Eyes on the Prize II*, interview with James Figgs, April 4, 1989, http://digital.wustl.edu/e/eii/eiiweb/fig5427.0488.051marc_record_interviewee_process.html.

18. Told to, and cited with permission of, Simon Cuthbert-Kerr.

19. Peter Joseph, *Good Times: An Oral History of America in the 1960s* (New York, 1973), 297.

20. "Marks March Has Rugged Start," *Memphis Commercial Appeal*, May 2, 1968, 4. The article reported the six arrested for disturbing the peace were Chester Thomas Jr. from Canton; Jimmy Wells, Marjorie Hyatt and Andrew Marrisett

from Atlanta; Major Wright from Grenada; and Marks local Dorris Baker. See also "Poor People's March Takes Emotion-Charged First Step," Gregory Jaynes, *Memphis Commercial Appeal*, May 2, 1968, 1; Larry Scroggs, "Emotion Outpaces Mules as Poor People's March Steps off from Fatal Spot," *Memphis Commercial Appeal*, May 3, 1968, 1; Jaynes, "Marks 'Stopover' May Be Longer," *Memphis Commercial Appeal*, May 3, 1968, 36. See also Earl Caldwell, "The Poor People of the South: Why Some Want to Join March to Washington," *New York Times*, May 7, 1968, 36.

21. Freeman, *Mule Train*, 100. "Alabama Towns Lie Ahead for 'Poor People's' March," *Memphis Commercial Appeal*, May 6, 1968, 21, reported 127 striking teachers. This increase in activism was occurring all over Mississippi and elsewhere in the South. See also "Negroes File Suit," *New York Times*, May 7, 1968, 37.

22. Resolution, May 2, 1968. I saw a copy in 1975 but it is now unavailable; probably in FIS Archives.

23. "'Poor People' Study Tactics," *Memphis Commercial Appeal*, May 4, 1968, 10.

24. Willie Thomas was involved in several voting suits. William Kunstler wrote to Joe that Mr. Thomas never let anyone intimidate him and was one of the best witnesses he'd worked with. Kunstler to Bateman, May 5, 2011.

25. Jaynes, "Young Hearts Sing Joyfully but Hope Is Phantom to Old," *Memphis Commercial Appeal*, May 4, 1968, 1.

26. Jaynes, "Philosophy of Brain Power Reaps Reward on Delta Farm," *Memphis Commercial Appeal*, May 5, 1968, 1.

27. "'Poor People' Study Tactics."

28. Ibid.

29. Also mentioned in Jaynes, "Marks 'Stopover' May Be Longer."

30. Cf. WATS Reports, August 5, 1964, 2, WHS, FIS WATS Report, August 1964, micro 780, reel 1, segment 6.

31. "'Poor People' Study Tactics."

32. Ibid.

33. Ibid.

34. "Washing Time in Marks Finds Drive on Doors," *Memphis Commercial Appeal*, May 5, 1968, 12.

Chapter 8. "We Was All So Determined"

1. Most discussions of the Poor People's campaign describe the Mule Train (see chap. 7, note 13, in this book), and marvelous images and interviews can be found in Roland Freeman, *The Mule Train: A Journey of Hope Remembered* (Nashville, 1998). The *Memphis Commercial Appeal*, the closest major paper to Marks, also covered it in depth (including photos). See "'Poor People' Also Lacking in 'Mulesmanship' Skills," *Memphis Commercial Appeal*, May 14, 1968, 10 (quotes Jack Franklin), 36; "Transportation Worries Stall March of Poor," *Memphis Commercial Appeal*, May 10, 1968, 8; "U.S. Gives OK to 'Poverty Camp' Site," *Memphis Commercial Appeal*, May 11, 1968, 14; "Marks March Is Gathering Steam," May 9, 1968, 18 (Marks marchers in Montgomery, Memphis, and Nashville); "Abernathy

Warns Congress Poor Will Stay Like 'Plague,'" *Memphis Commercial Appeal*, May 14, 1968, 1. For a 2016 interview of one Marks resident with the Mule Train, Eddie Lee Webster Jr., see "A Story of the Poor People's Campaign Mule Train," Mississippi Stories, http://mississippistories.org/story/a-story-of-the-poor-peoples-campaign-mule-train.

2. For more on Resurrection City, see Jill Freedman, *Resurrection City 1968* (New York, 2018); Morris Cunningham, "Mid-Southerners Help Build 'Resurrection City' in Park," *Memphis Commercial Appeal*, May 14, 1968, 10; and chap. 7, note 13, in this book.

3. *Eyes on the Prize II*, interview with James Figgs, April 4, 1989, http://digital.wustl.edu/e/eii/eiiweb/fig5427.0488.051marc_record_interviewee_process.html.

4. Cf. Collins interview in Freeman, *Mule Train*, 115–17.

5. Notes, now missing, from Jackson, Mississippi, law firm of Anderson, Banks, Nichols and Stewart.

6. Peter Joseph, *Good Times: An Oral History of America in the 1960s* (New York, 1973), 212–13.

7. The CC began as a support for the CDGM in 1965.

8. Mary Jones, Report, May 2, 1969, James Wilson Sr. personal papers.

9. Amzie Moore et al. to Rev. Oglesby, n.d. [1969], Wilson papers.

10. Keady from notes, now missing, from Jackson, Mississippi, law firm of Anderson, Banks, Nichols and Stewart. Order also cited in 1F.3d 1450, *Hull v. Quitman County Board of Education*, 91-1903, September 2, 1993, II.26, https://openjurist.org/1/f3d/1450/hull-v-quitman-county-board-of-education#fn2-1: "On July 24, 1969, after a finding that Quitman County local school authorities were operating an unconstitutional de jure segregated school system, the Honorable William C. Keady, United States District Judge for the Northern District of Mississippi, entered a desegregation order (the 'desegregation order'), which has never been set aside." See also *Cowan and U.S. v. Bolivar County Board of Education* 914 F. Supp. 2d 801, filed 1965; ruling 1969 https://www.clearinghouse.net/detail.php?id=13735#top and https://casetext.com/case/cowan-v-bolivar-cnty-bd-of-educ-4.

11. Ellis Statement, August 24, 1970, from notes, now missing, from Jackson, Mississippi, law firm of Anderson, Banks, Nichols and Stewart.

12. Richard Nixon, "Statement about Desegregation of Elementary and Secondary Schools," March 24, 1970, American Presidency Project, https://www.presidency.ucsb.edu/documents/statement-about-desegregation-elementary-and-secondary-schools.

13. Re Nixon's "southern strategy" and education, see Dean Kotlowski, *Nixon's Civil Rights: Politics, Principle and Policy* (Cambridge, Mass., 2002), which is more positive on Nixon's impact; Kevin McMahon, *Nixon's Court: His Challenge to Judicial Liberalism and Its Political Consequences* (Chicago, 2011); Chinh Q. Le, "Racially Integrated Education and the Role of the Federal Government," *North Carolina Law Review* 88, no. 3 (2010): 1–63; Erica Frankenberg and Kendra Taylor, "ESEA and the Civil Rights Act: An Interbranch Approach to Furthering Desegregation," *Russell Sage Foundation Journal of the Social Sciences* 1, no. 3

(December 2015): 32–49. Racially segregated education is even worse today: Gary Orfield, John Kucsera, and Genevieve Siegel-Hawley, "E Pluribus . . . Separation: Deepening Double Segregation for More Students," September 19, 2012, Civil Rights Project, http://civilrightsproject.ucla.edu/research/k-12-education/integration-and-diversity/mlk-national/e-pluribus...separation-deepening-double-segregation-for-more-students. In 2012, 74 percent of Black students and 80 percent of Latino students attended majority nonwhite schools; 38 percent of Black students and 43 percent of Latinos attended "intensely segregated" schools (at least 90 percent minority). A *Los Angeles Times* op-ed offered virtually identical figures for 2017: Beverly Tatum, "America Is More Diverse than Before, but Its Schools Are Growing More Segregated," September 12, 2017.

14. "John N. Mitchell Dies at 75; Major Figure in Watergate," *New York Times*, November 10, 1988.

Chapter 9. "Things Is Better in One Way and Worser in Another"

1. James Silver, *Mississippi: The Closed Society* (Jackson, Miss., 1964).

2. Andrew Kopkind, "Lowndes County, Alabama: The Great Fear Is Gone," *Ramparts*, April 1975, 8, reprinted in Kopkind, *The Thirty Years' Wars* (New York, 1995), 259–60.

3. In 1970, more than 60 percent of Quitman County residents still used outdoor toilets. "Howard U. Aiding Mississippi Poor," *New York Times*, October 4, 1970, 53.

4. U.S. Census data, IPUMS NHGIS, University of Minnesota, www.nhgis.org for 1970 (NT54), 1980 (NT55B). In 1970: 12 percent unemployment for Black men; 16 percent for Black women; 4 percent for white people. In 1980: 15 percent unemployment for Black men; 21 percent unemployment for Black women. See also *Mississippi Statistical Abstract 1971*, https://babel.hathitrust.org/cgi/pt?id=uc1.b3496446&view=1up&seq=265&skin=2021.

5. Overall in 1970 in Quitman County, 58.3 percent of all residents reported earnings under the poverty level. Despite higher unemployment, more government aid had dropped the poverty level to 41.4 percent—still far higher than both the state and the country. U.S. Census, "Population by Poverty Status by Counties," https://www.census.gov/data/tables/time-series/dec/census-poverty.html.

6. That was true for poor white families as well: according to the 1970 census, 26 percent of poor Black families and 24 percent of poor white families in Quitman County had only one parent in 1970, mostly female. U.S. Census, IPUMS NHGIS.

7. There were a number of state and federal housing programs that helped build affordable housing. I do not know the specific program Mrs. Weathersby was referring to, but see, for example, U.S. Department of Housing and Urban Development, *Housing in the Seventies: National Housing Policy Review* (Washington, D.C., 1974), https://www.huduser.gov/portal/Publications/pdf/HUD-968.pdf, esp. chap. 5.

8. U.S. Census, "Census U.S. Decennial County Population Data 1900–1990,"

https://www.nber.org/research/data/census-us-decennial-county-population-data-1900-1990.

9. *1974 Census of Agriculture*, County Data—Quitman, part 4, table 2. The total number of farms had also dropped, so the percentages were similar: 14 percent of farms were Black-owned in 1969; 13 percent were Black-owned in 1974. Another 35 percent were part owners in 1969, dropping to 20 percent in 1974.

10. See, for example, "Holmes County Civil Rights Movement," *Mississippi Encyclopedia*, https://mississippiencyclopedia.org/entries/holmes-county-civil-rights-movement.

11. Pesticides and other commercial farm practices also limit options for family farming. When a crop-dusting plane from the cotton plantations flew overhead, Mrs. Dean shook her head. "That the reason folks can't raise butter beans. That old poison get on the plants and kill them."

Chapter 10. "The Home House"

1. Sally Belfrage, *Freedom Summer* (1965; repr., Charlottesville, 1990), 210.

2. For more on churchwomen's activism, see Alysia Burton Steele, *Delta Jewels: In Search of My Grandmother's Wisdom* (New York, 2015), which documents "church mothers" across the Delta; Daphne Wiggins, *Righteous Content: Black Women's Perspectives of Church and Faith* (New York 2005); Cheryl Gilkes, *If It Wasn't for the Women: Black Women's Experience and Womanist Culture in Church and Community* (Maryknoll, N.Y., 2001); and Evelyn Brooks Higgenbotham, *Righteous Discontent: The Women's Movement in the Black Baptist Church* (Cambridge, Mass., 1994).

3. See Quitman County Development Organization, https://qcdo.org. For more about QCDO, see the epilogue.

Epilogue. "We Ain't Never Going Back to What We Was"

1. They now live elsewhere but still own land in Marks.

2. See "Quick Facts: Quitman County, Mississippi," U.S. Census Bureau, https://www.census.gov/quickfacts/fact/table/quitmancountymississippi,US/PST045219#; "Quitman County, Mississippi," City-data.com, http://www.city-data.com/county/Quitman_County-MS.html; and "Population by Race," CensusScope, http://www.censusscope.org/us/s28/c119/chart_race.html. In Quitman County, population had shrunk from just over 15,000 in 1970 to 6,176 in 2020, of which the Black population constituted 72 percent. In Marks, in 2020, 77 percent were African American and 1 percent Hispanic or multiple races. "Marks, Mississippi," City-data.com, http://www.city-data.com/city/Marks-Mississippi.html. Note that the 2021 population has declined further: World Population Review, https://worldpopulationreview.com/us-cities/marks-ms-population.

3. "Quitman County School District," Public School Review, https://www

.publicschoolreview.com/mississippi/quitman-county-school-district/2803810-school-district.

4. "Marks, Mississippi," City-data.com. In Quitman County, the highest proportion, 21 percent, worked in education and health services. Another 13 percent worked in public administration; roughly the same percentage in arts, recreation and food services; and 11 percent in manufacturing. American Community Survey (hereafter ACS), U.S. Census Bureau, Quitman County Table DPO3, 2020, https://data.census.gov/cedsci/table?q=quitman%20county,%20Mississippi%20Employment&tid=ACSDP5Y2019.DP03. To compare these occupation rates to those of 1970 see *Mississippi Statistical Abstract 1971*.

5. Crops' $133,575 value and $153,075 cost of production: "Quitman County, Mississippi," City-data.com. The average size of farms, 751 acres, reveals the extent of land consolidation. For more on land and dispossession, see chap. 1, note 7, in this book, especially Sydney Nathans, *A Mind to Stay*; and Vann Newkirk II, "This Land Was Our Land."

6. World Population Review; Marks, MS (Mississippi) Houses and Residents," City-Data.com, http://www.city-data.com/housing/houses-Marks-Mississippi.html. For more, see note 4. See also Mississippi Department of Health, Quitman County Health Profile (n.d.), 4, https://msdh.ms.gov/msdhsite/files/profiles/Quitman.pdf.

7. U.S. Census Bureau, 1990 Census, *General Population Characteristics*, "Mississippi 1992," esp. tables 1, 2, 5, 8, https://www2.census.gov/library/publications/decennial/1990/cp-1/cp-1-26.pdf. In 1970, unemployment in Quitman stood at 5 percent. "Mississippi Employment 1971–1975," in *Mississippi Statistical Abstract, 1971*, sections 5, 13. See also chap. 9. Poverty: in 1960, 93 percent of Black Quitman County residents and 72 percent of all the county's residents lived below the poverty line. See chap. 1 of this book.

8. "Reclaimed Project, Marks": https://www.reclaimedproject.org/marks-ms-1; Mississippi Department of Employment Security, "Summary of Employment Rates for the Years 1990 Forward: Quitman County," www.mdes.ms.gov/media/8735/urate.pdf; "Marks, Mississippi," City-data.com; World Population Review.

9. "Marks, Mississippi," City-data.com; World Population Review. Black county-wide poverty rate: 39.1 percent. Overall poverty rate: Marks, 27.1 percent; Quitman County, 37.6 percent (the second-highest percentage among Mississippi counties); Mississippi, 15.5 percent. For the county, just over 14 percent (ages 19–65) were unemployed. "Mississippi Poverty Rate by County, Index Mundi, https://www.indexmundi.com/facts/united-states/quick-facts/mississippi/percent-of-people-of-all-ages-in-poverty#chart; ACS, U.S. Census Bureau, Quitman County. See also "Challenges and Opportunities," Marks Project, https://marksproject.org/?s=statistics. In 1960, 94 percent of Black and 75 percent of all Quitman households were poor.

10. Marks poverty rate data: "Marks, Mississippi," City-data.com, http://www.city-data.com/poverty/poverty-Marks-Mississippi.html; ACS, U.S. Census Bu-

reau, Quitman County. Forty-four percent of all families with children and more than half of all single-parent households in the county are poor.

11. In 2019, 17 percent had no insurance; another 55 percent relied on public insurance. ACS, U.S. Census Bureau, Quitman County. Mississippi Department of Health, Quitman County Health Profile, 4, reported 20 percent lacked insurance in 2014.

12. Michelle Obama, "Remarks by the First Lady at Brinkley Middle School in Jackson, Mississippi," March 3, 2010, American Presidency Project, www.presidency.ucsb.edu/ws/index.php?pid=120724. See also David Kenney, "Michelle Obama Visits Brinkley Middle School," WLBT, n.d., [March 2010], *Mississippi News Now*.

13. It opened June 26, 2015. "Delta Regional Mule Train Farmers Market and Museum: Fit to Eat," Mississippi Public Broadcasting, July 31, 2015, https://www.youtube.com/watch?v=E5i9KiKsoSY. This emerged from the Quitman County Credit Union, now part of the Shreveport Credit Union.

14. Food statistics: "Quitman County, Mississippi," City-data.com (underestimate; supplemented with Google search). Salad: PBS, October 22, 2010.

15. Health rates: "County Profile: Quitman County, Mississippi," University of Washington Institute for Health Metrics and Evaluation, Seattle, Washington, 2014, http://www.healthdata.org/sites/default/files/files/county_profiles/US/2015/County_Report_Quitman_County_Mississippi.pdf. Obesity: of 3,142 U.S. counties, Quitman ranked 3,139 for women, 3,077 for men. See also Mississippi Department of Health, Quitman Health Profile, 6. According to City-data, just over 14 percent of residents there have Type 2 diabetes. It reports a 39 percent obesity rate, with no source.

16. "County Profile." Quitman: "Recommended Physical Activity": women ranked 3,140 of 3,142 counties, men 3,111.

17. Mississippi Department of Health, Quitman Health Profile, data from 2015; Institute for Health Metrics and Evaluation (IHME), "US Health Map," data from 2014, https://vizhub.healthdata.org/subnational/usa (also http://www.healthdata.org/data-visualization/us-health-map). IHME County Report: Quitman County's female life expectancy rate ranked 3,116 of 3,142 counties; the county's male life expectancy ranked 3,126 of 3,142.

18. "US Health Map."

19. Robert Wood Johnson Foundation, "Mississippi," County Health Rankings and Roadmaps, [2020], https://www.countyhealthrankings.org/sites/default/files/media/document/CHR2020_MS_v2.pdf.

20. Madison Shannon Palmer High School, http://www.qcschools.com/1/Home; "M.S. Palmer High School," Niche, https://www.niche.com/k12/ms-palmer-high-school-marks-ms; Mississippi Department of Education, Quitman County School District, https://msrc.mdek12.org/entity?EntityID=6000-000&SchoolYear=2019. Every source gives a different student body size.

21. See also "Marks, Mississippi," City-data.com, and Reclaimed Project.

22. The Mississippi Department of Education reported that 62 percent of the student body attended some post-secondary program.

23. QCDO, https://qcdo.org/. Shreveport Federal Credit Union, Marks, MS," http://www.usacreditunions.com/shreveport-federal-credit-union-11263/locations/marks-ms.

24. See, for example, Julia Cass, *"Held Captive": Child Poverty in America: A Children's Defense Fund Report* (Washington, D.C., 2010), chap. 1, https://www.childrensdefense.org/wp-content/uploads/2018/06/held-captive-child-poverty.pdf.

25. Reclaimed Project.

26. There are dozens of books on the political implications of the civil rights movement, including Ismail White and Cheryl Laird, *Steadfast Democrats: How Social Forces Shape Black Political Behavior* (Princeton, 2020); Steven Lawson, *Running for Freedom: Civil Rights and Black Politics in America since 1941*, 4th ed. (Chichester, UK, 2015); Kenneth Andrews, *Freedom Is a Constant Struggle: The Mississippi Civil Rights Movement and Its Legacy* (Chicago, 2004).

27. U.S. Census, "Voting and Registration in the Election of November 2020," Table 4b, "Reported Voting and Registration, by Sex, Race, and Hispanic Origin, for States November 2020," https://www.census.gov/data/tables/time-series/demo/voting-and-registration/p20-585.html. Eighty-three percent of Black Mississippi citizens and 79 percent of white Mississippians were registered to vote. Actually voted: 73 percent and 69 percent respectively.

28. For example, see "State Senator Arrested on Gun Charge in Quitman Election," *Y'all Politics*, Sept. 12, 2011, https://yallpolitics.com/index.php/yp/post/state_senator_arrested_on_gun_charge_in_quitman_election. For more on harassment of Black officials, see George Derek Musgrove, *Rumor, Repression, and Racial Politics* (Athens, Ga., 2012).

29. Pearl Stewart, "Freedom Summer Conference: Black Vote Still an Issue in Mississippi," *Diverse*, June 29, 2014, http://diverseeducation.com/article/65243. Ellipses in source. The conference celebrated the fiftieth anniversary of Freedom Summer. For more on Bob Moses, a pivotal figure in SNCC and Mississippi Freedom Summer, see Laura Visser-Maessen, *Robert Parris Moses: A Life in Civil Rights and Leadership at the Grassroots* (Chapel Hill, 2016); Eric Burner, *And Gently He Shall Lead Them: Robert Parris Moses and Civil Rights in Mississippi* (New York, 1994). Moses died in 2021. There are hundreds of obituaries and testimonials, many of which can be found here: "Robert 'Bob' Parris Moses (1935–2021)," *Historianspeaks*, July 25, 2021, https://historianspeaks.org/f/robert-bob-parris-moses-1935-2021.

30. Cochran retired in 2018.

31. See Federation of Southern Cooperatives / Land Assistance Fund, https://www.federation.coop/.

32. *Pigford v. Glickman*, 185 F.R.D. 82 (D.C. Dist. 1999).

33. Quoted in Mark Bittman, "Reimagining Detroit," *New York Times*, May 17, 2011. See also Mark Bittman, "Let's Help Create More Farmers," *New York Times*, June 10, 2015.

34. I let a Native American organization know about the destroyed mound so they could check on it. I was sorry I couldn't do more about it.

INTERVIEWEES AND FAMILIES

Although many made statements to me while I worked in Marks, I interviewed most people again in later years. In those cases, I list the interview date as well. In all cases I list the birthdates (and, when relevant, death dates) I know of. If I know someone has died but I do not know the date, I have simply put a D.

Rev. S. A. Allen, b. 1905. Interviewed 1975. D
Georgia Allen, b. 1909. Interviewed 1975. D

Jack Brown, b. 1885. Interviewed 1975. D

Sarah Ann Brown, b. 1920. Interviewed 1975. D
Willie Brown. (Later Mrs. Brown married Willie Thompson: see below)
    Betty Brown
    Martha Anne Brown

Joe Collins, b. 1909. Interviewed 1975. D
Lee Dora Collins, b. 1920. Interviewed 1975. D
    They had fifteen children. Among them:
    Clara Collins, b. 1944.
    Kay Collins, b. 1957. Interviewed 1975.
    Jeddie Collins, b. 1962. Interviewed 1975.

Gable Common, b. 1902. Interviewed 1975. D

Alec Dean, b. 1903. Interviewed 1975. D
Elnora Dean, b. 1900. Interviewed 1975. D

Ernestine Evans, b. 1926. Interviewed 1975.
J. D. Powells, b. 1945. D

Ruth Figgs, b. 1926, d. 1998. Interviewed 1975.
James Figgs, d. 2016.

The Franklins:
Jack Franklin, b. 1900. Interviewed 1975. D

Jessie James Franklin, b. 1918. Interviewed 1975. D
Jessie Franklin Jr., b. 1946. Interviewed 1975.
Man Franklin, b. 1948. Interviewed 1975.

William Franklin, b. 1910, d. 1989. Interviewed 1975.
Henrietta Franklin, b. 1927, d. 2014? Interviewed 1975.
Mae Ella Franklin
Ruby Franklin. Interviewed 1975.
Lenora (Wells), b. 1946. Interviewed 1975.
Presley (Azki Shah)
Hull Franklin, b. 1954. Interviewed 1975, 2010, 2013, 2015.
Jimmie Lee Franklin, b. 1960. Interviewed 1977.

Bernice Gates, b. 1933. Interviewed 1975.

Gilbert Hamer, b. 1910. Interviewed 1975.

Angela Marie Harris, b. 1968. Interviewed 1975.

Will Haynes, b. 1908. Interviewed 1975. D
Ella Mae Haynes, b. 1918. Interviewed 1977. D

Harry Hentz, b. 1959. Interviewed 1977.

James Herron, b. 1946. Interviewed 1975.

Robert Holland, b. 1958. Interviewed 1975.

Beatrice Humphreys, b. 1909. Interviewed 1975. D

Robert Jackson, b. 1955. Interviewed 2015 by Richard Arvedon.

Charles Jamison, b. 1948. Interviewed 1975. D

Lula Belle Johnson
Isabelle Johnson, b. 1933. Interviewed 1975.

Brother and sister:
Ruby Lee, b. 1953. Interviewed 1975.
Robie Lee, b. 1957. Interviewed 1975.

Samuel Lipsey, b. 1952. Interviewed 1975.

Rev. Willie L. Malone, b. 1909. Interviewed 1975. D

Junior Mayes, b. 1949. Interviewed 1977.

Elsa Mae Mitchell. Interviewed 1975.

George Nickerson, b. 1899. Interviewed 1975. D

Mrs. Ora Bea Phipps, b. 1927. Interviewed 1975, 2015.
Armstead Phipps, d. 1966.
  Geraldine Phipps, b. 1954. Interviewed 1975.
  Carol Phipps, b. 1961. Interviewed 1975.
  Cheryl Phipps, b. 1968. Interviewed 1975.
  Loretta Phipps, b. 1969. Interviewed 1975.
  Pete Phipps
  Armstead Phipps Jr.

Percy Phipps, b. 1928.
  James Phipps
  Leon Phipps, b. 1945?
  Bobby Phipps, b. 1953?

Bill Rucker, b. 1953. Interviewed 1975.
Clara Rucker. Interviewed 1977. D

Mittia Anne Smith

Dorothy Stanford, b. 1921. Interviewed 1975. D

Anne Belle Stuart, b. 1913. Interviewed 1975. D

Willie Thomas, b. 1907. Interviewed 1975. D

Willie Thompson, b. 1914. Interviewed 1975. D
  Jeanie Ruth Thompson. Interviewed 1975.
  Willie Edgar Thompson, b. 1958. Interviewed 1975.
  Johnny Thompson, b. 1950. Interviewed 1975.

Rev. Ezra Towner. Interviewed 1975. D

Lula Belle Weathersby, b. 1915. Interviewed 1975. D

James Wilson Sr., b. 1913. Interviewed 1981. D

Tommy Young, b. 1908. Interviewed 1975. D

No last names:
Sonny, b. 1962. Interviewed 1975. From Chicago, living with family in Marks.
Charles, b. 1963. Interviewed 1975. From Chicago, living with family in Marks.

Civil rights workers:

Richard Arvedon, b. 1947. Interviewed 1975, 2007, 2010–13, 2015.

David Harris, b. 1946. Interviewed 1975.

James Pete, b. 1948. Interviewed 1975.

Local white people:

Terry L., b. 1959. Interviewed 1975.

Danny Robinson, b. 1958. Interviewed 1975.

FURTHER READING

For readers who want more of the historical context in which *A Day I Ain't Never Seen Before* is rooted, this necessarily partial discussion offers a number of starting places. The scope of coverage is the southern civil rights movement broadly speaking. For those who wish to dig deeper into the histories of specific episodes and issues, from Emmett Till's lynching to Mississippi Freedom Summer, from Head Start to gender and civil rights, chapter notes at the point each topic is mentioned offer a guide to further readings on those subjects.

The achievements of the civil rights movement are certainly grounds for celebration, and a number of books take this more celebratory approach. These, however, tend to minimize the challenges facing activists or exaggerate the unity of the community or even of the activists themselves, and are not covered here. The work that follows is more nuanced. These authors grapple with complexities and assess disagreements, setbacks, and failures as well as unpack strategies and social forces that produced the movement's successes.

The richness of this literature of southern racial justice organizing is due in large measure to the wealth of voices contributing to the discussion—including, now, those from Marks—not just scholars and journalists but movement participants themselves. Committed to extending the struggle, these men and women (and often children) have written memoirs, offered reflections, and provided oral history interviews that have added immeasurably to the documentary evidence every scholar relies on. The discussion that follows therefore combines both primary and secondary materials to lay out the historical landscape.

Broad analytical histories of the movement, like Taylor Branch's magisterial *Parting the Waters*, Steven Lawson's *Civil Rights Crossroads*, and *There Is a River*, by Vincent Harding (himself both a civil rights activist and a historian), move beyond narrating the events to identify themes, patterns and interactions that shaped the movement as a whole. They in turn are undergirded by many equally important broad works of oral history like the wonderful *My Soul Is Rested*, edited by Howell Raines, and Henry Hampton's *Voices of Freedom*, which offer powerful activist voices, albeit with a limited contextual or narrative frame. Other oral history collections like the Civil Rights Movement Archives (crmvets.org), SNCC Digital Gateway (snccdigital.org), SCOPE 50 (scope50.org) (focusing on the SCLC and voting), and the SNCC Legacy Project (sncclegacyproject.org) are exclusively online collections, with links to hundreds of documents and other materials, including individual participant interviews.

The dozens of African American and white civil rights activists who have written their memoirs provide an overarching movement narrative of their own. Think of John Lewis's powerful *Walking with the Wind*, Ralph Abernathy's *And the Walls Came Tumbling Down*, and Mary King's *Freedom Song*, to cite just three. These writers range from movement leaders like Chuck McDew (*Tell the Story*) and James Farmer (*Lay Bare the Heart*) to rank-and-file activists including Sally Belfrage (*Freedom Summer*), John Reynolds of SCLC (*The Fight for Freedom*), and Peter Honigsberg, who describes his experiences as a movement lawyer in *Crossing Border Street*. Some are local residents swept up in the movement, like Tim Tyson's wonderful *Blood Done Called My Name* (in his case, in Oxford, North Carolina), and Melba Beals (*Warriors Don't Cry*), one of the Little Rock Nine, whose integration of Central High School required the use of U.S. troops.

Most of these books, whether memoirs or monographs, are set in urban centers like Birmingham (Diane McWhorter's *Carry Me Home* and Glenn Eskew's *But for Birmingham*), New Orleans (Adam Fairclough's *Race and Democracy*), and Selma (Bernard LaFayette Jr.'s *In Peace and Freedom* and Ronnie Barnes's *Amelia Boynton Robinson: A Biography*) where so much of the nationally televised events of the movement occurred.

Not all civil rights coverage is centered in urban places. Small towns like Marks do get attention, including Cynthia Griggs Fleming's *In the Shadow of Selma* and Hasan Kwame Jeffries's *Bloody Lowndes*, both set in rural Alabama. Robert J. Norrel's *Reaping the Whirlwind* looks at Tuskegee (whose 1,750 population in 1960 certainly qualifies it as small). The classic *Coming of Age in Mississippi* by Anne Moody describes life and organizing in the rural Mississippi Delta. Greta de Jong's *Can't Eat Freedom* explores southern rural activism after 1965 in Mississippi, Alabama, and Louisiana. Marks's hardships, its movement experiences, and its continued activism, fit well into this literature.

Thematic treatments also enrich our understanding of Marks, like the close examination of gender by Danielle McGuire and Steve Estes. McGuire's remarkable *At the Dark End of the Street* considers rape and other forms of sexual mistreatment of Black women as both a tool of racist control and a galvanizing force for activism, while Estes explored ideas of movement masculinity in *I Am a Man!* While no overt sexual violence occurs in Joe's story, these tensions are visible there, and Black women in Marks retain a memory of such experiences and even occasionally speak of it openly to whites. Monographs like Robert Mayer's *When the Children Marched* and James Marshall's *Student Activism and Civil Rights in Mississippi* and memoirs like Lynda Blackmon Lowery's *Turning 15 on the Road to Freedom* highlight the unique perspectives and pivotal roles played by courageous young people like Beals and so many in Marks. And building on Robert Williams's *Negroes with Guns* first published in 1962, Lance Hills's *Deacons of Defense* explores questions of self-defense versus nonviolence in Louisiana, a debate that played out in Marks as well. Akinyele Omowale Umoja focused on self-defense across Mississippi in *We Will Shoot Back*.

Other civil rights literature focuses on specific organizations like the Student Nonviolent Coordinating Committee (SNCC) and the Mississippi Freedom Democratic Party (MFDP), on specific strategies and actions like voter registration or sit-ins, on significant events such as marches and demonstrations, and on pivotal groups and individuals. These topics are covered more fully in chapter notes, but several are particularly relevant to Marks activists and so are worth highlighting here.

SNCC, which provided most of the staffing for Marks's projects, has been the focus of a great deal of both scholarly and activist writing. In fact, Howard Zinn, the first historian to look at the organization, published his *The New Abolitionists* in 1964, only four years after SNCC was founded. Scholarly interest has not slackened since then. But here too it is the SNCC workers themselves who have had the most to contribute to the ongoing discussion. Cleveland Sellers muses on, in his words, "the life and death of SNCC" in his autobiographical *The River of No Return*. So have John Lewis, Mary King, Chuck McDew, and so many others. Even more have reflected on their experiences in the online SNCC projects mentioned above and in conferences and reunions. *Hands on the Freedom Plow*, for example, highlights women's contributions in SNCC projects. The many panels and speakers at SNCC's twenty-fifth reunion at Trinity College in Hartford, Connecticut, can be found on recordings in the library's collections and in a volume Cheryl edited, *A Circle of Trust: Remembering* SNCC. Its fiftieth reunion has been compiled onto thirty-eight DVDs, available through California Newsreel. The sixtieth reunion, held in the fall of 2021, may produce still more materials about SNCC and its role in the broader civil rights movement.

The MFDP and Freedom Summer, central to the experiences of many in this book, have their own scholars and memoirists. Lisa Anderson Todd in *For a Voice and the Vote* describes her experiences with the party, for example, as does Kay Mills's biography of Fannie Lou Hamer, *This Little Light of Mine*. Bruce Watson, Susan Rubin, and Doug McAdam have all written books with the title *Freedom Summer*. John Dittmer used the same title for his brief history and collection of documents as do two books for young people. In addition to Sally Belfrage's book, Ed King told his story in *Ed King's Mississippi*, and Charles Prickett related his in *Remembering Freedom Summer*. (The deaths of Goodman, Schwerner, and Chaney at the start of the summer have received a great deal of coverage of their own.)

Others writers have used individuals as reflections of broader ideas and trends, like Barbara Ramsby's compelling *Ella Baker and the Black Freedom Movement*,

James Farmer's autobiographical *The Making of Black Revolutionaries*, and two books both entitled *Outside Agitator*: Adam Parker's biography of Cleveland Sellers and Charles Eagles's biography of Jon Daniels, the theology student killed while trying to shield Ruby Bridges in Alabama.

Many movement events directly involved Marks activists. For example, James Meredith's autobiography *A Mission from God* discusses his March Against Fear through Mississippi. Several Marks activists took part in that march; one died while marching, and Martin Luther King Jr. spoke at his funeral.

Studies like *Power to the Poor*, by Gordon Mantler, examine the SCLC's Poor People's Campaign. That effort launched with a "Mule Train" that originated in Marks. Marks residents drove mules or otherwise joined the trip, and many stayed in Resurrection City, the encampment that marchers set up in Washington, D.C. Photographer Roland Freeman's powerful book *The Mule Train* visually documents these events; some of his photos appear in this book.

What the Truth Sounds like, Michael Eric Dyson's discussion of Bobby Kennedy and the Justice Department's Civil Rights Division, comes to life in the words of Marks's William Franklin, who worked with Justice Department lawyers to challenge segregation in Marks's public schools and welfare services.

Perhaps most important for setting Marks in its context are studies of the movement in Mississippi—not just specific events like Freedom Summer or the Mule Train but broader explorations of activism there, such as John Dittmer's *Local People*. In addition to authors like Belfrage, Umoja, and Marshall, for whom Mississippi was the locus of action, several works explore local organizing traditions, including Charles Paynes's *I've Got the Light of Freedom*, Cheryl Reitan's *Thunder of Freedom*, and Neil McMillen's *Dark Journey*. Others drill down to the county level, work that proves especially useful in rural areas. In *A Little Taste of Freedom*, Emilye Crosby assesses the movement in rural Claiborne County; J. Todd Moye's *Let the People Decide* looks at the dynamics of organizing in Sunflower County. *Voices from the Mississippi Hill Country*, a series of interviews conducted and framed by Roy DeBerry, Aviva Futorian, Stephen Klein, and John Lyons, does the same in Benton County. Finally, a number examine broader policies and programs as they played out in Mississippi, like Polly Greenberg's *The Devil Wears Slippery Shoes*, which examines the Office of Economic Opportunity's controversial Head Start program in the Delta described by Joe and Marks residents.

These and so many others introduce us to activists few people know and even fewer people celebrate, but whose labor, persistence, and courage reshaped the South. As they all maintain, their fight is not yet over. The more deeply we understand the movement's underpinnings and processes, its successes and failures, the better we can continue that struggle.

INDEX